ENERGY,
THE ENVIRONMENT,
AND
HUMAN HEALTH

American Medical Association
Congress on Environmental Health

ENERGY,
THE ENVIRONMENT,
AND
HUMAN HEALTH

Asher J. Finkel, Editor

PUBLISHING SCIENCES GROUP, INC.
Acton, Massachusetts

Proceedings of a
Congress on Environmental Health

Sponsored by
Council on Environmental, Occupational, and Public Health and
Department of Environmental, Public, and Occupational Health
Division of Scientific Activities
American Medical Association

Printed in the United States of America.

International Standard Book Number: 0–88416–004–1

Library of Congress Catalog Card Number: 73–84167

CONTRIBUTORS

Robert J. Beyers, Ph.D.
Director
Savannah River Ecology Laboratory
Atomic Energy Commission
Aiken, South Carolina

Monte E. Canfield, Jr.
Deputy Director
Energy Policy Project
The Ford Foundation
Washington, D.C.

Joel Darmstadter
Senior Research Associate
Resources for the Future, Inc.
Washington, D.C.

Edward E. David, Jr., Sc.D.
Executive Vice President
Gould, Inc.
Chicago, Illinois

Garrett Eckbo
Architect
Eckbo, Dean, Austin, and Williams
San Francisco, California

Merril Eisenbud, Sc.D.
Professor of Environmental Medicine
School of Medicine
New York University
New York, New York

Erick A. Farber, Ph.D.
Professor and Director of Solar Energy
  and Energy Conversion Laboratory
University of Florida
Gainesville, Florida

Linnea C. Freeburg, Sc.B.
Administrative Assistant
Department of Economics
Carnegie-Mellon University
Pittsburgh, Pennsylvania

Marvin Goldman, Ph.D.
Director
Radiobiology Laboratory
University of California
Davis, California

John R. Goldsmith, M.D.
Head, Environmental Epidemiology Unit
California State Department of Public Health
Berkeley, California

Derek P. Gregory, Ph.D.
Assistant Director of Engineering Research
Institute of Gas Technology
Chicago, Illinois

Ralph E. Lapp, Ph.D.
Energy/Nuclear Consultant
Alexandria, Virginia

Lester B. Lave, Ph.D.
Professor and Head
Department of Economics
Carnegie-Mellon University
Pittsburgh, Pennsylvania

Daniel B. Luten, Ph.D.
Lecturer
Department of Geography
University of California
Berkeley, California

Peter A. Morris, Ph.D.
Director of Operations Evaluation
Atomic Energy Commission
Washington, D.C.

Joseph W. Mullan
Vice President of Government Relations
National Coal Association
Washington, D.C.

Frank L. Parker, Ph.D.
Professor of Environmental and Water
  Resources Engineering
Vanderbilt University
Nashville, Tennessee

Vic Reinemer
Staff Director
Senate Subcommittee on Budget, Management, and
  Expenditures
Washington, D.C.

David J. Rose, Ph.D.
Professor of Nuclear Engineering
Massachusetts Institute of Technology
Cambridge, Massachusetts

William E. Siri, Ph.D.
Trustee, The Sierra Club
Physicist, Donner Laboratory
University of California
Berkeley, California

Honorable John V. Tunney
United States Senator
Riverside, California

Alvin M. Weinberg, Ph.D.
Director
Oak Ridge National Laboratory
Atomic Energy Commission
Oak Ridge, Tennessee

Donald E. White, Ph.D.
U.S. Geological Survey
Menlo Park, California

H. J. Young
Vice President and Secretary
Edison Electric Institute
New York, New York

[+] Deceased

Contents

PREFACE

The Congress on Environmental Health that was sponsored by the American Medical Association and that concerned itself in April 1973 with problems of "Energy, the Environment, and Human Health" is presented here in book form because of its timeliness, its relevance to contemporary problems, and the thoroughness of treatment by the contributors and participants. This meeting was the most recent in a series sponsored jointly by the AMA Council on Environmental and Public Health, which late in 1972 was given the additional responsibility of Occupational Health, and the AMA Department of Environmental, Public, and Occupational Health in the Division of Scientific Activities. The scope of the interest that the American Medical Association has in environmental health is indicated by the range of topics that have been the subjects of recent AMA Congresses on Environmental Health: Human Habitat and Health (1972), Solid Waste Management (1971), the Population Problem and the Physician (1970), and Noise Pollution (1969).

The Council demonstrated considerable prescience and wisdom when in July 1971 it began to plan for the 1973 meeting and selected the interrelations of energy, environment, and health as the topics for discussion. The conflict, indeed the impending collision, between the social and economic demands for more energy and more power in this country and the growing voices of environmental concern, conservation, and consumerism were less apparent in 1971 than they are today. Moreover, the intensity of these public issues is likely to become more acute in the coming years. The papers presented at the April 1973 meeting have been gathered together in this volume in the hope that they may serve as a guide to the understanding of some of the very complex problems that American and world society face now and in the near and distant future.

The American Medical Association is grateful to the authors for their participation in the Congress and for their very substantial contributions to our collective knowledge. The success of the meeting was a tribute to the efforts of Mr. Frank W. Barton, secretary of the Council, and other members of the AMA staff. Special acknowledgement is made to Mrs. Lucille Morrisey for her careful editorial review of the typescript and to Mss. Margie Brooks, Katrina Cebrzynski, Diane Dale, Barbara Jansson, Christine C. Kelly, Linda LaBon, Mary Stelmach, and Leatha Tiggelaar for their diligence and devotion in the preparation of the typescript.

A. J. F.

INTRODUCTION

Many of you may be asking, "Why is the American Medical Association interested in energy production? Should we not be concentrating on diagnosis and treatment of diseases and leave energy to the engineers, the politicians, and the public?"

For one thing, the conversion of matter into energy—whether it is for space heating from a fireplace; for cooking meat to make it more palatable and free of pathogenic organisms; for electricity that can be utilized to aid in the production of food, clothing, and shelter; for transportation, business, or industry—is closely and inextricably interwoven into the physical and emotional health of human beings. Moreover, any method of production and utilization of energy in itself modifies the environment in which we exist.

Accordingly, it is to our benefit to see that alterations in our ecosystem by such modifications have a maximum of beneficial and a minimum of detrimental effects on a majority of the people.

The objectives of the American Medical Association are not, as some believe, solely to improve the professional education or the economic welfare of its members. The AMA is a multifaceted organization that for decades has spent a significant share of its financial and manpower resources on scientific and professional efforts to improve the health of the *public*. The AMA is not a "Johnny-come-lately" to efforts in the field of environmental health. We have not just jumped on the ecology bandwagon. From its creation in 1847, the American Medical Association officially expressed interest in, and concern for, environmental and public health matters; "the betterment of public health" was an objective in founding the Association.

As early as 1876 the AMA made recommendations on controlling water pollution. In 1924 it warned that a high disease and death rate from typhoid fever and other diseases due to the use of polluted water by the people of any municipality would imperil the country at large. In 1937 the AMA supported legislation to create a division of water pollution control within the U.S. Public Health Service.

In 1955, 1959, 1963, and 1965, the AMA supported certain important air pollution control measures then before the Congress. In the past few years, the legislative tempo on environmental quality has increased dramatically. Many AMA policy statements on specific air pollution bills have been submitted to the Congress in support of federal research and development programs, stricter standards, better abatement and control, and other measures to minimize human health problems associated with adverse environmental effects.

The AMA supported legislative proposals that were enacted as the Clean Air Act of 1953 and the Air Quality Act of 1967. These laws authorized the federal government to develop criteria for ambient air quality; the states were to develop both air quality standards in conformance with such criteria and plans for implementation and enforcement of the standards. In 1965 the AMA supported legislation, subsequently enacted as P.L. 89–272, the Motor Vehicle Air Pollution Control Act, to provide practicable standards to control emissions from new motor vehicles.

Ten years ago, in May 1963, the AMA Board of Trustees created a Committee on Environmental Health staffed by full-time personnel of the Department of Environmental Health. Over the past ten years there has been a variety of environmental topics highlighted by the Council, rather remote from the customary image that many people have of the AMA.

These topics have included national Congresses on Population Growth, on Air and Water Pollution, on Noise, on Pesticides, Radiological Hazards, Solid Waste Management, and Human Habitat and Health.

Adequate amounts and proper utilization of energy from a variety of sources are essential to the sustenance of human life on this planet. Any conversion of matter into energy has some detrimental effects on the environment as far as the human organism is concerned. The essential processes of life itself, converting ingested food and inhaled air into the energy reflected by human life and movement, pollutes the environment. Whenever air, water, or solid matter leaves a single human being (i.e., every time we exhale, perspire, urinate, or defecate), we modify our environment, frequently spreading potential sources of disease and injury. Each time we light a match; drive a car; turn on a light; burn coal, wood, gasoline; or boil water, we utilize energy and modify our environment. Sometimes the modification is to our benefit and at other times to our detriment.

It is the net balance between the harmful and beneficial effects of the production and utilization of energy on the majority of people involved that counts, and that is the theme of this Congress. We are attempting to spread the light of scientific knowledge of the environmental impact that energy production and utilization has on human health. Full factual disclosure and knowledge is essential to proper assessment of these effects. It is often the fear of the unknown that may lead to irrational behavior and to an improper assessment of the various factors involved. "Familiarity breeds contempt." We grew up seeing wood, oil, and coal being burned to provide energy, so we may not be fully cognizant of the environmental impact of the tons of carbon monoxide, sulphur oxides, and oxides of nitrogen that are products of this burning. On the other hand, the effects of invisible and unfelt ionizing radiation associated with the production of energy from newer processes of fission or fusion of the atom, which often have latent incubation periods of many months or years, are not fully known and are, therefore, frequently dreaded, possibly out of proportion to their overall effects when compared with the more familiar, older methods. It is not the function of this Congress to take one side or the other of the controversy—often a highly emotional one—over the expansion of nuclear fueled sources of energy. It *is* our function to help spread pertinent *facts* and scientific *knowledge,* relayed by persons who are expert in their fields—knowledge openly discussed and shared freely with all of us in this country and abroad.

I am hopeful that assembling and publicizing these facts will help us all to reduce the risks and maximize the benefits of prudent, but not profligate, utilization of energy.

Edward Press, M.D.

PROLOGUE

Monte E. Canfield

The name of my game is energy policy. I want to show you some of the relationships between overall energy policy and the problems that you have gathered here to discuss. I will not, therefore, go into the detailed aspects of environmental health. Let me instead show you some important links between national energy policy and your own work. The web is intricate, sometimes delicate, always fragile. But it is real, and only by seeing your own work in the context of overall national policy needs will you be able to make maximum use of what you are learning about the relationship of energy to the environment and human health.

People seem to be naturally inclined to think of growth and health together. The doctor is happy and the parents are proud when the baby doubles his birth weight in just six months. But common sense reminds us there are limits to healthy growth, and to healthy rates of growth. If the baby goes on doubling his birth weight every half-year he will weigh more than 7 million pounds when he is ten years old. And in that little example, we have learned much of what there is to learn about exponential growth.

As Ecclesiastes says, "For every thing there is a season." There is a time to grow and a time to mature. Today, I would like to share with you a few thoughts on our traditional American growth ethic and what it means in our use of energy. Ever-expanding use of fuels and electric power has brought us enormous benefits. But we have reached a point in our national life when we have to ask whether more and greater growth in energy consumption will bring us better social health. Or will it mean that, like the dinosaur, we will soon be straining the capacity of the earth and our economic system to feed our bulk? There is a fairly obvious lesson to be learned from the dinosaur: you don't see too many of them roaming around these days.

Let me say also that my comments today are tentative and personal. They do not necessarily represent the views of the Ford Foundation's Energy Policy Project, whose study is now in progress. When all the results are in, I may well change many of my ideas. But at the moment I am in the happy position of expressing my opinions without too much confusion from unexpected facts.

I have some very positive personal feelings about growth in energy use. I grew up in a corner of Kansas that must have been one of the last pockets of rural America to get farm electricity from the Rural Electrification Administration (REA). We lived on a tenant farm, and, lacking electric power, we hand-pumped our water from shallow wells, shallow enough that sewage often got mixed up with the water supply. The hazards to health under those conditions were pretty real. In winter we lived in the one room that the stove kept warm, and we left school at two in the afternoon in order to get home and milk the cows and slop the pigs before night fell. I well remember trying to work in the barn by kerosene lamplight; once I mistook gasoline for kerosene, and the ensuing explosion burned the whole barn down, from rafters to corn cribs.

Then, when I was about six or seven years old, the magic genie of electricity changed our world. With electric pumps to draw water, we could sink safe deep wells. My mother cooked on an electric range instead of a wood stove stoked with corncobs. No more barns burned down on the farm. Instead, we lighted the barn with Mr. Edison's invention and put electric motors in the repair shed to sharpen tools and work metal and wood. I can't count the hours and the labor we saved with the help of this nonhuman energy.

For the country as a whole, ever-growing energy use has given us prosperity, comfort, mobility, and a degree of freedom from brute labor that is hard to comprehend even today; and yet it is far too easy to take for granted. It has been calculated that the average American's use of energy provides him with the equal of 110 slaves toiling away for his pleasure and ease. Energy has shortened the work week, given us leisure and opportunities to travel, and helped preserve our health. It keeps us warm in winter and cool in summer. Most of the dank sweatshops of 50 or 70 years ago have given way to cleaner, healthier energy-intensive factories. In caring for the ill or injured, I hardly have to tell you that energy is a life-saver. Imagine a hospital without electric power.

These are some of the genuine good things that our high-energy civilization has brought us. But the question arises: If we go on redoubling our use of energy, will we go on reaping parallel benefits, from now to eternity? Will 220 energy slaves make our good life twice as good?

All I have left out of the picture so far is the toll it takes to keep pushing our energy consumption to ever higher levels. For a long time, since the Age of Energy began about a century ago, we paid scarce attention to the full social costs of energy use. Nature gave us a very generous share of the world's fossil fuels—coal, oil, gas, and oil shale. We blissfully ran through a large part of that patrimony without much thought for tomorrow. At the same time we used our big uncrowded country's earth, air, and water as a vast wastebasket for a growing pile of poisonous waste from energy use.

The fortune has dwindled now, and the wastebasket is overflowing. The simple growth ethic that served us well for the last hundred years, the ethic that says, "More is better," is, in many ways, out of step with present needs. We are face to face with the issue of whether more rapid growth in energy use is worth the mounting costs—the costs of very quickly using up irreplaceable resources, of degrading our environment, and of harming the health of the human beings who must live in it.

We can not escape the fact that something has disturbed our energy equilbrium. For several summers, heat waves have brought on brownouts. This winter's fuel shortages closed schools and factories in the Midwest, and now we are hearing predictions of gasoline shortages for the summer. Such shortages and dislocations are evidence of a growing conflict between very rapid growth in demand and the lack of equivalent growth in domestic supplies of acceptable clean energy. New environmental controls guard our earth and our health against pollution, but they also have limited rapid expansion of energy production. This conflict between goals—the traditional goal of growth in energy use and the goal of preserving the environment and human health—has handed us many problems that are new to us. Some have labeled these unfamiliar problems the "energy crisis." I believe that "crisis" is something of an overstatement. And while I do not see it as a true crisis, we are getting signals that the carefree days of easy growth have come to an end.

Let us take a quick historical look at growth patterns for energy, and see where we are now. Our total energy demand today is more than 15 times as great as in 1870, even though the population has only tripled. We got there by increasing our usage about 3% a year. That is pretty impressive growth, but in recent years we have outdone it. Since 1964 demand has risen by nearly 5% a year. That may not seem a very imposing figure, but, in fact, if we go on at that pace, we will double our consumption every 14 years. Alice, while traveling through Wonderland, came to a place very much like the one we are in. She found that she had to run faster and faster just to stay in the same place. So do we.

While energy use doubles and redoubles, supplies must keep up. But domestic productive capacity has failed to maintain the pace, and in the last decade we became a net energy-importing nation. Imports amounted to one quarter of our oil and gas needs last year, and this proportion must rise, at least for the short run, if we are to avoid shortages. By 1985 we will either import about 50% of our oil and gas or we will do without.

Yet we are not anywhere near a point of physical bankruptcy in our domestic energy resources. Though we have used our fossil fuels at prodigious rates, we do have enough of most of these fuels left for decades, even centuries. We are in trouble because we *are* beginning to run short of our cheaper, more accessible supplies, especially those that do not befoul our spaceship Earth, and threaten the health and lives of all of us who travel in it. And this brings us to the other half of the energy question.

In the recent past, we have begun to take very seriously our responsibility to preserve the earth and its inhabitants. We have made a commitment, in scores of laws and regulations, to safeguard human health and the environment. We said, in the Clean Air Act, that the Air can no longer serve as a free public dump for all the noxious wastes our cars and chimney stacks pour out. With the Coal Mine Health and Safety Act, we said that we value miners' lives and lungs above cheap coal. Our caution in opening federal lands in the arid West to strip mining shows a new respect for the fragile earth, and for the unknown consequences of disturbing it.

We are coming to realize that the more energy we use, the more problems of pollution we encounter. Whatever energy source we think of has its attendant dangers to the environment and to health. Coal mining has long been one of the most dangerous jobs in American industry; it has meant black lung, disablement, or death to many a miner. But strip mining, which is safer and cheaper, ravages the earth. In dry western lands where most of our low-sulfur coal and oil shale lie, there is a real question whether the land, once surface-mined, can ever be reclaimed. And regardless of where we get it, when we burn coal, with today's technology, it poisons the air, especially when burned in massive amounts in a concentrated area to generate electric power.

Most of our remaining oil and gas resources appear to be either in Alaska or in the Atlantic and Pacific outer continental shelves. Yet offshore drilling means building terminals and refineries on precious coastal lands. And it raises fears, whether justified or not, of accidental spills, polluted seas, and ruined beaches.

Importing more oil will mean more pollution in our seas, for tankers in their ordinary operations release small but certain quantities of oil into the oceans. Tanker accidents can cause massive spills. According to recent scientific reports, half the plankton in the Atlantic Ocean off our East Coast is now contaminated with oil. This tiny oceanic plant life has given the earth one quarter of its oxygen supply through the eons. We don't yet know what the long-term effects on plankton may be from absorbing so much oil.

And when we burn the oil and its products, especially in the super-extravagant internal combustion engine, we fill the air with carbon monoxide and the hydrocarbons and nitrogen oxides, which are ingredients for smog. Dirty, sulfur-laden fuel oil, which is often burned in power plants, adds sulfur oxides to the brew. Natural gas, the cleanest of our fossil fuels, is in shortest supply here in the United States. By the year 2000, economic reserves may well approach exhaustion.

Atomic energy has not yet provided the panacea we hope for since it has problems all its own, not the least of which are reactor safety, the hazards of radioactive waste management, the dangers of sabotage to nuclear plants, the possibility that plutonium may be stolen and used to make illicit weapons, and plutonium's extreme toxicity and persistence.

Clearly, it is not going to be easy for our mines, wells, and power plants to deliver enough clean safe energy to satisfy our demands. Does this mean we must give up and go back to the cave, or at least to one dark room heated by a Franklin stove? I think not. But it does mean that we must adopt new energy policies to meet new needs. The trick will be to strike a balance, a very delicate balance, between our genuine needs for energy and the jobs, warmth, health, and mobility it gives us, and our need to preserve the earth and its people. My own conviction is that efforts in two directions—conservation of energy and research and development for new clean energy sources—will help us to safeguard the environment without pulling the plug on our standard of living.

The purpose of the Energy Policy Project is to analyze carefully such issues and to develop alternatives from which we, as a nation, can choose to shape sensible energy policies. Let me give you some examples of the kinds of avenues we are exploring. Energy waste, and the possibilities for energy conservation, are critical questions for study.

Using a lot of energy is one thing; wasting it is something else. Ultimate consumers get about half of the energy content of our fuels; the other half is eaten up by distribution and conversion losses and just plain waste. I like to point out that the American Dream is wrapped in an electric blanket. Unhappily, the generation of electric power is only about 30% efficient. In our study we ask: What advances in technology can help us save energy? How can we get more usable energy out of our old-established sources, and what new sources can we find? How about solar energy, that clean inexhaustible source? (The sun will last as long as we do.) What can we expect from personal energy conservation? How can public policy encourage energy savings?

Another tough question regards energy imports. The growing worldwide demand for energy has profound effects on international relations. The problem we face in buying foreign oil and gas is more than just the simple matter of getting what we need at reasonable prices. We must also consider the effect of higher imports on trade balances and world monetary stability. Would dependence on foreign sources, especially Middle Eastern sources, subject us to unwelcome influence on our foreign policy? Or would the trade itself lead to lessened international tensions? What are the moral and political implications of our devouring such a Gargantuan share of the world's energy?

With only 6% of the world's population, we consume 35% of the world's annual energy supply. But it is sobering to reflect that we took an even larger share a quarter of a century ago—45% to be exact. The rest of the world wants and needs energy, too, and will compete more and more with us for it.

I cannot begin to list all the questions we are asking or to describe the more than 50 major areas our Project will review. But I would like to tell you about some of our work on the connections between energy and health.

The American Public Health Association is now conducting for us a large-scale study on health effects of different energy systems. We are exploring health hazards at every stage of production, transportation, and use of fuels and electric power. We are asking, for example, what health factors must be considered in siting power plants? What are the air pollution dangers from burning fuels in internal combustion engines? How serious is the possibility of catastrophic explosions from liquefied natural gas? If two liquefied natural gas (LNG) tankers should collide, and the gas escapes, it has been suggested that, under certain atmospheric conditions, the gas could form a compact cloud and drift over the city of Boston or New York and explode in a holocaust. Is such a concern real, or is it science fiction?

In the nuclear power field, we are investigating the dangers of radiation to uranium and thorium miners. And we are asking about the chances of accidents in transporting highly radioactive fuels and wastes from plants to storage points. And how about safety in storing those hot items? Are they likely to leak out from their containers to contaminate the environment? What sort of legacy are we leaving our great-great-great-descendants, when we pass along to them a pile of radioactive waste that must be tended for thousands of years? Plutonium, U-239, has a half-life of 24,000 years. How must we deal with such a fact?

Because of the paucity of existing data, we are studying two specific health and safety problems in greater detail in separate projects. First, what are the effects on human beings of breathing air that contains microscopic particles, bits of burned-out waste from fossil fuels that are small enough to escape all the "pollution traps" our technology has devised? Second, what are the dangers to people from highly radioactive plutonium? Preliminary evidence suggests that the developing fetus is especially susceptible to harm from plutonium radioactivity.

Another of our special study areas is oil spills at sea. While oil pollution of the oceans may not directly affect human health, its indirect effects could be momentous. How well can plant plankton do its job of using the sun's energy to make food, releasing oxygen in the process, when it is tainted with oil? What happens to the food chain, when oil passes along to larger and larger creatures of the sea?

Energy problems affecting human health and the environment, which sustains life itself, are among the most critical that we have to consider. We have neither medical nor technological solutions to most of these problems. In the meantime, it seems to me that a sensible response to pollution and health hazards, as well as to the shortages we are experiencing, is moderation in our use of energy. Slower growth can be part of the answer. Slower growth can buy us time—time to mount a massive effort in research and development of new clean energy sources, for finding methods of using present sources in less polluting ways, and for better understanding the dangers and probabilities of accidents. Finally, time will allow us to separate the fiction from the fact.

I believe that the time has come to start practicing real energy conservation. The second law of thermodynamics teaches us that some waste is inherent in the conversion and transmission of energy. But we need not waste so much. In fact, some experts have reckoned that we could save as much as one third of the energy we use and still get to work, keep warm, stay healthy, and enjoy the pleasures of civilized living.

Lyndon Johnson wasn't wrong about turning off the lights in the White House. One 100-watt bulb left burning unnecessarily for 24 hours will waste a full 12% of your total household electric consumption for that day. Home insulation matters too. Good insulation, which keeps heat inside instead of letting it seep out to heat all outdoors, could save at least one quarter on our use of fuels for space heating. Proper insulation also saves energy in air conditioning and lessens the load on power plants during heat waves.

We are only beginning to learn about some of the options for energy conservation in industry. Since industrial use accounts for 40% of all our energy consumption, savings in this sector could make a sizable impact. A few major firms have experimented with energy saving and found they can save 10% to 15% without major new investments. Redesigned rate structures for natural gas and electricity might provide powerful incentives for thrift in energy use. Another neglected possibility is recycling of waste materials. It takes far less energy to reclaim metals such as iron and aluminum from our mounting piles of trash than to produce them from raw ore. Recycling can save precious resources as well as energy.

Transportation requires 25% of our energy. Here the private automobile is the most blatant culprit, because it devours such a large slice of our energy—almost 13% of the total. And we use that energy with incredible inefficiency. We power a 2-ton vehicle at less than 10% fuel efficiency to carry one single 150-pound man to work. Perhaps I should change that to 200 pounds! The less the man walks and the more he drives, the greater that poundage is likely to be. This is one place where more energy use means worse health. If you walk a few blocks to catch the bus to work, or to run an errand, you save energy, and you may help save your health as well.

In general, buses and trains are about three times as efficient in energy use as private automobiles. Public policies that encourage mass transit are energy-wise. Driving a small car also helps to save energy. Fuel use varies directly with the weight of the car, so that a 1-ton compact vehicle uses just about half the gasoline a big 2-ton car burns.

Conservation and cutting back growth rates need not condemn us to a cottage economy or a spartan life. Better public transportation, tighter buildings, thriftier use of energy by industry need not threaten the essentials in our way of life. And we ought to recognize that even "no growth" in consumption still means a whale of a lot of energy use—at least what we are using today.

Conservation cannot solve all our energy supply and environmental problems. But it can buy time for us to perfect better technologies for protecting the earth and time to find new clean energy sources.

Yet, except for nuclear programs, we have illogically neglected our research and development opportunities in the last decade. Even today, research and development expenditures make up only about 1% of the $75 billion yearly revenues of the energy industry. What we need is a national commitment to an urgent effort for clean energy, the same kind of national commitment that put our men on the moon. Only the federal government, backed by the full participation of industry, has the resources to raise the money for such an effort. Federal funding of $1.5 to $2 billion per year—about three times the current level—is a minimum for adequate financial support.

Yet there remains a critical question: Can any effort, any potential solution to the energy problem, succeed without a reordering of our institutions that deal with energy? Among the more than 60 federal agencies that have a hand in energy problems, none is truly responsible for coordinating policy or for directing research.

What is lacking in energy research and development is not only the financial commitment but also effective leadership. Outside the Atomic Energy Commission, which deals with a limited area, there exists nowhere in government today that critical mass of technical talent that we need to "make it happen." In order to guide a new thrust for energy research and development, we need a fully responsible new agency, adequately funded, and with a firm sense of commitment. There is no doubt that many promising technical options for new clean energy sources, and for cleaning up existing sources, do exist. Some of them could be in operation by 1985, buying time to develop more options for the future.

Perhaps as a first step in providing overall leadership, a Council on Energy Policy at the White House level should be created to coordinate the work of numerous agencies and to reconcile their many conflicting views. Such an umbrella-type council would have to stand high in the pyramid of government, with its own independent staff, beholden to no one and promoting no specific fuel, technology, or industry. Whatever the direction of a new national energy policy, institutional reform will be a key to making it effective.

I believe we are going to see in the next few years a reconciliation in some of the conflicting goals that bedevil energy policy today. The environmental movement, which has sometimes seemed so stiff-necked to exasperated critics, has, after all, educated us. More than anywhere else, it has been a jolt for the energy industry, whose devotion to growth has helped build the very country in which we can afford to ask such questions. When most of us were hungry we didn't have either the time or the strength to ask them. Yet now we are being asked to shift gears and put environmental protection ahead of maximum production. It is a hard question to address, let alone answer. But I believe we are all learning together that careful husbandry of the earth is the first essential for man's survival.

I

ENERGY
REQUIREMENTS

1

World Requirements*

Joel Darmstadter

The contribution to civilization made by heat, light, and power—and hence the primary energy resources on which they are based—is undeniable. Of course, there are many countries low on the international income scale that are rich in energy resources, while others almost totally lacking such resources are among the most prosperous. These countries have managed to bridge their natural deficiencies with imports. The significant fact is that energy consumption and overall economic development have gone hand in hand. The higher a nation's gross national product (GNP), the higher in general is its energy consumption, in close even if not proportionate conformity. Some amount of electric generating capacity is obviously required in order to support a modern industrialized economy, or one on the move toward it. This input of energy may at first take the form of an increase in motorized capital equipment, endowing each worker with more power with which to increase his productivity. Then, advancing living standards will create new wants, the fulfillment of which is made possible only by more fuels and more power—the private passenger car, heating and air conditioning, numerous household appliances, and air travel are a few examples.

I want to focus first on world energy trends roughly over the last four decades, a period for which comparable national statistics are now available; I will then cite some projections of future world needs up to the year 2000 and say something about the adequacy of energy reserves and resources to meet these needs. Energy, as I have measured it, is made up of the following primary sources: solid fuels (bituminous coal, anthracite, lignite, and certain minor fuels, including peat); liquid fuels (crude oil and natural gas liquids); natural gas and hydroelectricity. Nuclear energy, even in recent years, has still been an insignificant source of commercial power before 1968. The various energy sources have been made statistically comparable by converting them to common units based on their respective calorific values.

---

* These remarks have been adapted from more extensive treatment in References 1, 2, 3.

3

PAST TRENDS

World-wide energy consumption more than quadrupled between 1925 and the late 1960s, as Table 1 indicates. During that period, annual growth rates of energy consumption greatly exceeded the growth of population in every region of the world. The increases occurred everywhere, although differences between the regions in per capita consumption have remained strikingly wide—a point conveyed by Tables 2 and 3.

Table 1
World Energy Consumption and Population
(selected years, 1925–1968)

Year	Total Energy Consumption (trillion BTU)	Population (million)	Energy Consumption per Capita (million BTU)
1925	44,249	1,890.1	23.4
1950	76,823	2,504.5	30.7
1955	99,658	2,725.6	36.6
1960	124,046	2,989.9	41.5
1965	160,722	3,281.2	49.0
1968	189,737	3,484.5	54.5

Average Annual Percentage Rates of Change

	Energy Consumption	
	Total	Per Capita
1925–50	2.2	1.1
1950–60	4.9	3.1
1960–68	5.5	3.5
1925–68	3.4	2.0

Source: Reference 3.

In addition to these quantitative changes, there was a marked shift in the role of the various fuels. The early preeminence of the British iron and steel industry, indeed the character of the Industrial Revolution as a whole, was closely tied to coal. Early industry in the United States made significant use of falling water. Subsequently the development and distribution of electricity as a commercial energy form revolutionized the organization of the factory system. Alongside there has been the pervasive influence of the "automotive age" whose emergence has proceeded hand in hand with the growth of the world's petroleum industry. Atomic fission, though quantitatively still insignificant, may well turn out to be responsible for the major shifts in energy sources during the last quarter of this century, after which fusion may perhaps become a practical energy source.

The major transformation in energy sources so far in this century, then, has been the marked long-term decline of solid fuels, concurrent with the rising importance of oil and natural gas. Although each of the energy sources increased

Table 2
World Energy Consumption and Population, by Major Regions, 1950, 1960, 1968

Region	1950			1960			1968		
	Total Consumption (trillion BTU)	Population (million)	Consumption per Capita (million BTU)	Total Consumption (trillion BTU)	Population (million)	Consumption per Capita (million BTU)	Total Consumption (trillion BTU)	Population (million)	Consumption per Capita (million BTU)
North America	36,860	166.1	221.9	48,701	198.7	245.1	68,594	222.0	309.9
Canada	2,707	13.7	197.6	3,885	17.9	217.0	6,162	20.8	296.3
United States	34,153	152.3	224.3	44,816	180.7	248.0	62,432	201.2	310.3
Western Europe	17,483	302.4	57.8	26,066	326.5	79.8	41,584	350.6	118.6
Oceania	890	12.2	73.0	1,398	15.4	90.8	2,240	18.3	122.4
Latin America	2,397	161.9	14.8	4,939	212.4	23.3	8,034	267.4	30.0
Asia (excl. Communist)	3,804	805.4	4.7	8,228	970.6	8.5	16,757	1,182.7	14.2
Japan	1,739	82.9	21.0	3,672	93.2	39.4	8,691	101.1	86.0
Other Asia	2,063	722.5	2.9	4,556	877.4	5.2	8,066	1,081.6	7.5
Africa	1,297	217.0	6.0	2,162	276.0	7.8	3,343	336.5	9.9
U.S.S.R. & Com. East Europe	12,842	269.8	47.6	25,973	312.9	83.0	39,843	341.9	116.5
U.S.S.R.	8,427	180.0	46.8	17,898	214.4	83.5	28,628	237.8	120.4
Eastern Europe	4,414	89.7	49.2	8,075	98.5	82.0	11,215	104.1	107.7
Communist Asia	1,250	569.8	2.2	6,579	677.5	9.7	9,342	765.2	12.2
World	76,823	2,504.5	30.7	124,046	2,989.9	41.5	189,737	3,484.5	54.5

Source: Reference 3.

Table 3
World Energy Consumption and Population, by Major Region, Percentage Distribution, 1950, 1960, 1968, and Average Annual Percentage Rates of Change, 1960–1968

Region	Percentage Distribution						Average Annual Percentage Rates of Change, 1960–1968		
	1950		1960		1968				
	Energy Consumption	Population	Energy Consumption	Population	Energy Consumption	Population	Energy Consumption	Population	Energy Consumption per Capita
North America	48.0	6.6	39.3	6.6	36.2	6.4	4.4	1.4	2.9
Canada	3.5	0.5	3.1	0.6	3.2	0.6	5.9	1.9	4.0
United States	44.5	6.1	36.1	6.0	32.9	5.8	4.2	1.3	2.8
Western Europe	22.8	12.1	21.0	10.9	21.9	10.1	6.0	0.9	5.1
Oceania	1.2	0.5	1.1	0.5	1.2	0.5	6.1	2.2	3.8
Latin America	3.1	6.5	4.0	7.1	4.2	7.7	6.3	2.9	3.2
Asia (excl. Communist)	5.0	32.2	6.6	32.5	8.8	33.9	9.3	2.5	6.6
Japan	2.3	3.3	3.0	3.1	4.6	2.9	11.4	1.0	10.3
Other Asia	2.7	28.9	3.7	29.4	4.3	31.0	7.4	2.7	4.7
Africa	1.7	8.7	1.7	9.2	1.8	9.7	5.6	2.5	3.0
U.S.S.R. and Com. East Europe	16.7	10.8	20.9	10.5	21.0	9.8	5.5	1.1	4.3
U.S.S.R.	11.0	7.2	14.4	7.2	15.1	6.8	6.1	1.3	4.7
Eastern Europe	5.7	3.6	6.5	3.3	5.9	3.0	4.2	0.7	3.5
Communist Asia	1.6	22.8	5.3	22.7	4.9	22.0	4.5	1.5	2.9
World	100.0	100.0	100.0	100.0	100.0	100.0	5.5	1.9	3.5

Source: Calculated from figures in Table 2.

absolutely between 1925 and 1968, their respective shares of energy consumed changed markedly. By 1968, liquid fuels accounted for 43% of world energy consumption, compared with 13% in 1925. The natural gas share went up from 3% to 18%. Hydropower rose as fast as oil, but with a 2% share of world energy consumed in 1968, it remains a minor factor in a global context. Virtually every part of the world reduced the proportion of coal in its energy balance while increasing the share of liquids, natural gas, and hydropower. Post-World War II trends appear in Table 4.

World crude oil supplies were boosted by major new supply sources. Six of the world's ten leading oil-producing countries in 1968 had virtually no recorded output in 1925. Many of the bigger Middle Eastern oil discoveries date only from the late 1930s, and those in the North African fields are still more recent. Although a few countries (principally the United States, Venezuela, and the Soviet Union) were prominent before World War II in global oil production and trade, it was only after the war, when the pervasive impact of oil surging from the newer oil fields in the Middle East was felt, that old patterns began to change. With respect to natural gas, enormous expansion of output took place in North America and in the Soviet Union, much of it occurring after World War II. Western Europe's onshore and offshore natural gas production did not get started until the late 1960s—and only now are the North Sea hydrocarbon resources being tapped.

The growing abundance of oil and natural gas presented energy users with fuels having a number of highly desirable properties. A ton of oil combined the dual virtue of possessing less volume than a ton of coal while yielding 50% more energy, so transportation costs fell substantially below those of coal. As a liquid, oil could be conveniently handled in loading, unloading, and storage, and it was far less subject to damage in transit than coal. It burned more cleanly and in a more controllable fashion than coal. In numerous applications its thermal efficiency was higher. Many of the desirable features of oil appear as well, and sometimes better, in natural gas: cleanliness, ease of use, and high calorific value to volume. With fewer polluting features than coal or oil, gas promises to offer even greater advantages in the future.

The rapid extension of oil and gas pipeline networks with progressively larger diameters and the ever-increasing size of tankers culminating in the arrival of the supertanker of several hundred thousand tons capacity are part of the energy story. The overland cost of transport for coal is the highest per ton-mile, and this disadvantage has grown as the pipeline costs for oil and gas have decreased markedly from their prewar levels. Ocean transport costs are more favorable for oil and coal by a wide margin.

REGIONAL SHIFTS

The declining world role of coal and the growing importance of petroleum has been accompanied by dramatic changes in the geographic distribution of world energy output and in regional energy supply-demand balances.

Table 4
World Energy Consumption, by Source and Major Region, 1950 and 1968

	1950					1968				
	Coal[a]	Oil[b]	Natural Gas	Hydro[c]	Total	Coal[a]	Oil[b]	Natural Gas	Hydro and Nuclear[c]	Total
				(trillion BTU)						
North America	14,013	14,264	6,226	2,357	36,860	13,968	29,734	21,032	3,860	68,594
Canada	1,100	775	76	756	2,707	639	2,682	1,468	1,373	6,162
United States	12,913	13,489	6,150	1,601	34,153	13,329	27,052	19,564	2,487	62,432
Western Europe	13,533	2,506	49	1,395	17,483	13,541	21,535	1,566	4,942	41,584
Oceania	581	243	0	66	890	958	1,086	0	196	2,240
Latin America	235	1,747	199	216	2,397	414	5,501	1,475	644	8,034
Asia (excl. Communist)	2,026	1,084	52	642	3,804	4,475	10,428	714	1,140	16,757
Japan	1,076	87	3	573	1,739	2,259	5,615	88	729	8,691
Other Asia	950	996	49	68	2,063	2,216	4,813	626	411	8,066
Africa	797	478	0	22	1,297	1,531	1,583	46	183	3,343
U.S.S.R. and Communist Eastern Europe	10,453	1,870	298	221	12,842	20,840	10,876	6,977	1,150	39,843
U.S.S.R.	6,369	1,660	207	191	8,427	12,294	9,167	6,140	1,027	28,628
Eastern Europe	4,084	210	87	33	4,414	8,546	1,709	837	123	11,215
Communist Asia	1,160	11	0	79	1,250	8,443	669	–	230	9,342
World	42,798	22,203	6,824	4,998	76,823	64,170	81,412	31,810	12,345	189,737

(percent of each region's total energy consumption)

North America	38.0	38.7	16.7	6.4	100.0	20.4	43.3	30.7	5.6	100.0
Canada	40.6	28.6	2.8	27.9	100.0	10.4	43.5	23.8	22.3	100.0
United States	37.8	39.5	18.0	4.7	100.0	21.3	43.3	31.3	4.0	100.0
Western Europe	77.4	14.3	0.3	8.0	100.0	32.6	51.8	3.8	11.9	100.0
Oceania	65.3	27.3	0	7.4	100.0	42.8	48.5	0	8.7	100.0
Latin America	9.8	72.9	8.3	9.0	100.0	5.2	68.5	18.4	8.0	100.0
Asia (excl. Communist)	53.3	28.5	1.4	16.9	100.0	26.7	62.2	4.3	6.8	100.0
Japan	61.9	5.0	0.2	32.9	100.0	26.0	64.6	1.0	8.4	100.0
Other Asia	46.0	48.3	2.4	3.3	100.0	27.5	59.7	7.8	5.1	100.0
Africa	61.4	36.9	0	1.7	100.0	45.8	47.4	1.4	5.5	100.0
U.S.S.R. and Communist										
Eastern Europe	81.4	14.6	2.3	1.7	100.0	52.3	27.3	17.5	2.9	100.0
U.S.S.R.	75.6	19.7	2.5	2.3	100.0	42.9	32.0	21.4	3.6	100.0
Eastern Europe	92.5	4.8	2.0	0.7	100.0	76.2	15.2	7.5	1.1	100.0
Communist Asia	92.8	0.9	0	6.3	100.0	90.4	7.2	—	2.5	100.0
World	55.7	28.9	8.9	6.5	100.0	33.8	42.9	16.8	6.5	100.0

Source: Reference 2.

Note: Dashes indicate "not available."

[a] Principally bituminous coal, but also includes anthracite, a variety of low-quality coals, and lignite.

[b] Including, where known, natural gas liquids.

[c] Also includes small quantities of geothermal electricity. The nuclear portion of this column for 1968 was (in trillion BTU): Canada, 8; United States, 130; Western Europe, 355; Japan, 11; Eastern Europe, less than 0.5 trillion; and U.S.S.R., unavailable. This column also includes net regional imports of electricity.

Regional shares of world energy output have shifted markedly away from the advanced parts of the non-Communist world to the newer oil-producing regions in the Middle East and Africa, which today account for a preeminent share of the world's petroleum reserves. North America, Western Europe, Oceania, and Japan accounted for nearly 90% of world energy production in 1925; by 1967 their share had dropped by nearly one half—a decline largely associated with the stagnation of coal mining in these regions.

It is striking how, in 1925, virtually all the major regions of the world met practically all energy needs from indigenous supplies. Four decades later, marked regional imbalances had appeared—notably in Western Europe, which by then imported 54% of the energy it consumed. The Far East had also evolved into another energy-deficit region, with Japan, in particular, experiencing a drastic long-term change in its energy position. The Communist group remained self-sufficient, at least partly as a consequence of autarkic policies. Latin America and the Middle East had become major suppliers. The United States, long a net exporter of, or self-sufficient in, energy, now faces the prospect of becoming significantly dependent on foreign supplies for at least some years into the future.

Table 5
Net Energy Imports or Exports in Relation
to Consumption or Production, by Region,
1925 and 1967
(percent of net imports in energy
consumption or net exports (–) in
production)

	1925	1967
North America	−0.6%	7.2%
Of which: United States	−3.1	7.2
Western Europe	2.0	60.8
Oceania	7.4	39.9
U.S.S.R. and Com. East. Europe	−12.5	−7.5
U.S.S.R.	−6.1	−11.7
Eastern Europe	−15.2	5.0
Communist Asia	6.8	−0.1
Latin America	−27.3	−45.3
Caribbean	−55.9	−61.4
Other Latin America	60.3	31.4
Asia	−5.7	−45.8
Middle East	−64.9	−87.8
Japan	...	80.4
Other Asia	3.4	18.1
Africa	28.5	−61.3

Source: Data derived from Table 13, Reference 1.

These trends in regional energy balances, summarized in Table 5, were accompanied by vast increases in world energy trade. In 1925, about 14% of the primary energy consumed had crossed foreign borders; by 1968, the proportion was up to 33%. For the interval for which comparable data exist, 1929 through 1965, world energy consumption increased at the average annual rate of 3.2%, while interregional trade among the principal areas of the world went up by over 6%.

In looking at the directional pattern of world energy flows that has emerged in fulfilling this web of interdependence, it is good to keep in mind the resulting geopolitical issues. This new dependency has produced in numerous fuel-deficient countries anxiety about the reliability and adequacy of their sources of energy supplies, while for major producing areas, such as the Middle East, North Africa, and the Caribbean, the assurances of stable and growing markets are a critical element in their aspirations for economic development. In view of recurrent political crises in the Middle East, as well as an almost chronic uncertainty over contractual relationships between host-country governments and the concessionary international oil companies, such considerations have assumed heightened importance in the last couple of years.

The most significant of these interdependencies is that of Western Europe and the Arab countries (along with Iran). In recent years Western Europe's imports of Middle Eastern and North African oil contributed to over 40% of the world oil flows, around 80% of West European oil imports, and 50% of Western Europe's *overall* energy requirements (i.e., oil, gas, coal, hydro, nuclear). The Middle East has figured significantly in West European energy imports for the greater part of the post-World War II period; the rapidly expanding role of North Africa, particularly Libya, dates only from the past decade. The paramount reliance of the Far East (chiefly Japan) on Middle East energy imports is also notable. United States imports of oil are beginning to approach 30% of domestic consumption—most of it still originating in Canada and Venezuela. But the share of the Middle East and other Eastern Hemisphere areas seems bound to rise above recent shares of 10% or so.

FUTURE PROSPECTS

What are the prospects for world energy demand and supply during the remainder of the 20th century? And in what ways will world needs be satisfied? Table 6, which is based on estimates by United Nations experts and others, summarizes some key projections.

Total world energy needs are bound to increase and will rise much more rapidly than the world's population, even assuming an almost inevitable escalation of real energy costs. World-wide population growth may hover around 2% a year, with energy consumption growing at between 5% and 6% during the next decade, followed perhaps by a gradually dampened growth rate thereafter. I have made no attempt to project the geographic distribution of world energy consumption all the way to the end of the century. However, during the next decade, I would anticipate declining shares going to the United States, Canada, and Western Europe; increasing shares going to Latin America, Asia, and Africa; and little change in the shares going to the Soviet Union and Eastern Europe.

Table 6
World Energy Consumption, Electricity Consumption, and Population:
Projections of Selected Data, 1968, 1980, 2000

	Unit	1968		1980		2000	
Energy consumption							
Coal	Percent and trillion BTU	33.8%	64,170	20.0%	68,931	12.0%	99,745
Oil	Percent and trillion BTU	42.9	81,412	48.6	167,637	44.1	366,284
Natural gas	Percent and trillion BTU	16.8	31,810	19.5	67,208	18.0	149,618
Hydro	Percent and trillion BTU	6.2	11,841	5.7	19,624	5.3	43,830
Nuclear	Percent and trillion BTU	0.3	504	6.2	21,257	20.7	171,732
Total	Percent and trillion BTU	100.0	189,737	100.0	344,657	100.0	831,209
Population	Million		3,484.5		4,419.0		6,439.0
Energy consumption per capita	Million BTU		54.5		78.0		129.1
Electric generating capacity	Mw		972,291		2,188,000		7,749,000
Of which: nuclear	Percent and Mw	1.2%	12,040	15.1%	330,000	41.1%	3,183,000
Electric generation	Billion kw-hr		4,203.8		9,901.2		37,605.4
Of which: nuclear	Percent and billion kw-hr	1.2%	49.9	20.5%	2,024.9	51.9%	19,515.0
Electric generation per capita	kw-hr		1,207		2,238		5,840
Resource input equivalent of electric generation	Trillion BTU		42,463		99,217		325,971
Share of energy consumption	Percent		22.4%		28.8%		39.2%

Source: Reference 2.

Future needs of the developing countries are bound to be large. Their high population growth rates, combined with the increasing energy requirements of their industrial advancement, will enormously increase world-wide energy demands. In Puerto Rico, for example, the shift between 1940 and 1970 from an agricultural, sugar-based economy to a relatively advanced industrial area was accompanied by an 18-fold increase in annual per capita electricity consumption—a rise from 100 kilowatt hours (kw-hr) to 1,800 kw-hr per person per year. The per capita gap among the regions, however, will certainly remain wide.

The most dramatic source of new energy will be nuclear, which is estimated to rise from a mere 0.2% worldwide in 1968 to maybe 10% in 1980, and over 27% by the year 2000. This is a conservative version of an International Atomic Energy Agency (IAEA) forecast, and it rests a good deal more on informed speculation and faith than on firmly anchored judgments. The IAEA's underlying assumption is that "nuclear power will dominate the market for new power plants in advanced countries by 1980 and almost everywhere by 1990."

Oil and gas are both projected to increase their shares of world energy consumption, at an average annual rate of about 6% between now and 1980. The potential market for automobile transport outside the United States remains huge, especially in the developing areas. The attractiveness of natural gas as a "clean" energy source—coupled with the growth of new supplies in such disparate areas as Algeria, Siberia, the North Sea, and Australia—and the feasibility (only now beginning to be realized) of transporting liquefied natural gas by specially designed tankers, with subsequent reformation to the gaseous state, points to a growing market. Beyond 1980, oil and gas are likely to have slightly falling shares of total energy consumption, since it is assumed nuclear power will have taken a strong hold by then. Nevertheless, both oil and gas may be expected to record significant growth in absolute terms in the closing decades of the century.

Coal's projected declining share may be cushioned by large-scale conversion of coal to pipeline gas and gasoline, a development whose technological feasibility has been demonstrated but whose economics remain in doubt. Estimates by the U.N. Economic Commission for Europe indicate a particularly sharp fall for coal during the next decade—from one third of world energy consumption in 1968 to one fifth by 1980. Beyond that date, the decline will be slowed, and, in fact, coal may revert to a phase of reasonable absolute growth because, to some extent, it is irreplaceable. For example, steelmaking will probably be an important market for coal for years to come, and, as mentioned, new uses might well develop.

THE ENVIRONMENT AND RESOURCE ADEQUACY

In any discussion of future world energy needs, environmental factors must be given serious consideration. Since that topic will be dealt with by others at this conference, I will be sparing in my comments. The world may well contain 6,500 million people by the year 2000. It will be a world that may consume about 4.5 times its present level of basic energy, may register an eightfold rise in total electric generating capacity, and may be compelled to handle the traffic of over 1,000 million automobiles. Such demands raise sober questions about the assimilative capacity of the earth's water, land, atmosphere, and other fixed, or at least relatively inelastic, endowments to cope with the environmental consequences resulting from such an expansion of energy demand. Thus, scientists are beginning to address the question of how fossil fuel combustion, through release of carbon dioxide, and how nonsolar energy utilization, in general, may, through heat emission, alter the earth's climate. The management of nuclear fuels and radioactive wastes is another obviously critical issue.

Will human institutions evolve the necessary flexibility to deal with these problems? Our ability to cope with many other environmental problems, such as waste disposal, may actually hinge to an increasing extent on the use of energy—which only makes the question more complex and paradoxical. Yet it is a sign of the progress that has occurred within the last few years that such questions are now being addressed. This recognition means that, henceforth, man's harnessing and use of energy resources must not be judged merely in the terms of their contributions to higher real incomes for increasing populations as has traditionally been the case. It must also be shown that the environmental consequences of energy use can be managed within socially defined tolerances.

There is, finally, the question of how these prospective levels of energy demand match up against the world's known stock of energy resources. It is at this juncture of a presentation such as mine today that one might normally be expected to produce graphic evidence that current, not to mention future, rates of energy utilization represent unsustainable claims vis-à-vis known reserves of the primary energy sources—oil, gas, coal, nuclear raw materials. Thus, the fact that world proved oil reserves are estimated at about equal to "only" a 35-year supply at current rates of production seems like ample evidence of oncoming world energy stringency. And even were the statistics more promising, there is the inescapable ultimate constraint of the nonrenewable nature of mineral fuels. Let me, in short order, check off some points bearing on this question—without, however, trying even remotely to come to grips with the enormous complexity of the underlying issues.

First, at a given point in time, the greatest certainty in resource appraisal applies to what in the case of petroleum, for example, is called "proved-up reserves"—that is, a stock of energy resources which can reasonably be assumed recoverable from known reservoirs under current economic and technological circumstances, and which producers have been induced to develop as a result of their calculations of changing market prospects and in response to specific commercial needs. The proved reserve concept is virtually useless for an analysis of the long-term adequacy of resources, since even in well-defined regions proved reserve figures do not begin to exhaust resources; on a world scale, oil and gas reserves have tended to more than keep up with production even though that has not been true in the case of the United States in recent years.

The second point, therefore, is that as one progressively relaxes both the economic and technological assumptions (for example, in the case of petroleum, to include an allowance for higher-cost marginal deposits or to allow for new recovery techniques), as well as assumptions about the degree of certainty (so as to allow for still undiscovered resources), far higher estimates of total resources of "ultimate probable reserves" can be derived.

These somewhat abstract formulations can be brought down to reality by citing a couple of concrete cases illustrating the economic and technological context for resource development. The technology for extracting the liquid energy content of U.S. oil shale deposits and Canadian tar sands is well enough established so that, with an appropriate rise in the price of crude oil above levels now prevailing, both of these essentially "new" and vast energy resources could come into production on a significant scale, provided their environmental consequences could be managed.

On the other hand, extensive coal deposits require further technological advances in liquefaction, gasification, desulfurization (pre- or post-combustion) processes before those could figure reliably in conjecture about future availability of energy resources.

As for the reserves of nuclear fuels, the adequacy of fissionable raw materials is not likely to be a critical factor. Probably more important than the known magnitudes of economically recoverable reserves of uranium (or thorium) ores will be the development of conversion technology for advanced reactors, including the likely development of breeders as one looks several decades or more into the future. The latter achievement would reduce the problem of nuclear raw materials to insignificance for a long time to come, since it enhances raw materials use by a factor of 50 or more compared to nonbreeder systems.

If (looking still further ahead) we assume that nuclear fusion can be controlled to produce power economically, the availability of the required resources (deuterium and lithium) appears to be still more staggering; alternately, or perhaps additionally, solar energy for power production looms as still another possibility for the long-run future. The possible realization of such opportunities clearly demands varying degrees of government-supported research and development activity. The time horizons are too distant, the proprietary payoffs too uncertain, the investment sums too vast for private sector institutions to assume most or all of the burden.

This cautiously optimistic assessment of the world's capacity to meet its growing energy requirements should not obscure the fact that there is continuing—perhaps increasing—concern with the specter of absolute physical exhaustion of world energy resources, even if that point is centuries removed from our own vantage point. It would be cavalier and presumptuous—indeed, ignorant of the laws of nature—to try to allay that fear: the growth of economic activity and its associated utilization of energy cannot be maintained forever. Man's scientific capabilities can at best postpone the consequences of such growth. But, as a colleague of mine recently expressed it: ". . . knowledge that growth must eventually cease is of no practical consequence by itself. The relevant question is *when?* It makes an enormous difference for policy today whether the 'we' who must limit growth is mankind alive today or some far-off future generation."[4] This raises the appallingly difficult issue of the intergenerational transfers of resources and their benefits and costs—a subject which is really central to much of the current debate over growth and equity, environment, and raw materials depletion.

In the meantime, and closer to the immediate subject of this paper, the technology and the economic cost of exploiting various energy resources, and the environmental constraints governing their production and use, will pose significant questions in the years ahead.

Another matter, not emphasized by the global perspective in which we have framed our discussion, is the uncertain prospect for particular fuel-deficit regions of the world. Because of spotty geographical occurrence, particularly of oil, the world aggregates I have been referring to cannot be expected to relieve the concern of regions whose satisfaction of fuel and power needs may be dependent on what are judged undependable supplying regions, or whose dependence on energy sources from abroad may impose severe foreign exchange burdens. Indeed, these very uncertainties may in themselves prompt energy-deficit areas to engage in the search for fuel deposits and new ways in meeting their energy needs, and this could, in unforeseen ways, alter the world's energy resource picture as it appears today.

References

1. Darmstadter J, et al: *Energy in the World Economy*. Baltimore, Johns Hopkins University Press, 1972.

2. Schurr SH (ed): *Energy, Economic Growth, and The Environment*. Baltimore, Johns Hopkins University Press, 1972.

3. Ridker RG (ed): *Population, Resources, and The Environment*, Vol. 3 of *Research Reports of The Commission on Population Growth and The American Future*. Government Printing Office, Washington, DC, 1972.

4. Ridker RG: *Must We Limit Economic Growth*. American Association for Advanced Science Symposium, Washington, DC, 1972.

2

United States Requirements

Daniel B. Luten, Ph.D.

With respect to the energy requirements of the United States, the first reality we must face is that the costs of energy, which have diminished throughout our lifetimes and also, I should think, through those of our immediate ancestors, are destined to increase throughout the lives of our children. This is one of our legacies to them. A corollary can be phrased rhetorically by asking: How much energy will Americans buy as its price rises? Inklings of the answer to this are beginning to appear.

A second reality is to forget the myths of "energy as the ultimate resource," of the "unlimited energy" that will let us recover everything we need from the earth despite the progressive depletion of its riches. This is the economists' myth, shyly assented to by the technologist, that technology's capabilities will increase faster than resources are depleted and that, accordingly, the product of waxing technology times waning resources will never cease to grow. And so they say, "Everything will come out all right; follow me as sheep and I, the good shepherd, will lead you into green pastures, and you shall not want." But what if they be false prophets? What if, having followed the pied piper, there be no salvation? Who is to pay? Has anyone posted bond? No. In fact, you are on your own and will have to make up your own minds.

(Looking back on that delightful paragraph, I can reflect that about the only privilege a generalist is granted in this society of specialists is to mix metaphors in a manner to outrage scholars!)

Technology, in fact, will not continue to expand as it has during this century. If the growth of the postwar production rate of scientists and technologists were to continue, by the end of the century, I am told, all of the children of this society would have to become scientists and technologists.

BACKGROUND

Let me begin with a little history of American energy practices, magnitudes, and trends. First, we have the matter of units. In energy discussions a decade ago you heard from "coal-equivalent" men, "BTU" men, "millions of

17

barrels per day" men, "millions of tons per year" men. Now, you hear from "kw-hr" men, "kw" men, and a few more. Presently, "joules" will be the word. And we have all heard of calories, large or small. Everyone says we must go metric, and I suppose we must. But do not imagine this will help much. Diverse manifestations of energy are truly incommensurable and cannot be entirely reconciled simply by a better choice of units (Fig. 1).

Worse, all of the numbers are so huge that everyone, except engineers in their detailed proposals, slips a decimal place—or two or three—now and again. The first task is to reduce the numbers to magnitudes where one has a chance to cope with them. Palmer Putnam, 20 years ago, defined a new and huge unit suitable for national and world energy economies. He called it Q and set it at 10^{18} BTU.[1] One BTU, a British Thermal Unit, is the heat required to warm a pound of water through one degree Fahrenheit. Q, a quintillion BTU, is ten times the world's energy use in 1950, five times it in 1970. That is, mankind's present energy use is 0.2 Q or, we might say, 200 milliQ. A supplementary and very helpful device is to reduce national energy use to a per capita and a per day basis. The numbers are still large but are more manageable. We will use both in this chapter.

Next, take a passing look at our uses of energy. We need it for only two purposes, warmth and work. We use heat for space heating and process heating; to keep our houses warm; to cook; to refine oil; to run blast furnaces, smelters, kilns, and many more processes in our industries. We convert a portion of it to work in our power plants. In contrast, we use work to lift, to move, to pump, to transport, to fabricate, to shape, to mill, to grind. We use it in our homes to run electric motors, which pump heat out of our refrigerators and out of our houses, which move heat from our furnaces into the rooms we wish warmed, and we convert it to light so that we may see. We use it in electric motors in industry to run elevators and grinders and presses and pumps. We use it in electrochemical processes to reduce alumina to aluminum. Electricity is work. We also convert heat to work in gasoline and diesel engines and use it to overcome friction and inertia and to transport things. So, we have, broadly speaking, domestic and personal consumption on the one hand and industrial and commercial consumption on the other. Each of these is divided into warmth and work but the work, for convenience, is divided again into electricity and transport.

One more preliminary item: In our management of energy, we must deal with seven unit operations, not always in the same sequence, not always entirely evident, but pretty much so. These operations are discovery of a resource, harvest, transport, storage, conversion, use, and disposal. Most of our energy resource is discovered as latent chemical energy, the energy that can be converted to heat by burning. Discovery comprises drilling an oil well in the right place. There is also latent nuclear energy, the energy that can be converted to heat in a nuclear pile. Another portion we discover in the form of potential energy when we appreciate the possibility of harnessing a waterfall. We harvest energy by mining coal, by running water through a turbine. We transport it in

Figure 1
Order of Magnitude and Conversion Chart

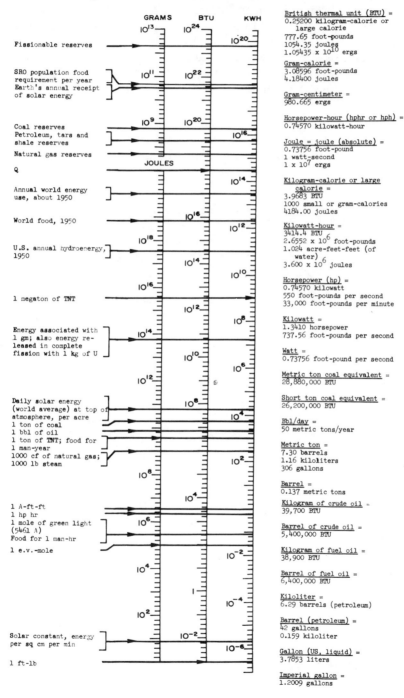

British thermal unit (BTU) =
0.25200 kilogram-calorie or
large calorie
777.65 foot-pounds
1054.35 joules
1.05435×10^{10} ergs

Gram-calorie =
3.08596 foot-pounds
4.18400 joules

Gram-centimeter =
980.665 ergs

Horsepower-hour (hphr or hph) =
0.74570 kilowatt-hour

Joule = joule (absolute) =
0.73756 foot-pound
1 watt-second
1×10^{7} ergs

Kilogram-calorie or large
calorie =
3.9683 BTU
1000 small or gram-calories
4184.00 joules

Kilowatt-hour =
3414.4 BTU
2.6552×10^{6} foot-pounds
1.024 acre-feet-feet (of
water)
3.600×10^{6} joules

Horsepower (hp) =
0.74570 kilowatt
550 foot-pounds per second
33,000 foot-pounds per minute

Kilowatt =
1.3410 horsepower
737.56 foot-pounds per second

Watt =
0.73756 foot-pound per second

Metric ton coal equivalent =
28,880,000 BTU

Short ton coal equivalent =
26,200,000 BTU

Bbl/day =
50 metric tons/year

Metric ton =
7.30 barrels
1.16 kiloliters
306 gallons

Barrel =
0.137 metric tons

Kilogram of crude oil =
39,700 BTU

Barrel of crude oil =
5,400,000 BTU

Kilogram of fuel oil =
38,900 BTU

Barrel of fuel oil =
6,400,000 BTU

Kiloliter =
6.29 barrels (petroleum)

Barrel (petroleum) =
42 gallons
0.159 kiloliter

Gallon (US, liquid) =
3.7853 liters

Imperial gallon =
1.2009 gallons

20

coal trains, power lines, pipelines, tankers. We store it in reservoirs, in oil tanks, in liquefied natural gas tanks and, with plutonium, in safes. We rarely find it in the form we wish it to be in, and so we must convert it: from latent chemical energy to heat in a fire, thence to electricity in a power plant, thence from work to light in a light bulb (Fig. 2). Often discovery is really the discovery of a conversion process. A pile of wood is cold comfort until one knows how to start a fire. Uranium was cold comfort until Fermi's first pile, on the University of Chicago campus, just a generation ago.

Figure 2
Conversions Among Five Basic Manifestations of Energy

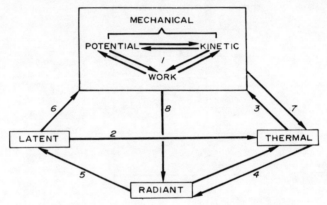

1. Pendulum, flywheel, electrical generator
2. Fire, nuclear pile, respiration
3. Heat engine: power plant, gasoline engine
4. Radiation behaviour
5. Photosynthesis
6. Muscle, battery
7. Friction, electric heater, brake
8. Electric light

Disposal, disposal of anything, hardly bothered us until recently. We simply threw away what we were through with. After all, it was a big empty world and probably infinite; trash would never be a problem. In most cases, heat disposal is still adventitious and accidental. We trap it in our houses and then it leaks out. Only in our power plants, which convert a third of the latent heat transported into them into electricity, must we make systematic provision for the other two thirds which is rejected as heat. That gives rise to primary thermal pollution. Nonetheless, all of the energy we bring into our cities ends up warming the entire region, and that is a secondary thermal pollution.

Ultimately, all of this heat warms the entire earth and then is radiated from it. Fortunately, the earth can get rid of a lot of additional heat with little extra warming. Virtually the only energy resource that does not lead to such warming is solar energy and its derivatives: hydropower and wind power. Tidal power, although trivial, falls in the same class, so, perhaps, does geothermal power. These resources would be converted to heat, anyway; we have just detoured them to our advantage along an inevitable course.

WHERE WE ARE

Currently (1970), mankind's annual use of energy is about 0.2 Q. The United States, with 5.7% of the world's people, uses one third of its energy. If everyone were to come up to our level, that 0.2 Q would rise to about 1.15 Q. If, on the other hand, present use were uniformly divided, our share would be much less. Instead of our current 850,000 BTU/day/capita, we would have 150,000, about one sixth as much.

We obtain three fourths of our energy from petroleum (37%) and natural gas (38%) in almost equal shares, one fifth from coal (21%), and 4% from hydropower. Nuclear power and other contributors are still trivial.

We use one fourth of it to generate electricity. Of that, perhaps one third (9% of the total) is used in households and the balance in commercial and industrial establishments. Another one fourth is used for transportation, three fifths of it personal. The remaining one half is used for space and process heat, one sixth of the total in households, the balance in industry and commerce.

	Industry	Commerce	Household or Personal	Total
Electricity (input)	12	6	9	27
Transport		10	15	25
Heat	28	5	15	48
Total	40	21	39	100

Perhaps the most important point to make of this distribution is that about two fifths of our energy consumption is subject to our personal control: how we elect to heat and light our houses, what appliances we use, how far we drive our automobiles and in what fashion. Three fifths is determined indirectly by our other habits: whether we frequent brilliantly lighted stores and are drawn by electric advertising, how much we fly, whether we buy exotic or local products, how much we support industry by our purchases. But it is unrealistic to imagine that we have much short-term control over such matters other than in terms of our general affluence and total spending patterns.

That is the present state. How has it come about? How has it grown? Two patterns are clear: First, total energy growth has been dramatically small and has been at a remarkably steady rate of 2.7% per year since 1850 (Fig. 3). Until about 1900 it paralleled population growth. Then population growth slowed, but the energy continued. Its sources have changed. Until 1850, we had a fuelwood energy economy. After the Civil War, we began to change to coal and had about completed that when petroleum became important. Coal ceased to grow and oil, and then gas, carried the burden of growth (Fig. 4).

Figure 3
United States Total Energy Consumption and Population Growth

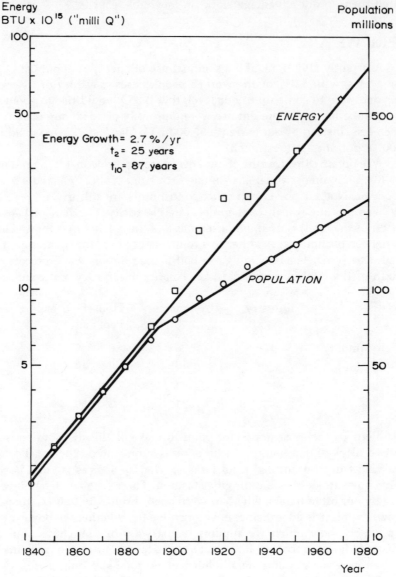

Energy
BTU x 10^{15} ("milli Q")

Population
millions

Energy Growth= 2.7 % / yr
t_2 = 25 years
t_{10}= 87 years

ENERGY

POPULATION

Year

That 2.7% per year was surprisingly small. Cogent reasons for it to be so small included a diminishing extravagance in the use of fuelwood as the forests of the Ohio Valley were cleared for agriculture and, to a lesser degree, the increasing efficiency of the steam engine. Growth was promoted by a growing population, an increasingly urban and industrial economy and, in this century, by the mechanization of all mobile activities, in part by internal com-

Figure 4
Sources of Energy in the United States

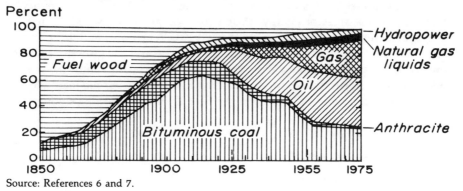

Source: References 6 and 7.

Figure 5
Growth Patterns of Fossil Fuels in the United States

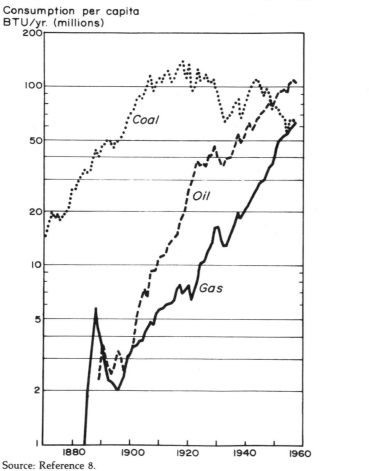

Source: Reference 8.

24

bustion engines and in part by electricity. Little vocational muscle remains in the American scene.

In contrast to this overall picture, a second pattern is the rapidity of growth of new sources of energy. When coal was replacing wood, its use increased at better than 8% per year (1870–1910). When automobiles came in, petroleum grew at 9% per year (1900–1925) (Fig. 5). And the growth of electric power was 8% per year almost from its first recording in 1902 until the present time. Surely, with such a record, it must continue (Fig. 6). As the man who fell off the skyscraper said while passing the fifth floor, "Everything's going fine, so far."

Figure 6
Growth of Consumption of Electricity in the United States

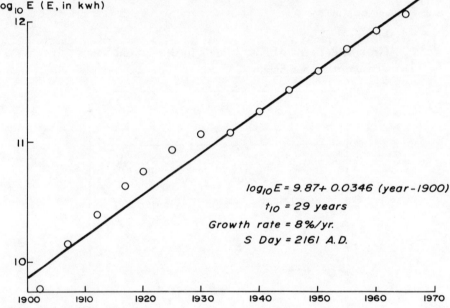

$$\log_{10} E = 9.87 + 0.0346 \; (year - 1900)$$
$$t_{10} = 29 \text{ years}$$
$$\text{Growth rate} = 8\%/yr.$$
$$\text{S Day} = 2161 \text{ A.D.}$$

Source: References 9 and 10.
Note: "S Day" is when the rate of human use of energy equals the energy received from the sun.

THE FUTURE

Until quite recently, the people of the industry, the growth economists, the growth engineers all talked as if the future were straightforward and clear, 8% growth per year for electric power, doubling every nine years, increasing tenfold every 30 years through the foreseeable future. It was, in fact, a most thoughtless, unreflective, and emotional attitude. Do not let anyone tell you American businessmen are cold-blooded keen thinkers. Instead, they are the most hot-blooded and emotional of our people. Is love of beauty, love of the landscape an emotion? What, then, is love of money? What is the insecurity that drives men to squirrel their money away—is it intellect or emotion?

Figure 7
Extrapolation of U.S. Energy Growth

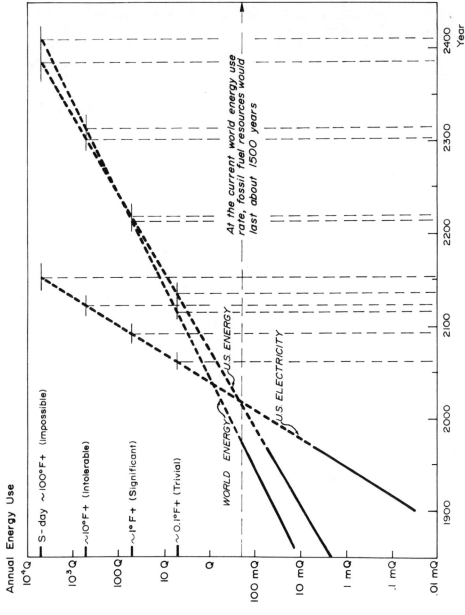

Note: At "S Day" the world would be about 100 F hotter than today and would be uninhabitable; accordingly, the condition is unrealizable. At one tenth the S-day energy use, the earth would still be 10 F hotter and much of it uninhabitable, an intolerable condition. Note how long it is before even trivial heating occurs and how quickly it worsens.

But in a finite world, growth must end. Twenty-five years of a growing literature (which itself must stop growing) has almost persuaded the American public that population growth must end. Now the argument has turned to economic growth—which also must end—and a part of the argument is that the energy economy's growth must end. The simplest, if least persuasive, argument was that continued growth, at present rates, of American electricity consumption would lead in less than two centuries to an outpouring of heat that would cook the entire earth (S Day, Fig. 7).

A second constraint has been argued by Hubbert over a period of 25 years.[2-4] He has by now almost convinced the fossil fuel industry that these resources are finite and that the probable pattern of consumption is one, first, of exponentially increasing use, then of a lesser growth to a maximum production at about half exhaustion of the resource, all followed by a decline in similar pattern. He has, for a number of years, forecast that American petroleum production would reach its ultimate peak at about 1970 (Fig. 8). As it looks now, he may have hit it just about on the nose. Unquestionably, we are well on our way to becoming one of the great have-not nations as far as petroleum is concerned.

Figure 8
Hubbert's 1949 Representation of the "Age of Fossil Fuels"

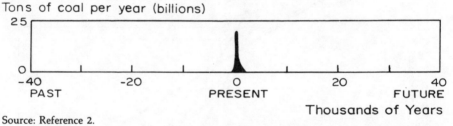

Source: Reference 2.

Finally, a third constraint is that if present growth patterns for electric power were to continue, we would find ourselves handing over entire paychecks for electric power. Somehow economic resistance will insure that no single activity dominates the entire economy.

These three constraints are inescapable. But what this debate has achieved thus far is barely an admission that the historical patterns of growth must end. We have not really come to the second stage of the argument: will this fearful condition arise in my lifetime or can I continue in my traditional growth patterns secure in the knowledge that not I but my children will have to cope with it? The third stage will be an appeal: can we in good conscience persist in our addiction to growth and then, having addicted our children, tell them in our wills to kick the habit? No. If we can foresee this problem, we must begin to attack it now. If mankind has any special talent, it is an extra degree of foresight, a more pervasive concern for the future, a willingness to work on problems, even those that will not be the death of us until tomorrow. The question, "My grandchildren, what have they ever done for me?" is a denial of humanity (Fig. 9).

Figure 9
Conceivable Alternatives in Consumption of the World's Fossil Fuel Resources

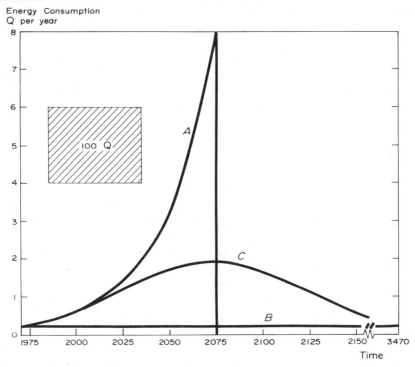

Energy Consumption
Q per year

A — At present world growth rate of about 3.5% per year it will all be gone in 105 years
B — At present consumption rates, it will all be gone in 1500 years
C — Under Hubbert's hypothesis, it will mostly be gone in 200 years

REQUIREMENTS AND NEED

For several decades now, most of us could not have cared less about energy costs. We built our houses with picture windows; we kept them at whatever temperature was the going pattern; when the architects told us insulation could not be justified we left it out. We bought electric appliances according to our capacity for monthly payments. We bought as much premium gasoline as our tanks would accept and went where we wished. With other expenses we might seek a bargain, but energy was a social expense dictated by location and social class. Some of us, yes, bought economy cars, but the industry learned how to compromise our targets. Some of us bought discount gasoline, but not many.

We believed the myths about not turning off fluorescent lamps, that leaving the furnace on overnight cost less than to warm a cold house in the morning. We were drawn to the bright lights, whether on theater marquees or in daylight-bright supermarkets. We subsidized and encouraged energy-extravagant truck transport over rail freight. We turned to the single-occupant car for urban transport. We destroyed rail passenger service in one brief decade and turned to the air and more energy, again, for interurban transport.

Does anyone remember the electric interurban cars of two generations ago? The Traction Terminal in Indianapolis had eight tracks each long enough to load four or five of those rambling electric cars, and spewed them out in all directions at the rate of dozens per hour. They used little energy. But you could not do that today. When you got to Lafayette, or Wabash, or South Bend, how would you get around? Walk? Automobiles have rebuilt our cities so that only with automobiles may they be occupied. We ask ourselves the whimsical question: Who's in charge, men or automobiles? Do cars go where men wish, or do men dutifully come forth in the morning to guide automobiles to their tidy mid-day conclaves? Recall Thoreau's, "For we are the tools of our tools."

But automobiles are not solely to blame. Look farther afield; look at new patterns of home ownership that made it possible for an ordinary guy to become attached to a house, and to the automobile that permitted him to keep the house despite changes in direction and distance of the journey to work. So, not merely Detroit, but the Federal Housing Authority is part of the energy crisis.

If anyone had suggested the resource was limited, we would have laughed. We knew it was infinite, just as we had known all along that all of this great new world was infinite. Some had carped, yes; some were Cassandras, conservationists even. They had told us back in the 1920s that we only had enough oil for ten years. They said it again in the forties, in the fifties. But each time we defiantly doubled our use, and still it came forth. They called wolf so many times—how could it ever end? Our entire world was built on cheap energy; it was the basic myth of America.

But it *is* ending; the world *is* changing. We *are* beginning to concede it to be finite. While we really do not know how big the resource is, Hubbert has told us clearly that, as long as we remain addicted to growth, resource magnitude makes little difference. We have also heard it, clear and explicit, in the book by Meadows, et al, *The Limits to Growth.*[5]

And presently we will be ready to ask, how much do we really need?

Enough to keep us warm.
Enough to run our households.
Enough to provide us with mobility, but not in Cadillacs; nor
    to commute, one per car. But we do need mobility; such
    individuality as we still have may be preserved in considera-
    ble measure by our freedom to move.
Enough to operate a reasonable industry and commerce.
    Growth here must end, too.

Enough to mitigate a number of insults to the environment. But while some of this will cost (especially smog control in the next generation of cars), other measures may save more than they cost, for example, the recycling of aluminum, paper, and glass.

Enough so that we are not cramped into mass institutions for the sole purpose of saving energy, for the purpose of better serving a cramped economy. We must always remember that this society does not exist to serve its economy; the economy exists to serve the society and when it does not do this well, it must yield and reform.

And, in fact, the economy is changing. Economists are willing now to internalize the externalities, to assent that industry should pay the costs of cleaning up effluents, of straightening out land uprooted in the grubbing for coal, and to agree that perhaps industry should stay out of beautiful places.

But still, why should natural gas remain such a bargain because of a strange combination of the technology of its transport, a public power tradition in a regulating agency, and the still enduring shadow of the "invisible hand" of Adam Smith. Is there no way for us to recognize the very special value of this resource and to insure that it not be used where other fuels suffice?

Will we perhaps one day come to agree that the society still has some title to the resource, that the resource has an intrinsic value, and that a severance tax large enough to insure that use is moderate and selective is an appropriate measure? This is a far cry from our tradition of giving our natural wealth to the first comer in order to stimulate development. But that was an infinite world; this one is finite. Such a system of severance taxes large enough to discourage growth and to encourage selective use would be clumsy and full of inequities and would require repeated adjustment. Nonetheless, it could hardly fail to be superior to the present mess.

To sum up on the issue of "need" and "requirement," no matter how much we rail at our past and our lack of vision, no matter how humanistic our phrasing, we must still set prices that will lead to acceptable demands. How much do we "require"? Only as much as we are willing to buy at the prevailing price. It is hard to say we require more. It is easy to say it would be nice to have more; it is easy to say it would be nice for us to get along on less. But in the absence of clear principle, we must rest on the empirical test and must find ways to set prices so they will serve our purposes.

RESPONSE TO CRISIS

As these difficulties build up, one tends to become depressed, to believe the society cannot manage its affairs. But, in fact, we do respond.

First a feeble literature appears, based on uncertain fact, confused thought, obscure principle. It generates a limited academic and public concern and then more voluminous writing. The first recognition that something may be happening is the appearance of counterattacks, of a defense of the status. After several rounds of this back and forth before an increasing public, suddenly, quite suddenly, one of the mass media, usually television, senses an issue that will bear watching. Then with the rush to center stage, the confrontations come on, wave after wave. We see it happening now; in this case it is industry versus conservationist. The conferences come on in legions, promoted by both sides, but also by the middle. Policy statements are issued by everyone, and steadily, carefully, they become clearer, more competent. A new literature of careful inquiry begins to appear. It is much easier to learn today how we use our energy than it was five years ago. The economists are beginning to sense how demand will be affected by price. We are beginning to understand where we are extravagant in energy use, where prudent. Pamphlets appear telling us how to apply this information.

The institutions begin to bend; pricing regulations for natural gas are changing; big electrical customers are not being given the advantages they have traditionally had. We can, in fact, look forward now to a steadily spreading overhaul of all of those institutions of infinity.

SOME WARNINGS

Let me conclude with a small budget of warnings. Those that I have already argued for, I will only mention now.

Take a skeptical view of:

1. The myth that if we do not build more power plants we will end up living in caves. Do we consume power plants or just power? If we build no more power plants we will still have as much power as we have ever had. The industry that has generated this myth sounds more driven by emotion than intellect.
2. The myth of national security. Which provides better security—a land of undeveloped oil resources or one of wells pumped dry? If it is security we want, then let us drill up all of the fields and shut them in still unused. They tell us we need a trans-Alaska pipeline for national security. Ask them to guarantee that the oil will not go to Japan.
3. The myth that says to leave the fluorescent lights on and the heat on overnight. They have little substance.
4. The myth that environmental quality will demand vast new energy developments. The next generation of cars will, yes, require more fuel. Thereafter, I would suspect not. For water quality, mass transport, recycling, there would be an increase of a few percent, nothing near a doubling.
5. The mystical phrases of "foreseeable future," "need," and several others are almost always used to stop you from

thinking and are self-serving. Whenever they are used, ask for elaboration, explanation, justification.

You should also:

1. Be warned against the all-electric home. It costs a bit less, it may end up the winner a century ahead, but for the middle run it is going to hurt every month when the power bills come in.
2. Be warned, of course, against the exponents of growth.
3. Be warned against the exposition of growth as a panacea for the poor. Poverty is a relative thing; recent growth hardly seems to have eliminated it. Poverty may stem more from the complexity of this society than from its overall affluence or lack of it. There is little reward nowadays for those who only understand simple things, for those whose virtue is to work hard. If we really seek to do something for the poor we will have to look elsewhere than at growth.
4. Be warned against dependence on the Middle East for oil. Most of the world's oil seems to be there and we may have it for our pledge. Economists are now guessing that we might end up owing the Middle Eastern states as much as $150 billion by the time that oil is gone. What would the Middle East do with all that foreign exchange? What else could they do but buy $150 billion worth of productive America. So with the oil gone, the United States would be committed to provide the Middle East with, say, half a dozen billions a year in foreign exchange to the end of time. And what would we get for it? Merely, 10 to 20 years of relaxation. If we are to resolve the energy problem, let us get at it now, and in high gear. Let us get at a crash research and development program to bring fusion and solar energy within practical research at the earliest possible moment. The Manhattan Project of World War II and the space programs are reasonable models of how to go about it. We have had enough of penny pinching research in this area.
5. Be warned against the "energy ethic," the theory that we need to learn to use energy more carefully because it is right to do so. This is quite true, and we should, but it is not enough. We must also have a pricing policy to persuade the unethical.

CONCLUSION

My general thesis has been that we have paid too little for energy, that we have created institutions to encourage the profligate use of energy. We cannot continue; neither can we turn back. Now, we must find a new path. I suggest that we set our minds to getting along on no more than our present consumption of energy. We will overshoot this target but if we do not go too far over, we can come back. When, finally, our population comes down to a level which can be sustained at a decent level on our portion of North America for perhaps 100 million of us, there will be enough energy.

References

1. Putnam PC: *Energy in the Future.* Van Nostrand, NY, 1953. See, especially, pp 77 ff.

2. Hubbert MK: Energy from Fossil Fuels. *Science* **109**:103–109, 1949.

3. *Energy Resources: A Report to the Committee on Natural Resources.* National Academy of Sciences/National Research Council Publ 1000-D. Washington, DC, 1962.

4. *Resources and Man,* Committee on Resources and Man. (National Academy of Sciences/National Research Council, Washington, DC). WH Freeman and Co, San Francisco, 1969. Chapter 8 on "Energy Resources" pp 157–242.

5. Meadows DH, et al: *The Limits to Growth.* New York, Universe Books, 1972.

6. Schurr SH, Netschert BC: *Energy in the American Economy, 1850–1975,* Baltimore, Resources for the Future/Johns Hopkins Press, 1960.

7. Landsberg HH, Schurr SH: *Energy in the United States,* New York, Random House, 1960, 1968.

8. Potter N, Christy FT, Jr: *Trends in Natural Resource Commodities.* Baltimore, Resources for the Future/Johns Hopkins Press, 1962.

II

ENERGY
SOURCES

3

Fossil Fuels

Joseph W. Mullan

Let me begin by congratulating whoever expressed the theme of this discussion in three key words—energy, environment, and human health—instead of the usual two. The last word is what makes the others worth discussing in the first place. Unless we relate energy production and environmental protection to basic human needs, we cannot assign a proper value to either of them, and we certainly cannot order our priorities when energy and the environment are—or appear to be—in conflict. Certainly, we will get nowhere by drawing a hard line between energy and the environment as if they were mutually exclusive ways to the better life. With apologies to both sides, neither way is perfect. A man struck by lightning could complain equally against energy and nature.

Obviously, all of the fuels and energy industries will have to factor stricter environmental protection considerations into their planning and operations to prevent permanent damage to our elemental resources of air, land, and water. The sheer growth and sophistication of modern civilization are putting enormous pressures on resources that to earlier generations appeared limitless. At the same time, environmentalists must stop thinking in terms of increasing restraints on energy production and use and start thinking more in terms of progressive resource management if they expect to preserve a world in which man can live on more than a subsistence level.

Providing people with an adequate supply of energy is serious business, as we are learning all over again this spring. I do not recall that anyone has yet complained that he had to put aside his electric toothbrush or turn off his neon sign or postpone his automobile tour of the national forests. But during the past winter I heard of cold homes, closed schools, and threats to essential rail, truck, and airplane traffic plus other assorted problems that demonstrate the real value of energy to our way of life. This is not to deprecate other human—and even planetary—needs for an environmental cleanup. It is merely to wring some of the emotional extremism out of the energy-environment issue. We are not really facing a choice between the Garden of Eden or Disneyland.

What the United States does face is a hard, protracted, and expensive struggle to meet the legitimate energy demands of its people without either devaluating their lifestyle or debasing their natural habitat. Ironically, the more fervid environmentalists must allow the nation to rebuild a flourishing energy economy if they ever hope to repair the accumulated damages of man and nature to the environment—or expect people to give priority concern to their efforts. In our common experience, when people tighten their belts, they frequently lower their sights. The nation must make a balanced response to its energy needs and its environmental aspirations at a bad time for energy. Taking stock of our energy resources is a sobering exercise that I would recommend to anyone who still thinks that coal is a throw-away fuel.

DOMESTIC FUEL RESOURCES

Proved reserves of natural gas—the most environmentally prized fuel because of its minimal sulfur content—have been steadily declining in recent years. Conversely, demand for gas has been going up, under the double attraction of its clean-burning characteristic and its relative cheapness under federal wellhead price regulation. Now there is simply not enough gas to go around, and the Federal Power Commission has proposed a rationing system to give priority to residential and small commercial customers, with the biggest volume industrial and electric utility users dropping to the bottom of the list. While new natural gas reserves are waiting to be found and developed, they are likely to remain statistics unless the natural gas industry receives from government a bigger incentive to mount the required massive and enormously expensive search program with risk capital. In any case, a gas industry study has indicated that our lower 48 states will need about 433 trillion cubic feet more of natural gas than the industry will produce during the rest of this century.

Like the gas industry, the oil industry has been living on declining proved reserves. Crude oil production has peaked, but according to the Department of the Interior, the nation is still short by at least 3 million barrels a day of capacity to produce all the oil we now require, and demand is growing by at least 750,000 barrels a day each year. The lag in U.S. refining capacity is threatening to compound the problem of production shortfalls. We could find ourselves in the ambiguous position of importing crude oil that we still could not refine to the finished products that our scheme of life demands.

The only fossil fuel that the United States has in abundance, not only for the short term but for the longest term any self-respecting energy prophet would consider, is coal. And our huge coal reserves are not probable, but proved; they represent 88% of fuel resources, fossil and nuclear, that we know are on hand and 74% of the fuels that we ultimately expect to find. Best of all, this vast store of coal is immediately accessible.

Before I get into coal's problems—which are strongly, although not exclusively, bedded in environmental concern—I should complete the roll call of our major energy options with atomic power. If any energy source other than natural gas started life with a good environmental press, it was the peaceful atom. Atomic power was not only hailed at its birth as the energy source that would make coal burning obsolete, it was even optimistically foretold at a time when coal dominated the energy market like a Colossus. Back in 1926, Dr. James F. Norris, then president of the American Chemical Society, predicted that the energy of the atom would be harnessed, giving a "limitless supply of energy" that "will make over the world." With the same unabashed optimism, the Atomic Energy Commission much later saw the first atomic generating plants to go into operation as the first step in making the deserts bloom through plentiful cheap power.

Here in 1973, we know that there is still a long way to go to the promised land. Atomic power now supplies the nation with a mere fraction of its energy needs, and it is all in the form of electric power. In view of the fact that about 90% of the nation's energy use is nonelectric, atomic energy is of small help in stemming the depletion of our oil and natural gas reserves and is far from ready to replace coal in the power market. In fact, the atomic energy industry has borrowed far more power from coal to convert its limited uranium ore to usable reactor fuel through the enrichment process than it returned to the national energy supply in the first 25 years of its life.

Atomic power has not expanded up to now at the optimistic pace proclaimed even in the last decade. It is currently face to face with growing problems—increasing capital costs, commonly accepted delays in plant construction, snags in both the supply and reliable operation of equipment, and, finally, a groundswell of environmental opposition based on charges of thermal water pollution and radioactive emissions. I suspect that at least part of the environmentalist's present bitterness toward atomic power is not that it has not produced unlimited power but that it has not eliminated coal.

Even spokesmen for the Atomic Energy Commission have freely acknowledged that both coal and uranium will have to supply the great bulk of our future staggering electric energy demands, not as antagonists but partners. And in the realistic meantime, increased coal use is the only bridge available to the atomic future, which has already stretched beyond the painful growth years of fission power to the still more distant promise of fusion power. There is nothing essentially wrong in being optimistic—even to the extent of looking forward to clean, limitless solar power—provided that we keep up our daily energy strength, and coal is clearly the only guarantee that we can stay on the course.

SULFUR CONTENT LIMITATIONS

Speaking of health, the coal industry must have that, too, if it is to be expected to support the United States through its energy crisis. An industry that is hedged in with restrictions on the production and use of coal is not in very good shape to grow to the heroic stature that will be required of it by the nation's need not only for electric power but synthetic replacements for spent oil and gas. The government's hastily conceived environmental policies are serious obstacles to coal industry growth.

Air pollution control policy is very much to the point. As embodied in the Clean Air Act and implemented by the Environmental Protection Agency (EPA), that policy is progressively reducing our usable coal base by tightening the limits on sulfur content. With those limits already down to 0.7% sulfur, and in some cases as little as 0.3%, the great bulk of our historical coal supply faces an outright ban. Data from the Bureau of Mines show that only about 8% of coal reserves east of the Mississippi could meet the 0.7% sulfur standard without additional means of controlling sulfur oxide emissions.

But sulfur limits have been set without regard for the current state of emission control technology, which, despite a speedup and significant advances, has not yet reached the proved, commercially ready stage. So the only immediate response to the arbitrary rule has been the use of low-sulfur fuels. This is the point at which reality has reared its head—if we are short of most fuels, we are shortest of those naturally low in sulfur. There is simply not enough natural gas available to eliminate the sulfur emission problem at any price, and there is not enough low-sulfur domestic oil either.

We do have large reserves of low-sulfur coal, but they are predominantly in the distant West, generally beyond the economical transport reach of the heavily industralized East. Even the dedicated Environmental Protection Agency has lost some of its assurance that fuel sulfur limits can survive low-sulfur fuel shortages. It recently acknowledged that, if proposed state plans to meet federal air quality standards go into effect as scheduled in 1975, there may be a shortfall of more than 300 million tons of coal with less than 0.7% sulfur. That shortage, EPA said, would have to be met either by importing more low-sulfur residual oil, at a cost that might increase the U.S. balance of payments deficit by $3 billion a year, or by modifying state implementation plans in many states, primarily in the Midwest. EPA has stated that this, the second option, which still would require meeting the nation's health standards, would have the least economic impact on the nation. This is an encouraging sign that EPA recognizes the realities of the energy crisis and the need for flexibility even in the clean air crusade.

AN ENVIRONMENTAL TRADE-OFF

The immediate answer to this dilemma is twofold; more precisely, there are two answers that are reasonably complementary and will serve both the needs of short-term energy supply and the interests of continuing environmental protection. The government must greatly accelerate the development and demonstration of commercially effective systems to remove sulfur dioxide from the stack gases of coal-burning plants—and it must modify its air quality demands to allow desulfurization technology time to catch up with the most stringent standards. That is certainly a reasonable compromise, since EPA has already conceded that complete implementation of state air quality control plans may not be attainable by the 1975 deadline in any case.

Coal's long-term solution to its air pollution problem rests heavily, of course, on the redemption of high-sulfur coal through its conversion to clean synthetic gas and oil and to new products such as solvent-refined coal that can be burned as a solid or a liquid virtually free of sulfur and ash. But if the coal industry is to stay vigorous enough to take on a second big job of supporting the emerging synthetic fuel industry while still underwriting a major share of our electric power supply, Congress and the public will have to work with the coal industry to solve the environmental problems associated with strip mining.

Responsible coal companies are effectively reclaiming the land they mine and have been increasing the acreage restored by making reclamation part of the mining cycle. The National Coal Association has supported federal legislation realistically designed to help the states and the coal industry to do a better job of reclamation and to insure that all coal operators join in the effort. But we cannot, for the life of the industry, settle for the simplistic idea that less strip mining or none is a form of instant reclamation. That is not resource management but resource neglect, at the very time when our coal resource is most urgently needed and our prospects for recovering it compatibly with good land use planning are the brightest.

The nation's energy stake in strip mining is crucial. This method of mining now accounts for about half of our annual bituminous coal production, and that share must grow steadily for such basic reasons as recoverability, economy, and safety. It is not merely the easiest way to mine coal but, in many areas, the only way, and it is largely the key to necessary development of the underused coal deposits in the West that are just starting to produce long-range power and will play a substantial part in realizing the coming synthetic fuel industry. At present, coal accounts for 44% of all the electricity generated in the nation, and three fourths of the coal shipped to electric utilities comes from surface mines.

The easiest way to prove that reclamation will not work or that the coal industry will not practice it is to remove the opportunity. A bad idea dies hard, as we should have learned from trying to legislate clean air. The opponents of strip mining who blithely propose that we make up strip coal losses with substitute fuels have lost touch with our hard times. Underground coal mines are not built in a hurry or out of petty cash, and our other fossil fuels are a forlorn hope. Every lost ton of coal saps the strength of the other fuel industries and our total energy effort. In our choice of substitutes, we are down to brand X—imported oil.

The coal industry is heartily tired of the forced confrontation of energy and the environment. And I suspect that you, too, who are born energy consumers even if you are devoted ecologists, are also growing weary of being faced with a simplistic either-or proposition. What you naturally want is the best of both worlds, but life has conditioned you to the necessity of trade-offs. Right now the United States needs its old reliable domestic coal resource in the worst way—but it has an opportunity to use it in the best way through the aid of redemptive research. If coal offends our new environmental sensibilities, our energy sense recommends that we refine it, not discard it. Coal is not only our uniquely abundant fuel, but a highly versatile hydrocarbon that can serve us in solid, liquid, or gaseous form. To neglect its full development because of temporary environmental shortcomings would be a tragic waste of an incomparable national energy asset.

4

Nuclear Fuels (Fission-Fusion)

David J. Rose, Ph.D.

This is a relatively nontechnical sketch of nuclear power and its prospects. In order to put it in perspective, I first quote a few numbers.

Consider first the total scale of the energy business in the United States. Total electric power sales are about $24 billion per year; gasoline sales are about $15 billion; heating and industrial fuels account for many billions more. In addition to those very straightforward energy costs, which total altogether perhaps $70 billion per year, I think it reasonable to include some modest fractions from other sectors that are direct consequences of our national cheap energy policy—that is, some small fraction of our interstate highway system, some small fraction of our buildings (because cheap energy leads to types of construction that minimize capital cost and increase the need for space conditioning), etc. Half of what we transport is fuel. Thus it is possible to arrive at a figure of about $100 billion per year, give or take a little, as the total handle on our national energy business. This represents one tenth of the gross national product (GNP), and it cannot be considered apart from its intimate connectivity with the rest.

I turn now to the role of nuclear energy. First, the principal use by far of nuclear energy will be for producing electric power in large generating stations. To be sure, nuclear reactors are used to power aircraft carriers and submarines, and reactors might be used in the future to power a civilian merchant fleet. Here and there a nuclear reactor might be used just as a source of heat energy—say, for industrial processing or even simple heating. But all those applications taken together will be small compared with the electric generating role, at least during the next 30 years. I think that will also be true later on, but it is harder to be sure.

Let us then look at electric power generation for a moment. At present, it takes about 25% of all fuel resources used in the United States. With this fuel we generate some 300,000 megawatts (Mw) of electric power on a more or less continuous basis.

Now to the sources of fuel for this power: a little over 40% is coal, 24% is natural gas, some 15% to 20% is liquid petroleum, about 15% is hydropower,

43

and presently about 4% is nuclear. So about 14,000 Mw out of the total 300,000 is now being generated by nuclear power, but that fraction, now small, is expected to grow rapidly. At present, 140,000 Mw of nuclear reactors are on order, to be completed between now and the very early 1980s. The capital investment represented in that commitment is large—over $40 billion of nuclear-fueled electric power plants. These investments represent purchases almost entirely within the United States.

What does the future hold in this business? Nuclear energy could, in principle, be expanded to satisfy all future electric power demands, but there are many caveats. First, look at some predictions. Typical maximum predictions for electric power demands in the year 2000 are about 1.7 million Mw—some six times the present value, and the minimum believable predictions for that time have been 1 million Mw. Using the upper value for discussion, projections have it that about half of the 1.7 million will be nuclear; thus, in that scenario, we are left with some 800,000 electric Mw still to be produced by fossil fuels in the year 2000. If all that power were to be produced by petroleum, using plants of present efficiency, the petroleum products needed would be more than now used in the United States for every purpose.

Will things go that way? Very probably not:

1. The very welcome movement toward more efficient energy utilization will trim the growth rate—that is, better technology, better design, possibly new regulations that penalize energy waste.
2. Coal gasification and liquefaction will come in as new strategies of provision making coal, once it is mined in environmentally acceptable ways, a more attractive fuel again.
3. Energy is clearly going to cost more than it did in the past.
4. The nuclear sector may be stimulated to grow more rapidly.
5. The energy growth rate may be lower from other causes (e.g., environmental pressures).

Just how things turn out depends on policies to be decided upon and followed; all these matters are now lively subjects for discussion.

But several things seem pretty clear:

1. Nuclear power can speak to only one sector of our energy needs—electric power production. That is, to be sure, the fastest growing sector, doubling every ten years until now. Depending on how the country decides, some trade-offs are possible between electric generation and other traditionally nonelectric uses; for example, electric cars of much expanded electric mass transit would take some of the load from transportation fuels. But even so, nuclear power cannot be any-

thing like a real substitute for most fossil fuel uses, at least for a long time.

2. The predictions of overall energy growth, not just electric power growth, in the U.S. are such that more fossil fuels will be needed in other sectors too.

3. All fossil fuel reserves are quite limited, for the long term, and these national resources will be more valuable as chemical stock than as mere material to burn. Thus, all that I have said so far has applicability in the short term—say in the next 30 or 50 years. But for longer times, the question of substantial depletion of our main fossil stock—coal— becomes paramount; then we must have an energy strategy that does not depend upon fossil materials. The only options seem to be nuclear, geothermal, or solar energy; and of those three, only nuclear energy presently holds sure promise.

With that, I now turn more toward nuclear power itself. In the long term, nuclear power may come from either nuclear fission or nuclear fusion; but at least until the year 2000, it will all be fission power. Thus I concentrate on that topic, but will put in a few remarks about fusion at the end.

RESOURCES

The first question one might ask concerns the reserves of fissionable material. Table 7, taken from work by my excellent colleague Professor Manson Benedict of MIT, shows one estimate of how things are. Expressed in units of 10^{15} British Thermal Units (BTU) to the nearest order of magnitude, reserves of natural gas (1,000), liquid fuels (1,000), and coal (20,000 to 40,000) are to be compared with uranium and thorium reserves each over 1 million, when 75% utilized in efficient breeder reactors.

Table 7
U.S. Energy Reserves

Material	10^{15} BTU
Natural gas	850
Petroleum liquids	638
Oil shale	464
Coal	18,090
	38,070
Uranium, costing under:	
$15/lb U_3O_8, assuming 1% utilization in nonbreeding reactors	972
$100/lb U_3O_8, assuming 75% utilization in breeder reactors	1,125,000
Thorium, costing under:	
$100/lb ThO_2	1,665,000

The numbers in Table 7 are to be compared with total U.S. energy consumption of 66 X 10^{15} BTU in 1970 and a projected consumption of 150 X 10^{15} BTU in 2000. Thus we surmise that only coal and uranium and thorium in breeder reactors are available in sufficient quantity to serve as principal fuels in the 21st century, and that only uranium and thorium can satisfy energy needs into the distant future. I am not speaking here of the possibilities of solar or geothermal power, which are by no means negligible; you will hear of those matters from other sources. And fusion power comes later in this presentation.

Now these estimates are of more or less proved reserves, and even here we see that the amount of cheap uranium, even if inefficiently used in present-day nonbreeding reactors, will suffice to keep us going at present expansion rates until, say, the 1990s. Actually I think (but cannot prove) that matters are even better off than Table 7 indicates. Each of the two times that the U.S. has gone looking for uranium within its boundaries—in the 1950s and the 1960s—plenty turned up, and the search was called off when the supply seemed adequate for about a 20- to 30-year need. It just wasn't economic to search for more. Since, in fact, relatively little effort has been spent in discovering uranium (compared, say, with that going toward oil and gas discovery), I suspect that the real supply is several times as large as the numbers shown. Thus even with present-day conventional nuclear reactors, uranium supply will not be a serious problem before the year 2000, when we will surely have a breeder reactor of some type.

When a breeder reactor comes along, it will be able to utilize not only the rare uranium isotope of atomic weight 235 (which present reactors utilize almost exclusively) but also the common uranium isotope of weight 238 which constitutes over 99.3% of all uranium. Thus the available resource increases by a large factor not only because of more efficient utilization, but also because we can afford to pay more for the ore (because we will use virtually all of it). Thus we have the large ratio of over 1,000 in the two estimates of reserves in Table 7. Actually, things are probably even better: for a good breeder reactor, we could afford to pay $200 or $300 per pound for uranium oxide. At that price, the reserves are almost indefinitely large—enough to last us probably millions of years.

In summary, I think that the domestic uranium reserves will be adequate for our demands for a long time, if used wisely. My estimates are more optimistic than those presently being made by our Atomic Energy Commission (AEC). Of course, the availability of appreciably more cheap uranium would make early development of a breeder reactor a somewhat less urgent matter. My views are shared by some others outside the AEC, both here in the United States and abroad.

COSTS OF NUCLEAR VERSUS FOSSIL FUEL OPTIONS

In judging nuclear versus other generating options, which in this case means fossil fuels, the relative costs of the various schemes are important. Thus I turn now to some ideas about costs, not being at this stage of the discussion too specific about differentiating one nuclear reactor scheme from another.

Present predictions have it that present-day nuclear power stations will be cheaper than coal-burning ones in all areas where coal costs more than about $9 per ton. Nuclear fuels cost next to nothing to transport compared with coal. The $9 per ton cost seems likely to be met in the late 1970s only at or near low-cost coal mines. Petroleum costs for equivalent amounts of energy are predicted to be—and now are—even higher, and gas is out of sight, except for a few special locations. Thus, according to these ideas, nearly all future electric generating plants should be nuclear. That would probably be the case, except for certain social and institutional issues that have been raised about nuclear plants, especially in populated areas. Without wishing in any way to appear as an apologist for the Atomic Energy Commission, I think that many of the nuclear critics wear their intellectual clothes inside out.

Under normal operating conditions, a nuclear reactor emits no smoke, particulates, or noxious chemicals. It *does* emit more waste heat than fossil fuel plants, because of its generally lower thermal efficiency, but the difference is not at all overwhelmingly large. The radioactivity release is truly negligible. What, then, are the hazards? They are of accidents occurring during reactor operation, of releases during nuclear fuel reprocessing at separate reprocessing plants, of mining uranium, and of manufacturing nuclear fuel elements. In an excellent article L. A. Sagan estimates that the principal hazards actually come from uranium mining and manufacturing, not from reactor operation at all.[1] With his figures for the cost of a human life ($300,000), he concludes that the annual total societal cost from a 10,000-Mw nuclear industry is just over $2 million.

That is a very interesting number; 10,000 Mw about equal the electric power generated in New York City. Two years ago, in reading epidemiological reports about conditions in New York City in 1968, I concluded, on the basis of what little evidence was then available, that the additional 1968 deaths attributable to coal-burning regulations then in effect were very much larger. And such figuring ignores the societal cost involved in strip mining coal, transporting oil, etc.

The national discussion on these matters is out of joint. Where have matters gone wrong? I ventured the opinion two years ago that the nuclear criticism came about because the nuclear issues were better illuminated, and that criticism of fossil fuel systems was still subdued because people had not yet recognized their much greater hazards—people had lived and died with those systems for a long time, and had gotten used to them. Thus, perversely, much of the nuclear criticism arises because the AEC had brought both the nuclear technology and its main societal consequences to the stage where the main costs and benefits were clearly visible. For example, our understanding of the biological effects of nuclear radiation was developed at a research cost of over $1 billion. The issues were plain for all to see.

As a corollary, I predicted that fossil fuel generation would suffer increasingly severe criticism as its true societal costs were discovered; that now seems to be coming true. Unfortunately, neither the AEC nor some other agencies seems to have fully understood these sociotechnological issues.

To summarize this part of the discussion, I aver that narrowly structured economic analyses show that nuclear-powered electric plants are cheaper than fossil-fueled ones, when the fuel costs are considered. Even more, I aver that including the societal diseconomies and nonmarket costs will generally accentuate this difference. Thus, a potentially large item in the use of fossil fuels has to do with societal awareness about the costs and benefits of nuclear versus fossil fuels. This issue probably transcends the small details of the cost of one present-day fission reactor versus another.

PRESENT FISSION NONBREEDING REACTORS

Now I turn briefly to present-day fission reactors. In the U.S. nearly all installations until now have been so-called light-water reactors—where ordinary water is both the moderator of the neutrons produced by the nuclear reaction and the medium by which heat from the reactor is removed. Two different types of light-water reactors exist. First, there are pressurized-water reactors, wherein the water does not boil at all but is pumped at high temperature through a heat exchanger to boil water and make steam in a secondary circuit; the steam then drives a conventional turbine, which turns the generator. The second type is the boiling-water reactor; as the name implies, the water inside the reactor boils, and its steam runs the turbine directly. Advantages and disadvantages exist for both types, but the differences are not essential for our purposes here today. Both reactors are well developed—with some improvements and hazards protection still to be incorporated. Thermal efficiency of each is about 32%, a relatively low number by modern standards for turning heat into electricity. These reactors also regenerate some new nuclear fuel, from absorbing neutrons into the common isotope uranium-238 (U-238), to produce fissionable plutonium. In these reactors, the ratio of "fissionable fuel made" to "fissionable fuel used" is about 0.6. Thus fissionable reserves are extended, but the reactors are a long way from being breeders.

The other reactor now coming into use is the high-temperature gas reactor, a quite different animal. It uses solid graphite as a neutron moderator and helium gas at high temperature and pressure to remove the heat. The hot helium then passes through a heat exchanger where it boils water for the turbine as before. The high-temperature gas reactor has certain advantages:

1. Its thermal efficiency is nearly 40%, as good as the best fossil-fueled plants.
2. It regenerates nuclear fuel much better than did the light-water reactors—a ratio of 0.8 or more, compared with 0.6. (Since it is the difference between these numbers and 1.0 that is significant, we see that the high-temperature gas reactor is significantly better in this respect.)
3. Some accident modes believed conceivable (but very unlikely) in the light-water reactors are absent in this particular design.

Against these advantages lie, as usual, some disadvantages:

1. Fuel reprocessing is not yet as neatly worked out as it is for the light-water reactors.
2. The makeup nuclear fuel is almost pure uranium-235 (U-235), the very stuff from which nuclear weapons are made. Thus, it requires exceptionally close guarding to prevent criminals and deranged people with antisocial ideas from stealing it.

BREEDER REACTORS

Now, briefly also, I discuss breeder reactors. These devices all lie in the future, but the future lies not far ahead. When I was a student, it seemed to me an intriguing mystery how a nuclear reactor could produce more fuel than it burned. Perhaps this audience is similarly intrigued; and so, as a short entr'-acte, I will describe how reactors can do this.

Figure 10
Simple Chart of Nuclear Fission

URANIUM

+   ⟶ FISSION

NEUTRON

⟶ ENERGY
+
⟶ FISSION PRODUCTS (WASTE)
+
⟶ 2.3 MORE NEUTRONS

Figure 11
Better View of Nuclear Fission

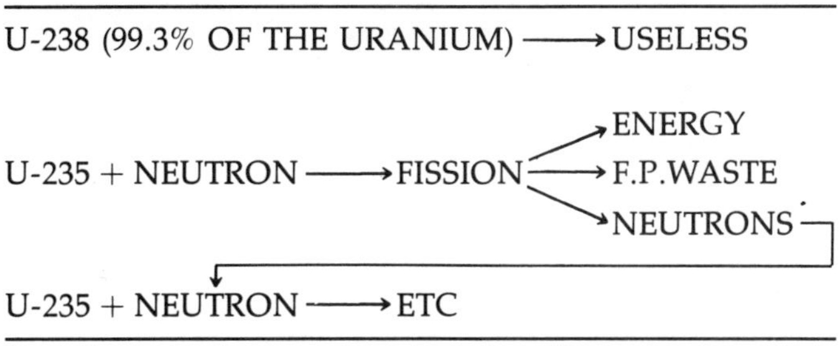

U-238 (99.3% OF THE URANIUM) ⟶ USELESS

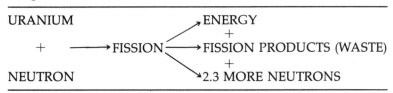

U-235 + NEUTRON ⟶ FISSION

⟶ ENERGY
⟶ F.P. WASTE
⟶ NEUTRONS

U-235 + NEUTRON ⟶ ETC

Figure 10 shows the basic idea of fission. Uranium plus a neutron undergoes a nuclear reaction—fission—to produce a lot of energy, elements made from the broken-up uranium nucleus (such as strontium, barium, and so forth) and more neutrons. If we had more uranium available, these neutrons would initiate more reactions, and on we go.

But matters are more complicated, because most uranium atoms—over 99%—do not do this. Only the rare isotope of atomic weight 235 does this, as we see in Figure 11. Here, the vast bulk of the common isotope U-238 goes along

50

for the ride, and the U-235 fissions as I described. But with care, and by enriching the nuclear fuel with this U-235 isotope, one can make a chain reaction, as I start to show on the figure. So nuclear reactors are possible and get built.

The complications are in fact greater than that, because the large unreacting component U-238 does something in real fact, which we see in Figure 12. The uranium-235 business goes on as before, but the U-238 absorbs neutrons to make the new element plutonium. This is basically what happens in present-day fission reactors, the sort I described in the previous section.

Figure 12
Essentials of Fission Burner Reactors

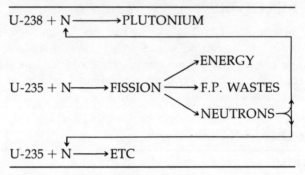

Figure 13
Essentials of Fission Breeder Reactors

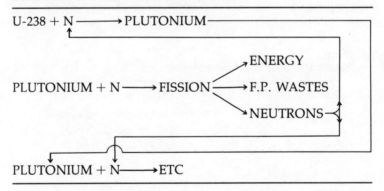

Formation of plutonium would make no difference to things were it not for one important matter: plutonium itself will fission, although the parent U-238 would not. Thus we are led to Figure 13, where we capitalize on this fact to make a nuclear reactor that utilizes the plentiful U-238 isotope. Note that plutonium now does the fission work, the role formerly played by the rare isotope U-235, and the process breeds its own fuel—hence the name breeder reactor. From the figure, we clearly need more than two neutrons per fission event: one at the top to make new plutonium, one at the bottom to initiate the next reaction, and a little bit more to make up for the inevitable losses to nonproductive reactions that I have not shown. Anent that point, one of the early important questions asked was whether the neutrons per fission exceeded two. The answer was about 2.3, whereupon breeder reactors were recognized as scientifically possible. It turns out that similar things are possible using the element thorium; thus uranium and thorium are our nuclear fission resources.

The status of breeder reactors at present is this: the so-called liquid-metal fast-breeder reactor (LMFBR) is the presently favored type. In this design, the nuclear fuel elements—made of plutonium and uranium—are immersed in a large tank of liquid sodium metal; the liquid sodium is circulated through the reactor, and takes the heat to a succession of heat exchangers, where eventually steam is generated to power the turbines. The Soviet Union is testing a large prototype LMFBR; the United Kingdom and France are not far behind. The United States has proposed to build a 300-Mw demonstration plant near Oak Ridge, Tennessee, at a cost of over $300 million, to be completed before 1980. Thereafter, in the AEC's view, LMFBRs would be increasingly adopted by the nuclear industry, with the first commercial introduction to start in the late 1980s. With the total capital investment in nuclear-powered generating stations being estimated as about $300 billion during the period between now and 2000, we see that there is a lot at stake. Penalties for wrong decisions—too early, too late, wrong type, etc.—are severe, both economically and societally. The USAEC presently supports the LMFBR program at $260 million per year, the largest single research and development item anywhere in the energy field; and the AEC also supports the program indirectly via many more auxiliary activities.

I do not doubt that an LMFBR can be developed that is safe, reliable, and effective. Thus we could find relief from present-day less efficient and more resource-wasteful reactors by the mid or late 1980s. The uncertainty involves the cost, for one can in these matters achieve almost any arbitrary degree of safety, depending on what one wants to pay. The uncertainties are therefore more subtle, and opinions about the LMFBR vary. Obviously the proponents think it is a very good thing. On the whole, I think it is too. On the other hand, I have reservations, *not* relating to simplistic views of catastrophe. The advantages would be real: an efficiency of 40% or more, low-pressure operation (using liquid sodium as the coolant) so that a number of failure possibilities are truly eliminated, and it *is* a breeder. The disadvantages relate to such things as acceptance by the power companies; all that liquid sodium is troublesome in itself, and tests the acceptance of the utility companies, who have a remarkable history of conservatism in the face of innovation. Then too, maybe one of the *other* breeder options might turn out more societally desirable, when more is known. Here I mention the existence of another possible breeder type, the gas-cooled fast-breeder reactor, a very interesting extension of the high-temperature gas-cooled reactor concept. In the opinion of its developer, the Gulf General Atomic Company, it could be made just about as soon as the LMFBR, for less money ($200 to $300 million total of government expenditure), and it would be a better reactor. The USAEC disputes these claims and supports the concept at a relatively low level. In my opinion, the gas-cooled fast-breeder reactor could, with a few hundred million dollars of financial input, be explored in depth to the full feasibility stage by about 1980.

In summary, then, we can and will have a breeder reactor by the 1980s, but the cost is still somewhat uncertain. And it is not clear to me that, for the long term, concentration on the LMFBR almost exclusively has been a good thing. But all things taken together, this country could, with its various nuclear fission options, satisfy most future electric generating requirements and do so without using fossil fuels, except for what I believe to be a number of serious institutional and social issues.

CONTROLLED NUCLEAR FUSION

Now let me turn briefly to controlled fusion reactors. I cannot show you a schematic diagram of an operating one because none exists yet, and it won't for a long time. As with fission, I do not think that the basic fuels (deuterium, and also lithium as the raw ingredients of a deuterium-tritium controlled fusion cycle) are scarce. Deuterium is plentiful; and lithium is not much searched for yet. The lithium is required to generate tritium, which does not occur in nature, via an auxiliary nuclear reaction. So *that* most likely fusion reaction can be looked upon as a breeding process too.

The worst disadvantage of fusion is the sheer difficulty of bringing it about. By their nature, nuclear fusion reactions require that the reactants be heated to an ignition temperature of between 100 million and 1 billion degrees, which exceeds substantially the temperature at the center of the sun. Thereafter, the "plasma" must be confined long enough for an appreciable fraction of the nuclear fuel—deuterium-tritium, deuterium-deuterium, or whatever—to "burn." That confinement for long enough is what has occupied the attention of the scientific community for so long and has taken most of the money. A cheerful result of all this is that several different scientific groups now imagine that they will in a few years be able to demonstrate experimentally to the world that adequate plasma confinement has been achieved.

The stage of demonstrating scientific feasibility must be followed by increasingly expensive stages of technological development and, finally, demonstration of economic and societal acceptability. While good hopes exist for successful completion of these stages, no guarantees exist. I think that the development stages will proceed to the year 2000 at least, and its ultimate feasibility won't be known even by the early 1980s. Thus controlled nuclear fusion does *not* represent at present a viable alternate to the breeder program. It *might* be an alternate option to a second generation or improved breeder reactor, and it will probably have to compete by breaking into a more or less established breeder technology.

CONCLUDING REMARKS

Although I was asked to discuss the nuclear alternatives for energy provision, which hopefully was done on the preceding pages, I cannot refrain from commenting a little more. Some of these remarks relate to material I submitted in briefings before the Congressional House Task Force on Energy, in the spring of 1972.[2]

Energy has been viewed mainly as the business of providing it—oil production, electric power production, coal mining, etc. Our annual research and development expenditure, amounting to perhaps $1.4 billion total in public and private sectors, reflects such an attitude, because nearly all of it relates to providing energy.

Such a program is unbalanced and leads to trouble. Every bit of energy provided is used somewhere, and that use is quite often inefficient or ill-planned or societally disadvantageous in some way. It has been estimated that the energy used for transportation, and for heating and cooling of buildings, could be reduced substantially through more rational design and operation. Various analyses show that reductions of 25% to 50% would be possible without significant discomfort to us as members of the consuming public. Furthermore, the dollar savings from using less energy would more than pay for the modest added sophistication of the articles or structures in question. Waste not, want not, as the saying goes.

Other large benefits would accrue from a more careful energy policy. Most atmospheric pollution—more than 80%—comes from processes directly related to the transformation of energy. Half the sulfur oxides come from coal-burning electric power stations; the vast majority of carbon monoxide and particulates comes either from power plants or the engines of transportation. To these more obvious effects can be added others that I think are not less important. To put it cynically, it is energy that permits us to turn raw material resources into junk at an ever-increasing rate. Thus we contemplate dust from rock crushing, smoke from burning dumps, rivers not only too acid from coal mine runoffs but filled with unwanted chemicals—all products of a too-cheap energy policy. The latter represent an excess of what scientifically could be called free energy, but that adjective begins to take on a hollow ring. In a social and economic sense, it is an unwanted leakage from our high-energy system.

Much of our present environmental quality drive relates to energy and its uses—in particular, to the problem of plugging leaks in our energy system, things such as hydrocarbons and nitrogen oxides, excess active fertilizers, waste reactive chemicals, and so forth. Hitherto, societal pressures to plug these leaks have been low; now they are high. We must put energy in its proper ecological niche, so to speak, rather than let it run around so freely where it causes trouble.

The environmental and health costs of energy are large: that is what this meeting is all about. I expect to learn here as well as instruct, and I look forward to having discussions on all these nonengineering matters which will serve to put the national debate on energy into better perspective.

54

References

1. Sagan, LA: Human costs of nuclear power. *Science* **177**: 487–493, 1972.

2. Rose, DJ: Rational Development of Options: Energy as an Example. Briefings before the House Task Force on Energy, Committee on Science and Astronautics, U.S. House of Representatives, 92nd Congress, vol 2, pp 77–104.

5

Geothermal Resources*

Donald E. White, Ph.D.

Geothermal resources involve the distribution of temperature and thermal energy beneath the earth's surface. Present-day technology emphasizes production of electricity from geothermal steam; requirements now include reservoirs of high temperature (greater than 350 F), depths of no more than 10,000 feet, natural fluids for transferring the thermal energy from the reservoir to the power plant, adequate volume and permeability of the reservoir, and no insurmountable environmental, chemical, or physical problems. Technological developments in the future may greatly change these requirements.

Temperatures generally increase with greater depth in mines and wells and are estimated to be as much as 1,800 F at the base of the crust of the earth. Thermal energy flows from the hot interior to the surface by conductive flow through solid rocks and convective flow in circulating water.

Where conductive heat flow is dominant, temperatures always increase with depth, but the rate of increase varies, depending on the quantity of heat flowing from an area and on the thermal conductivities of the rocks. "Normal" heat flows and conductivities yield gradients that generally range from about 20 F to 135 F per mile of depth. Most "normal" conduction-dominated areas are not attractive sources of geothermal energy at present prices and technology.

Abnormally high thermal gradients result from high conductive heat flow and/or low rock conductivity. In favorable environments conductive gradients range from 135 F to 200 F per mile of depth, and even higher near magma bodies. Very high gradients are attractive in searching for concealed permeable reservoirs, but projection of a shallow measured gradient to great depth is not justified until rock conductivities and any effects of circulating water can be evaluated.

---

* This chapter is a summary of a paper with identical title and supporting bibliography in *Geothermal Energy; Resources, Production, Stimulation,* Paul Kruger and Carel Otte (eds), Stanford University Press, Stanford, 1973.

55

PRODUCTION SYSTEMS

Present production of geothermal power is entirely from large subsurface hydrothermal convection systems. In such systems heat is transferred by circulating water or steam, a process which tends to heat the rocks near the surface while rocks at the bottom of a convection system are cooled. One consequence is that thermal gradients in such systems are generally highest near the surface but decrease greatly with depth.

Two major types of hydrothermal convection systems are recognized: hot-water systems and vapor-dominated systems.

Hot-water systems are relatively abundant; various subtypes are based on temperature relations, salinity, presence or absence of insulating cap rocks, and importance of convection versus conduction. With present technology, temperatures at depth must be much above surface boiling (permissible because of the high pressure). With flow up a well, water starts to boil when pressure decreases sufficiently; at the surface the steam fraction is separated from residual water and is used to generate electricity. Vapor-dominated systems are rare (probably less than 5% of all convection systems with reservoir temperatures above 400 F). The best known are Larderello, Italy, and The Geysers, California, which are characterized by reservoir temperatures near 450 F and steam pressures near 450 pounds per square inch (psi) to maximum drilled depths. Wells drilled into such systems produce dry steam, all of which can be used in generating electricity.

TECHNOLOGICAL DEMANDS

Extensive utilization of geothermal resources is confronted by many problems of various kinds.

1. The very attractive vapor-dominated systems are evidently very rare.
2. Such systems probably require surface leakages for flushing out gases other than steam; completely concealed systems may not exist for future discovery.
3. Present technology converts only about 1% of the stored energy of hot-water reservoirs into equivalent electrical energy.
4. Waters of many hot-water systems, when flash-erupted, deposit silica and/or calcium carbonate in wells and surface pipes.
5. Some hot waters are corrosive.
6. Many hot-water systems do not have adequate reservoir volume, temperature, or permeability.
7. The waste water from hot-water systems is commonly high in salts, boron, ammonia, arsenic, and some other metals and is thus a potential environmental hazard that requires

underground reinjection or some other means of satisfactory disposal.

8. Some hot water effluents will react chemically with subsurface waters, and this reaction precipitates minerals and decreasing permeability in reinjection wells.

9. "Steam-lift" (production by means of erupting like a continuous geyser) is not dependable for producing most geothermal waters so that pumping or some other method will be required.

10. Desalination will result in precipitation of SiO_2, $CaCO_3$, and perhaps other constituents from most waters; each water will differ, but general principles need to be developed.

11. Thermal, noise, and air pollution (principally H_2S) will commonly require control.

12. Subsidence of the ground surface will occur over massively produced hot-water reservoirs, especially if the rocks contain much clay, shale, or overpressured sand.

13. Reinjection sufficiently massive and local enough to offset subsidence may decrease the temperature of produced water except, perhaps, in very large permeable reservoirs.

14. Earthquakes may be caused by reinjection into some hot-water systems, so that monitoring and special attention will be required.

Some of the above problems may be inherent, with no obvious solution regardless of cost (1, 2, 6?); most others can probably be solved or avoided by alternate technology, perhaps with only modest increases in costs. The most serious problems, in my opinion, are likely to include numbers 4, 6, 7, 12, 13, and 14. The recent surge of interest in geothermal energy provides hope that these problems will be solved at costs that are competitive relative to other energy sources.

The most significant "break-throughs" needed for large-scale use of geothermal energy include:

1. Binary fluid heat-exchange methods for utilizing the heat of fluids at temperatures down to 220 F, or less. Such methods are especially needed for utilizing the heat that is stored in deep sedimentary basins or other permeable rocks of modest temperature.

2. Successful multipurpose developments that include desalination and/or chemical recovery to share total costs.

3. Low-cost mechanical, chemical, or nuclear fracturing of hot dry rocks to increase permeability so as to permit the introduction of a heat transferring fluid for utilizing the stored energy.

4. New methods for drilling low-cost holes to great depth.

5. New technology or other developments that favor direct use of geothermal energy for space heating, horticulture, refrigeration, and product processing.
6. Solution or control of the most serious geothermal problems at no greater hazard and cost than for alternate sources of power (each of which has corresponding problems). If proposed research and development are sufficiently successful, geothermal energy can provide a substantial part of our future energy needs (10% or more).

Geothermal reserve and resource estimates differ tremendously (by about 1 million times!), mainly because of differences in assumed technology, the rate and cost of discovering new geothermal fields, the productivity and spacing of individual wells in a field, the relative abundance of favorable vapor-dominated systems in new discoveries, and confidence that all associated problems can be solved at low cost. In my personal opinion, world geothermal power production is likely to exceed 30 million kw only after one or more of the above "break-throughs" occur.

6

Solar Energy

Erich A. Farber, Ph.D.

Our present civilization has been built upon the energy provided by fossil fuels (coal, oil, and gas), resources which have been provided for us by nature through rather inefficient conversion of solar energy. This is nature's way of storing energy through plant life and just the right conditions of oxygen starvation, high pressure, and temperature coupled with millions of years of time.

This energy source can be compared with the savings account of a family. Knowing how much is consumed each day, simple arithmetic will reveal how long the family can survive by drawing upon their savings, or how long civilization can live as it has become accustomed to before running out of these energy deposits.

Everyone agrees with the above, and the only differences of opinion arise from the question as to when this will occur. Not much is gained by arguing about the exact time since we do not know how much of these resources exist—we can only estimate—and no one can predict how sensibly and effectively we are going to utilize them.

One further observation should be made, namely, that these fossil fuels are also the source of our chemical industry, our medicines, preservatives, etc., and if they are burned for energy they will be unavailable for those other uses equally essential for life.

Not much energy had been used per person for thousands of years until about 100 years ago. With the increase of energy consumption each person has effectively multiplied the number of "servants" working for him so that quantities of goods and the standard of living increased rapidly. The richer a country is in energy and the more it uses, the faster is its climb to the heights aspired to by mankind as expressed by its standard of living.

The well-being of civilizations will parallel the availability and consumption of energy. With fossil fuels being used at a tremendous rate and becoming scarcer, we will have to curtail our activities and possibly even accept a decline, or find other sources and methods to provide for our energy needs and requirements. We will have to develop nuclear energy and, especially, learn to live off solar energy, our only energy income, to conserve our energy savings.

For these reasons, the University of Florida Solar Energy and Energy

59

Conversion Laboratory was established about two decades ago to study the feasibility of providing the forms of energy needed for our daily life by the conversion of solar energy. The conversion is to be done in the fewest possible steps along the most direct route. The activities of the laboratory cover the monitoring of solar radiation, the determination of solar properties of materials, solar water heating, swimming pool heating, house heating, air conditioning and refrigeration, solar cooking and baking, solar distillation, high temperature applications such as solar furnaces, solar power generation both mechanical and electrical, solar sewage treatment, liquid waste recycling, and solar-electric transportation.

The laboratory has a solar house where many of the devices developed in the laboratory are being used and their performance is observed. It also has a solar-electric car, which is driven by a staff member daily to obtain "in use" performance information. In the following pages, some of the larger of these projects are discussed.

USE OF SOLAR ENERGY

Fossil fuels, which are really stored solar energy, will have to be supplemented by other energy resources, especially by the direct use of solar energy, the output from an old, large, and safe nuclear plant. Solar energy is the only energy income we have, it is well distributed, it is free and does not add anything degrading to the environment through its conversion and utilization. The end product is heat, whether conversion steps are interposed or not. It arrives at about 1 horsepower (hp) per square yard, so that the amount of energy that falls on the roof of a typical house is several times as much as could possibly be used inside.

Since solar energy is intermittent, available only during the day, storage or another source must be provided for nighttime operation. Technically it is possible today to convert solar energy to all the forms of energy needed. Some of these conversion methods are more competitive economically than others. Fossil fuels and nuclear fuels can best and most efficiently be converted to energy in large central stations. Even though large conversion units have been proposed for solar energy, it is questionable whether its basic characteristics match these schemes. It might be better to convert solar energy in small units at the location of use rather than collect it somewhere else, convert it, and then transport it to locations where it is found in the first place.

About 100 stations in the United States monitor the amount of incoming solar radiation continuously so as to provide the necessary information for utilization at a specific location.

SOLAR PROPERTIES OF MATERIALS

The University of Florida Solar Energy and Energy Conversion Laboratory has extensive facilities for the study of solar properties of materials. The most flexible instrument is the solar calorimeter, which provides almost all the information on solar characteristics of fenestrations published in the GUIDE of the American Society of Heating and Air-Conditioning Engineers, which is used extensively by all architects and engineers.[1] It is essentially a well instrumented black cavity that allows the mounting of materials to be studied. Extensive instrumentation with hundreds of thermocouples allows the measurement of incoming energy of high and low wave length radiation, convection and conduction, and delicate heat balances. The instrument can be oriented in any desired position with respect to the sun, it can simulate walls and inclined or flat roofs, or it can be made to follow the sun.

A small weather station and an instrument building go with the calorimeter. It is possible to simulate winter conditions by use of a refrigeration system, summer conditions by means of electric heaters, or ambient conditions as desired. Utilizing the real sunshine rather than artificial sources has been found to be of considerable value since simulations did not seem to be very reliable. Blowers on the instrument can simulate wind conditions for the tests. Photospectrometers and hot and cold boxes are also available.

Materials such as glasses (plain, tinted, coated, laminated, multilayered), plastics (transparent and translucent), glass brick, venetian blinds (some of them water cooled), drapery materials, sun screens of all kinds, etc. have been investigated.[2-5]

In addition to the determination of solar properties, the laboratory has exposure test facilities to evaluate the weathering properties of materials. This is often done before studying the materials in detail. Two 5-foot diameter solar furnaces are used for high temperature work. Once the true properties of materials are known, the best can be selected for the conversion of solar energy into the required forms.

SOLAR REFRIGERATION AND AIR CONDITIONING

One of the real needs is the ability to preserve food. This can be done by solar refrigeration, which is ideally matched to the energy supply since cooling is needed most when the sun shines hottest. Solar energy can be used to drive an engine and then a compressor to provide compression refrigeration, or the heat from solar energy can be used in an absorption refrigeration system. These and a few other systems have been developed in the laboratory.

Steam jet refrigeration was tried at one time, and oil heated by the sun was used to replace the gas flame of a gas refrigerator. These methods worked but were not considered to be the best since they required concentration and thus could not utilize the diffuse portion of the solar energy on cloudy days.

For this reason emphasis was put on flat plate solar collectors for providing the energy to operate absorption refrigeration and air-conditioning systems. Flat plate solar absorbers heat water, which is the energy source for absorption refrigeration or air-conditioning systems. In an ammonia-water system the heat drives the ammonia from solution. The ammonia is then condensed and the liquid expanded. This makes it very cold and able to absorb heat and thus provides the cooling. The warmed vapor is reabsorbed in the water and circulated back to start its cycle over again. The process can be carried out intermittently or continuously.[2,7,8]

Storage can be provided in the form of hot water, ammonia, or ice. The latter has the advantage that it can be moved to different locations and thereby service other than just the immediate area. The ice machine has a 4 ft X 4 ft solar collector, which serves at the same time as the ammonia generator, not requiring solar water heaters. Its conversion is slightly better since no heat is lost in heat exchangers.

A water driven air-conditioning system is the easiest to combine with a solar heating system, and this combination permits double use of many parts.

SOLAR POWER GENERATION

A rather extensive program in the laboratory deals with power generation. Many engines of different designs and operating on different principles have been designed and evaluated. Some of them do not have moving parts. However, at this time it seems that the vapor and hot air engines have the most promise. A number of fractional horsepower vapor engines and hot air engines have been built and used to pump water, drive machinery, or drive electric generators to charge batteries for night use or for transportation in the solar-electric car.

The closed-cycle hot-air engine shown in Figure 14 can develop about $1/3$ hp, the limitation not being the engine but the concentrating mirror which is about 5 feet in diameter. A larger mirror would allow the engine to put out more power. These engines only need a source of heat and therefore can be operated with wood, coal, gas, or oil if nighttime operation is required. In the closed-cycle hot-air engine, the enclosed air is alternately heated and cooled when brought in contact with the hot and then the cool walls. When the air is hot, the pressure is high and the power piston is pushed down; when the air is cool, the flywheel returns the power piston against low pressure. A plunger moves the air back and forth between the hot and cool walls.[2,9,10] In the closed-cycle engine, the speed of the engine is controlled by the speed with which the air can be heated and cooled.

In order to separate the speed of the engine from the heat transfer characteristics, open-cycle engines were designed. Figure 15 pictures one of those engines. In the open-cycle hot-air engine, the air is taken in and compressed. It is then moved through a heater where it reaches high temperatures. From the heater it flows through the engine where it expands, does work, and is then exhausted to the atmosphere. The engine and the compressor are coupled together. By this method the engine speed and the heat transfer characteristics are independent.

These two engines require concentration of solar energy and thus need rather good sunny days for operation. Vapor engines have been designed

Figure 14
The Closed-Cycle Hot-Air Engine

Figure 15
The Open-Cycle Hot-Air Engine

and built that use flat plate absorbers to generate vapor at relatively low temperatures and use it in vapor cycles.

SEWAGE TREATMENT

Among other applications of solar energy is the treatment of sewage. It was found that solar energy can be used to keep the sewage digester temperature up to provide more efficient bacterial activity. In this manner the sewage handling capacity of digesters can be considerably increased.

THE UNIVERSITY OF FLORIDA SOLAR HOUSE

Approximately two years ago the conversion of the University of Florida Test House into a solar house was started. This was done step by step as time and funds permitted.

The reasons for utilizing this house were many, the most important ones being that information existed over the last 16 years as to how different conventional systems performed in supplying the hot water, heating, air conditioning, energy for cooking and other activities while the air quality in the house was monitored. All the data in this thoroughly instrumented house were obtained while a married student couple lived in this house with all modern conveniences provided.

In the early stages of the project, walls, windows, and insulation in the house were changed to evaluate their performance and later the systems serving the house were evaluated (i.e., oil, gas, and electricity were used at different times to provide the energy to water heaters, air conditioners, heat pumps, and cooking systems). Overhead or attic air distribution systems with different diffuser outlets were compared with underfloor distribution systems.

These years of data and experience, under actual lived-in conditions, gave a wealth of information and a firm basis for absolute comparisons of different systems serving the same house under the same conditions.

The house is a conventional, typical block construction dwelling similar to many found in Florida and elsewhere. It has three bedrooms, two baths, kitchen, living and dining rooms, utility and laundry rooms, and a carport with enclosed storage space. The laundry room, besides holding a washing machine and dryer, is used for all the instrumentation monitoring the many activities and systems of the house. The road approaching the house comes from the east so the solar energy equipment is not seen until one walks around the house. All the solar energy equipment installed in the solar house was developed and evaluated in the University of Florida Solar Energy Conversion Laboratory.

The first unit that was added to the house was the solar water heater. The collector was put on the roof with the hot water tank behind it. The first visitors to the solar house were disappointed that they did not see the solar equipment, and it was too hazardous to take them up on the roof. For educational reasons it was decided to place the rest of the solar energy conversion equipment next to the house in the open, rather than to incorporate it inside, so that visitors can walk around the equipment, touch and photograph it and, in general, get a good idea of what such equipment is like.

Further, two swimming pools were added, one heated by solar energy and the other by standard means for comparison. Also added was a house heating system with a large storage tank, above ground rather than buried, with plans to use the solar collecting and storage parts also for the air conditioning; a small liquid waste recycling system; a small solar-energy-to-electricity conversion unit; and a solar-electric car which is part of the overall system. In the near future, solar air conditioning, refrigeration, and cooking will be added.

Adaptation of Conventional Systems

WATER HEATER. The solar heater consists of a 48 ft^2 solar collector and an 80-gal well-insulated hot water storage tank.[3,13-17] The solar absorber is a galvanized sheet metal box having 1 inch of styrofoam insulation inside in the back. In front of the insulation is a copper sheet with two parallel circuits of sinusiodally arranged tubes soldered onto it. Both sheet and tubes are painted with a good absorbing paint. The box is covered by glass having good solar energy transmitting properties.

The hot water delivered by this unit flows by free convection to the hot water storage tank which is well insulated to reduce heat losses.

HEATED SWIMMING POOL. To truly evaluate the effectiveness of heating the swimming pool by solar energy, two identical pools were installed, 15 feet in diameter and 4 feet deep. One was heated by various methods utilizing solar energy, and the other was used as standard for comparison.

Both pools were well instrumented with many thermocouples in each. One pool, the unheated one, was left to itself. The other was heated by solar energy in a number of ways. The simplest method was to float a transparent sheet of plastic on its surface. Two sheets of the air-mattress design do a better job, or bubble sheet can be a reasonably good collector and a good inhibitor to heat losses. The solar absorbers of the house heating system described below were also used at times to heat one of the pools. The latter system is economical only as a combination between house and pool heating.

The simple plastic sheet could keep the average pool temperature 20 F above the average air temperature and 10 F above the unheated pool temperature. Utilizing the house heating absorbers, the pool temperature could be kept about 40 F above the average ambient air temperature.

HEATING SYSTEM. The solar house heating system is basically a hot water system that was selected over the air heating system since the former is easier to use as the front end of a solar air-conditioning system. Ten solar absorbers, similar to the one used for the solar hot water system and comprising 350 ft^2 of absorbing surface provide hot water which is stored in a 3,000-gal tank with 4 inches of insulation around it.

Water from the storage tank is circulated by a small pump through the baseboard heating system in the house as required to keep the temperature of the house at the desired value. With 140 feet of baseboard heaters, 60,000 BTU per hour can be delivered with supply water of 130 F, which is the design load for the house to meet the maximum heat requirement under extreme conditions in Gainesville, Florida. With the water hotter, more heat can be delivered, and cycling controls the actual amount of heat delivered.

The flow rate through the solar absorbers can be controlled so as to deliver water at the desired temperature that is stored in the upper part of the storage tank. The delivery to the house is thermostatically controlled. The storage tank is larger than actually needed but was used to allow long-time storage to carry the house through bad weather conditions. For only 1 F water temperature drop in the storage tank, 25,000 BTU can be delivered to the house.

LIQUID WASTE RECYCLING PLANT. Since fresh water is becoming more and more difficult to obtain and is also getting more expensive, a small liquid waste solar recycling plant has been added to the house. This solar distillation unit (Figure 16) has a liquid holding tray area of 27 ft^2 and can produce up to about 3 gal of fresh water on a good day. This unit is also designed to collect rain water which, in Gainesville, just about doubles the output.[18] This plant is not able to handle all the liquid waste of the house, but one could be built any desired size depending upon the recycling requirements.

Figure 16
The Liquid Waste Recycling Plant

SOLAR-ELECTRIC CONVERSION UNIT. Most of the energy today in a house is used for water heating, house heating, and air conditioning. The real need for electricity is only a small fraction of the total energy requirement. It is really only needed for radio, T.V., lights, and some small appliances. Figure 17 shows the small unit used to convert solar energy, by means of solar cells, into DC electricity and store it in NiCd batteries. The energy from the batteries is then converted as needed by a DC-to-AC solid state converter to operate lights, radios, T.V., and small appliances. The cost of this unit is certainly not competitive at this time, but it demonstrates the feasibility of providing electricity.

Figure 17
The Solar-Electric Conversion Unit

AIR CONDITIONING, COOKING, AND REFRIGERATION. When the solar house heating system was designed, it was done so that the solar absorbers and the storage system can be used to drive a specially designed air-conditioning system during the cooling season. The hot water is used in the winter for heating the house and in the summer for air conditioning. Systems described earlier have been designed in the University of Florida Solar Energy and Energy Conversion Laboratory for use in this manner.[7,8,19,20] The systems operate with water as low as 120 F.

The air distribution system to be used with the solar air-conditioning system is already in the house, so that only the absorption system has to be

68

added. It is being designed to fit the needs of the house, and, once it is installed, air conditioning will be the next step.

After the air conditioning is incorporated into the solar house, a concentrator from the Solar Energy Laboratory will be moved to the house to provide oil at high temperature which will be stored in a tank. This oil will then be circulated as needed around burners of a stove and in an oven so as to allow cooking very similarly as with an electric stove. The electric elements are replaced by coils of copper tubing.

Such an experimental system was operated a number of years ago in our Solar Energy and Energy Conversion Laboratory. At that time, the hot oil was also used to operate a refrigerator in which the gas flame was replaced by a hot oil bath. A better and more effective solar refrigerator has, however, been developed since.

THE SOLAR-ELECTRIC CAR. The solar-electric car of the laboratory (Figures 18, 19), which can go about 60 mph and has a range of about 100 miles, is part of a system providing the energy requirements for a family, both in the house and for necessary transportation. All this comes from solar energy directly and is pollution free.

Figure 18
The Solar-Electric Car

For transportation, solar energy at the present time is converted into mechanical work by a hot-air engine which, in turn, drives an automobile generator that can charge the batteries of the electric car. This type of conversion from solar energy to electricity is much less expensive than the use of solid state conversion.[12]

A network of "filling stations" each having such conversion systems and using them to charge up banks of batteries could, instead of filling the gas tank of a car with gasoline, exchange run down batteries for charged ones to provide the needs of the traveler.

Figure 19
The Battery-Engine Compartment

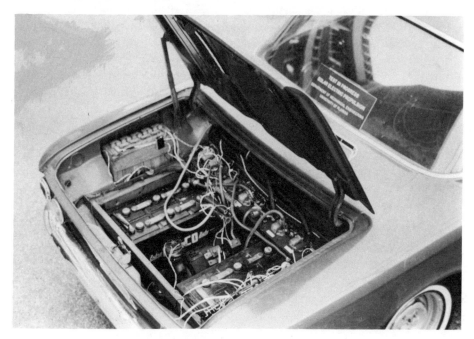

OUTLOOK FOR THE FUTURE

The fact that fossil fuels, nuclear fuels, etc. are fixed in quantity may in itself not be the limiting factor in their utilization. Pollution, inherent in the conversion of these fuels, may instead force the curtailment of their use. In the Los Angeles basin, limitations have been put upon the building of new power plants. The only alternative in this case may be to limit the consumption per person. "Rolling Black-outs" have been suggested as one solution. The basin can be divided into regions and the power to each region can be cut for 1 hour out of a 24-hour period, the blackout moving consecutively from region to region.

Gas rationing was suggested for the Los Angeles basin during the last part of 1972 to reduce the pollution and smog problem. This limiting of the energy supply is due not to shortage or unavailability of fuel but to the consequences of using it.

Solar energy is the only large source of energy that can be pollution-free. Its use does not add or subtract anything from the environment; it only interposes additional steps into the conversion from solar energy to heat, which is the end product even if it is not used. This can be likened to a river which, on its way from the mountains to the ocean, drives a water wheel and thereby provides useful energy. The water flows from the mountains to the ocean whether energy is extracted or not.

In summarizing it may be stated that, in this writer's opinion, we will always need fossil fuels for certain applications but, since they will become scarcer and more expensive, other fuel sources will have to be drawn upon if we wish to continue to enjoy the standard of living whch we are enjoying now and if the rest of the world is to raise its standard of living.

So we will move from a "Fossil Fuel Society," in which we are at present, to an interim "Nuclear Society," at which time a considerable portion of our energy requirements will be met by this source. But since the above sources of energy have to be classified as savings they cannot last forever, and society and civilization will have to move toward a source that is well distributed, pollution-free, and inexhaustible, and thus classified as income. Ultimately, we will, by necessity, become a "Solar Society." When all this will come about depends upon our actions, wise or unwise, dictated in many cases by economic and political decisions.

References

1. Pennington CW: University of Florida-ASHRAE Solar Calorimeter. *ASHRAE Journal,* vol 8, March 1966.

2. Farber EA: Solar Energy: Conversion and Utilization. *Building Systems Design,* June 1972.

3. Farber EA: Selective Surfaces and Solar Absorbers. *Journal for Applied Solar Energy,* April 1959.

4. Farber EA: Theoretical Effective Reflectivities, Absorptivities, and Transmissivities of Draperies as a Function of Geometric Configuration. *Solar Energy,* vol 7, No. 4, Oct-Dec 1963.

5. Farber EA: Experimental Analysis of Solar Heat Gain Through Insulating Glass with Indoor Shading. *ASHRAE Journal,* Feb 1964.

6. Farber EA: Crystals of High Temperature Materials Produced in the Solar Furnace. *Solar Energy,* vol 8, No. 1, Jan-Mar 1964.

7. Farber EA, et al: Operation and Performance of the University of Florida Solar Air-Conditioning System. *Solar Energy,* vol 10, No. 2, April-June 1966.

8. Farber EA: A Compact Solar Refrigeration System. *ASME Paper* #70WA/SOL4, Dec 1970.

9. Farber EA, et al: Closed Cycle Hot Air Engines. *Solar Energy,* vol 9, No. 4, Oct-Dec 1965.

10. Farber EA: Hot Air Engines. *Mark's Mechanical Engineers' Handbook,* 7th Ed, McGraw-Hill Book Co, New York, 1966.

11. Farber EA: The Application of Solar Energy to Sewage Digestion and Liquid Waste Recycling. Proceedings of the Third National Convention of the Institute of Plumbing, Australia, March 1973.

12. Schaeper HRA, et al: The University of Florida Solar-Electric Automobile. *Mechanical Engineering,* Nov 1972.

13. Farber EA: Practical Applications of Solar Energy. *Consulting Engineer,* Sept 1956.

14. Farber EA: Solar Water Heating; Present Practices and Installations. *ASME Paper* #57-SA-45, June 1957, and *National Engineer,* Aug 1957.

15. Farber EA, et al: Solar Energy to Supply Service Hot Water. *Air-Conditioning, Heating and Ventilating,* Oct 1957.

16. Farber EA: Solar Water Heating and Space Heating in Florida. *The Journal of Solar Energy Science and Engineering,* vol 3, No. 3, Oct 1959.

17. Farber EA: The Use of Solar Energy for Heating Water. U.N. Conference Proceedings on New Sources of Energy, Aug 1961.

18. Garrett CR, et al: Performance of a Solar Still. *ASME Paper,* Dec 1961.

19. Farber EA: Solar Water Heating, Space Heating and Cooling. *Journal of Applied Solar Energy,* Aug 1960.

20. Eisenstadt M: Tests Prove Feasibility of Solar Air-Conditioning. *Heating, Piping and Air-Conditioning,* June 1960.

7

Hydrogen Energy Systems

Derek P. Gregory, Ph.D.

We are living in an exciting and rather frightening period in the history of mankind. In the last 30 years, we have used as much energy as was used by the whole of mankind in all of its previously recorded history. We will use the same amount again in the next 15 years, and the same again in the following 7 years. Until now, almost all of this energy has been derived from the sun and stored for our use by Mother Nature as wood, oil, coal, gas, or water power. Because our storehouse of energy is showing signs of running dry, we have to develop new sources, such as nuclear energy or different forms of solar energy. Unless we learn to do this, we cannot maintain even our present standards of civilization, let alone improve them.

In spite of this obvious and urgent need, the introduction of novel energy sources is not taking place at a fast enough rate to satisfy U.S. domestic needs. The nuclear energy program is not proceeding as fast as was originally planned, and we are having to import very large amounts of oil to supply our demands. The direct use of solar energy has not found extensive economic use up to the present. This paper discusses a concept that may help us to overcome some of the difficulties encountered in introducing these novel power sources and, at the same time, allow us to continue to use energy in our conventional and traditional ways without condemning our environment. This concept is the use of synthetic hydrogen as a universal fuel.

For some time, the Institute of Gas Technology has been investigating the technical and economic feasibility of converting, at some time in the future, the nation's natural gas distribution system to operate on a synthetic fuel that could be manufactured in unlimited quantities by use of nuclear or solar energy. This work is supported by the American Gas Association. So that we do not run headlong into a pollution problem, we have carefully selected our choice of synthetic fuel, limiting it to one that, upon combustion, does not produce any product that cannot be rapidly accepted by the atmosphere. At the same time, we have ensured that the fuel is synthesized from materials that are in abundant supply.

To meet these requirements, we are restricted to consider compounds of hydrogen, oxygen, nitrogen, and possibly carbon. Carbon can be obtained in abundance from limestone rocks (carbonates) or, with some expenditure of energy, from the carbon dioxide in the atmosphere, where it is present in small concentrations but in enormous quantities. Hydrogen can be obtained from water, which is present in abundance, while oxygen and nitrogen are, of course, major constituents of the atmosphere.

Therefore, we can consider synthesizing such fuels as ammonia (NH_3), hydrazine (N_2H_4), methane (CH_4), methanol (CH_3OH), or hydrogen (H_2). The simplest and cheapest of these to make, and the cleanest in use, is hydrogen itself. For these reasons, we selected hydrogen as the best candidate for a synthetic fuel.

THE HYDROGEN FUEL CONCEPT

In summary, this concept is one in which hydrogen, derived with nuclear or other energy forms, is used for supplying all the demands commonly met today by fossil fuels (including industrial, commercial, residential, and vehicular power), as well as for generating electricity on a local level. Such a concept has been termed a "Hydrogen Economy" [1] or an "Eco-Energy" [2] system. Studies carried out at the Institute of Gas Technology [3] and elsewhere [4] have established that there would be no insuperable problems in the transmission and distribution of hydrogen or in the use of hydrogen for domestic and commercial heating and cooking. For many industrial uses, it represents an ideal fuel and/or reducing gas. The application of hydrogen as a vehicular and aircraft fuel seems to depend on solving problems concerned with the tankage and transfer of fuel rather than with the engine itself.

The economics of producing hydrogen from nuclear or solar power can be assessed fairly accurately. For the simple case of electrolytic hydrogen, it is obvious that the hydrogen energy must always cost more than the electricity from which it is made unless unexpected allowances can be made from the sale of by-product oxygen or heavy water. It is the relatively less expensive transmission and distribution of hydrogen compared with electricity that makes its use so attractive. Its extreme cleanliness in use—only water vapor is produced on combustion—makes it even more attractive on environmental grounds.

The concept appears to present an economically attractive alternative to the "all-electric economy," in which the nuclear and solar power stations of the future will generate electricity and transmit it to the load centers. Some of the problems of using electricity are concerned with the very long distances likely to be involved between the power stations and the load centers, the public's opposition to overhead transmission lines, their high cost, and the need for an energy storage system to even out the variations between production rates (constant for nuclear, periodic for solar) and demand (widely variable on daily, weekly, and annual cycles).

HYDROGEN PRODUCTION

Hydrogen can be made today by the electrolysis of water. This process is used industrially where specific conditions make it most attractive; for large-scale production this requires cheap electric power. Large-scale plants are in operation in Canada, Norway, and Egypt. As a result of fuel cell technology, advances in the cost and efficiency of electrolyzers have been demonstrated on a small scale. Much remains to be done to fully exploit the potential for electrochemical improvements in electrolyzers. With power costs at 4 to 7 mills per kilowatt hour (kw-hr), hydrogen costs of $2.00 to $3.00/million BTU are predicted. With reasonable assumptions on the results of long-term research improvements to the electrolyzer, costs of $1.50 to $2.50 can be proposed (compared with today's costs of liquefied natural gas imports at about $1.00/million BTU, which are expected to rise significantly over the next 10 to 20 years).

These hydrogen costs take no credit for the value of the oxygen produced in very large quantities as a co-product. Oxygen is valuable in water-treatment and waste-disposal processes as well as being highly important to the metallurgical and other industries. It might be sold at a price sufficient to lower the selling price of hydrogen by about $1.00/million BTU.

An interesting possibility exists for the splitting of water into hydrogen and oxygen by using the heat from a nuclear reactor or a solar furnace, without going through the electricity generation stage. The temperatures required to split water directly are too high for today's materials, but stepwise chemical processes, which achieve the same objective, have been proposed. Research is still in the earliest stages, and it is not yet possible to assess either costs or efficiencies.

Today, industrial hydrogen is made from natural gas and other fossil fuels by reaction with steam. The conversion of coal, shale, and low-grade fuels to hydrogen is technically possible today and could certainly make a significant addition to the sources of hydrogen fuel in the near term. In this way, hydrogen could act as a common fuel to bridge the gap between the fossil fuel age and the nuclear or solar age.

HYDROGEN TRANSMISSION AND STORAGE

Transmission of hydrogen in pipes is routinely carried out over relatively short distances in refinery operations. Longer pipelines do exist: one about 50 miles long is in the Houston area, and a network of about 130 miles is in West Germany. Thus, hydrogen pipeline technology at pressures of 500 to 1,000 pounds per square inch (psi) is demonstrable. For long-distance transmission, however, compressors are needed at intervals along the pipeline, and no direct experience with hydrogen is available. Natural gas, of course, is routinely transmitted in this way for distances of 1,000 to 2,000 miles. The knowledge gained from this technology can be used to predict the costs of moving hydrogen. The transmission costs of natural gas, electricity, and hydrogen can conveniently be compared in terms of units of energy moved.

The cost of pipelining gas is considerably less than typical electric power transmission costs. For example, a typical 36-inch natural gas pipeline is capable of moving energy at a rate of about 1 billion BTU/hr, or 12,000 Mw, at a cost of about 1¢ to 2¢/million BTU/100 miles. Compare this with a high-voltage overhead transmission line that can carry up to 2,000 Mw at a cost of 9¢ to 20¢/million BTU/100 miles. Underground power cables are likely to cost between 10 and 40 times as much as overhead lines.[5] Estimates of the cost of hydrogen transmission in bulk pipelines that have been made [3,6] range from 3¢ to 4¢/million BTU/100 miles. This is only about one hundredth the cost of underground electricity transmission.

The storage capability of hydrogen is of extreme importance if it is to be of use in evening out both daily and seasonal peaks. Natural gas is stored in huge quantities in underground porous rock formations, in depleted gas fields, and in aquifers. There seems to be no reason why hydrogen cannot be similarly stored. An aquifer storage area near Paris, France, stores 13 billion cubic feet (cu ft) of manufactured gas that contains 50% hydrogen. In areas where underground storage of gas is geologically impossible, a recent trend has been to liquefy natural gas and store it in refrigerated tanks. The technology for the liquefaction and storage of hydrogen as a liquid is well developed thanks to the aerospace program; there seems to be no technological reason why this technique cannot be applied to hydrogen in the quantities required. The largest tank for liquid hydrogen has a 900,000-gal capacity and is located at Cape Kennedy.

UTILIZATION OF HYDROGEN

The use of hydrogen as a fuel presents some problems together with some distinct technical advantages. There seems to be no reason why pure hydrogen could not be used for all the purposes served by natural gas today. It burns smoothly and easily when mixed with air on burners closely resembling today's gas burners. Natural gas burners would have to be modified to account for the different combustion properties of hydrogen, but the data required to do this are available. The combustion products would be water vapor and traces of nitrogen oxides.

An exciting possibility exists to make hydrogen an absolutely clean fuel, eliminating even the trace nitrogen oxide emissions that occur when any fuel is burned in air. This can be achieved by the technique of catalytic combustion.

If the temperature of combustion is kept below about 2,200 F, no measurable amount of nitrogen oxides can form, on basic thermodynamic grounds. In a free flame, it is difficult to reduce combustion temperatures to this low level. However, hydrogen and air mixtures combine smoothly and spontaneously on an active catalyst surface at quite low temperatures, even at room temperature. If the catalyst temperature is allowed to rise above about 1,100 F, a flame occurs, and conventional combustion takes place. However, if the heat of reaction is conducted or convected away fast enough, the catalyst cannot reach this temperature; thus no flame occurs, and the only product of combustion is water vapor.

Simple appliances operating on this principle have been constructed in the laboratory and demonstrated in such applications as space heating, water heating, and cooking. It appears that operation without a vent or flue can be made perfectly safe, but some form of humidity control would be required in the house. In general, it will be relatively easy to maintain living and working environments at a fairly high humidity level in winter.

Engines operate well on hydrogen. Already, several teams are converting automobile engines to run on hydrogen. The main modifications required are to carburetion and ignition. It has been shown [7] that a laboratory engine operating on hydrogen has far less nitrogen oxides emissions than a gasoline engine. No other pollutants are possible. The main problem concerning hydrogen as a vehicle fuel is that of tankage. Compressed hydrogen tanks are too heavy and bulky to be seriously considered. Liquid-hydrogen tankage at present is expensive and rather bulky, although technologically quite feasible. A promising area is the use of chemically bound hydrogen in metal hydrides, which can be decomposed by the heat of the exhaust to provide pure hydrogen.

Gas turbines can be converted to hydrogen fuel with little trouble. This was done quite successfully in the 1950s. Indeed, a B-57 aircraft flew with liquid-hydrogen fuel several years ago. Hydrogen has such a weight advantage over kerosene (only about one third of the weight to supply the same energy) that it is receiving considerable attention as a candidate for the aircraft fuel of the future. As an additional advantage, most of the pollution problems associated with today's jet aircraft would thus be eliminated.

Hydrogen is a raw material for the chemical industry of vast and growing importance. It is used in the manufacture of fertilizers and foodstuffs, for upgrading petroleum fuels, and for many other purposes. Its use as a direct metallurgical reductant (for example, in producing iron from ore) has been technically proved, but it has only been used in special cases, such as where hydrogen happens to be cheaper than coke. As fossil fuel prices rise, more use of hydrogen with its attendant decreases in pollution levels will take place.

Hydrogen is an ideal fuel for fuel cells, eliminating the need for the fuel-conditioning stage required for hydrocarbon fuels and increasing the efficiency somewhat. Local or dispersed generation of electric power by fuel cells is under active study at present by both the gas and electricity industries. Hydrogen is also an attractive fuel for more conventional electricity generation techniques that use advanced gas or steam turbines.

HYDROGEN SAFETY

Perhaps the most controversial issue concerned with the use of hydrogen is that of safety. Hydrogen is a hazardous and dangerous material, but it has been used so extensively in industry and in aerospace that very clearly defined codes of practice have been developed. Compared with natural gas, its lower flammability limit in air is about the same (4% and 5%, respectively), but its flammability range is far higher (up to 75% for hydrogen and up to 15% for natural gas). Hydrogen has a very low ignition energy, so that a static spark will ignite it, and also has a very high flame speed. Compared with propane and gasoline, its lower flammability limit when mixed with air is higher, and it is far lighter than air so that it diffuses away from a leak or spill. With odorization to make leaks easily detected and with proper handling techniques, pure hydrogen should be no more hazardous than the old "town gas" or manufactured gas, which was composed of 50% hydrogen and which had the added hazard of toxicity because of its carbon monoxide content.

CONCLUSION

Hydrogen thus appears to be a very promising universal fuel. Its price today is high compared with that of fossil fuels, but hydrogen from nonfossil sources should become relatively cheaper as the fossil fuels become more expensive. It has very considerable advantages in pollution and in energy transmission. An energy system centered around a hydrogen transmission and distribution system is attractive because hydrogen could be introduced to the system from a wide variety of sources—nuclear, solar, geothermal, wind, and tide power—as well as from low-grade fossil fuels, while the consumer would experience no changes in his fuel quality. Such flexibility will be of very great importance to the energy industry in the next 50 years or so when very considerable changes in energy sources must be made. Hydrogen is a clean chemical fuel that can be produced from wholly domestic energy sources, without importation. While interest in this concept is rapidly growing within the energy industries, the problems in implementation of such a system are immense and would have to be thoroughly planned well in advance.

References

1. Gregory DP: The Hydrogen Economy. *Sci Amer* **228**:13–22, 1973.

2. Hausz W, Leeth G, Meyer C: Eco-Energy, Paper *729206.* Intersociety Energy Conversion Engineering Conference, San Diego, Sept 1972.

3. Gregory DP, Wurm J: Production and Distribution of Hydrogen as a Universal Fuel, Paper *729208.* Intersociety Energy Conversion Engineering Conference, San Diego, Sept 1972.

4. Winsche WE, Sheehan TV, Hoffman KC: Hydrogen—A Clean Fuel for Urban Areas, Paper *719006.* Intersociety Energy Conversion Engineering Conference, Boston, Sept 1971.

5. The Transmission of Electric Power—A report to the Federal Power Commission by the Transmission Technical Advisory Committee, p 123, Feb 1971.

6. Winsche WE, Hoffman KC, Salzano FJ: Economics of Hydrogen Fuel for Transportation and Other Residential Applications, Paper *729213.* Intersociety Energy Conversion Engineering Conference, San Diego, Sept 1972.

7. Murray RG, Schoeppel RJ: Emission and Performance Characteristics of an Air Breathing Hydrogen Fueled Internal Combustion Engine, Paper *717009.* 1971 Intersociety Energy Conversion Engineering Conference, Boston, Aug 1971.

Discussion

Dr. Boyle: Mr. Mullan, apparently you believe that the air quality standards for sulfur dioxide are too stringent. Yet of all the standards we have for which the health hazards are recognized, this is probably the one for which we have the greatest scientific basis.

Mr. Mullan: I cannot argue with the primary ambient air quality standards that were established by the Environmental Protection Agency (EPA). What I argue with are the fuel emission limitations that have been established by the states and regions to meet the secondary standards in a time frame much faster than the Clean Air Act requires. The states have been directed by the Clean Air Act to meet the primary standard in 1975 and to meet the secondary standard at some reasonable time in the future. Most of the states have written into their legislation requirements for meeting the secondary standard as well as the primary standard in 1975. This action has imposed an undue burden on the energy industry in this country. The Clean Air Act also says that states should establish regions where more stringent standards are required than would be needed in the rest of the state. Yet, most states have chosen to set the standards for the worst situation in the state and make them statewide. This can only serve to compound the environmental demands and also to compound the energy problems of each of the states.

Q: Mr. Mullan, can you give us some idea of how much is going into research on the burning of coal, both from governmental sources and private sources? Second, what does your industry feel in regard to the possibility of new methods of using coal? I get the feeling from listening to Mr. Mullan that he would like to see SO$_2$ standards relaxed in places; he does not come before us and say we are on the verge of being able to correct this situation. I am trying to get some feel of the prospects of the industry's research programs into other means of using coal. My reason is that I think that there are five more plants coming on line west of Colorado, each of which will burn at least 25,000 tons of coal a day. This is a really major problem and, if the industry does not have some method of coming to grips with this, we are facing a terrible problem.

Mr. Mullan: The question, as I understand it, is that you want to know, first, how much money, both governmental and industrial, is involved in methods of burning coal and, second, other uses of coal. The proposal that I just stated to modify the standards of the time frames is not mine alone. In fact, it was proposed by Mr. William Ruckelshaus when he was director of the Environmental Protection Agency. I think it is the end result of EPA's taking a long look at the energy situation and the environmental situation in this country. I think he accomplished back in November 1972 what I would hope would be the result of this particular meeting. There is an environmental concern and there is an energy concern, and there has to be some way to balance them. Mr. Ruckelshaus feels that protecting the public health has to be first, and I agree with him completely. At no time did I say that we should violate the primary standards, and I do not think that you will find any of us in the coal industry, and in the utilities industry, talking about any violation of the primary standards. The problem we face is the speeding up to meet the secondary standards, which are the public welfare standards, without regard to the availability of equipment. The equipment is not here today. Now there is a lot of technology that has been developed in the last year and there are about 25 or 30 SO_2 removal systems that have been installed for demonstration. None of them has worked for any long period of time except for one in Japan, and I am aware of that particular installation. A duplicate of that unit is being constructed and is just started here in this country. We hope these removal systems will run on U.S. coal and that they will be ready before 1980. The thing that concerns me is the construction capabilities of the companies that produce these devices. The SOXTECH report on sulfur oxide technology said that the biggest problem was the capability of the equipment industry to produce the SO_2 control devices at a speed fast enough to solve the problem.

Q: I would like to once again emphasize the importance of the biological end points here. If you remember that these standards that industries are trying to meet are set up, at least in principle, to protect the public health, then you have to ask the question, "How good are these numbers?" In short, with the possible exception of radiation (where they may be over-conservative in some cases), and perhaps in the case of plutonium (where they are very uncertain), these numbers are terrible. Although the numbers are here and they are real, the biology behind them is awful. I feel that, as a group of physicians, we should be more aware of the need to understand the biology so that the numbers with which we all have to live and to which industry had to adjust are more realistic than just good guesses. In the case of nuclear power, for example, imagine how free one would be to exploit a plutonium economy if there were no great biological hazards from plutonium on the loose. I recognize that safeguards are another problem. Similarly, if the standards that are set for sulfur emissions really should be phrased in terms mostly of sulfur particulates, for which there is a little bit of indication, it might be possible now with appropriate forms of combustion to use some high sulfur fuels without great public health hazards. Our ignorance is what is holding us back now.

Mr. Mullan: The point that is raised is valid since most of the research that went into establishing these standards was for sulfur dioxide, alone, and the particulates, alone, without any real concern for the synergistic effects of the two. Also, much of it was based on animal studies as opposed to epidemiological studies.

Dr. Boyle: I simply have to challenge the observation that there is not a sound scientific basis for picking the numbers as far as air quality standards are concerned. There may be a need for more information but there was a sound basis for those standards. I think that some of the air pollution disasters that have occurred probably attest to that, particularly with respect to SO_2.

Dr. Forrest E. Rieke: You skipped rather lightly over the question on strip mining. I get the impression in the West, where I live, that some of the coal companies are not really very anxious to pay much attention to the environmental problem, unless somebody ties their hands pretty quickly in Montana. Where does the industry find itself in this relationship to the big argument about stripping and not restoring the land?

Mr. Mullan: I believe I made the statement and, if I did not, I will make it now: if you cannot reclaim it, you should not strip it. It is that simple.

Dr. Rieke: Does the whole association believe this?

Mr. Mullan: Yes sir. There are companies that do not belong to the association, but those are very few.

Q: Dr. Rose, as I understand it, the fission reactors produce about 1 to 10 curies of tritium a year, and with the fusion reactors we are talking in terms of 300,000 or so. How are we going to handle that problem?

Dr. Rose: The one substantial radioactive material in controlled fusion is tritium. Tritium in fission reactors is a relatively minor radioactive effluent that has a half-life of about 12 years. It is relatively harmless per curie of radioactivity, although none of the radioactive materials is really harmless, of course. Tritium is the one hazard of controlled fusion. There have been some estimates of how much there is in a fusion reactor. There would be several kilograms of tritium, which is a large amount, and this might be in the order of 10^8 curies of tritium. Nonetheless, if you ask what the biological hazard is of that much tritium compared with a fission reactor, it is several orders of magnitude less in terms of a threat to your existence. There are problems of keeping it in that are not solved, because fusion reactors are still in people's minds, not in reality. The technology is not fully worked out but the prognosis is, I think, fairly good.

Q: One of the frightening prospects of nuclear energy is the stockpiling and storage of the spent materials. I wonder if Dr. Rose would have a comment on that issue, especially as it relates to the problem of stockpiling it in salt mines in Kansas or sending it down to Antarctica.

Dr. Rose: The Kansas salt mine proposal was less than adequate for the purpose. In effect, what happened was that the Atomic Energy Commission consulted its contracting laboratories; together they convinced themselves that this was the best option and should be explored almost to the exclusion of any others. Putting things in salt mines is not in itself a reprehensible thing. The arguments that have been made in favor of that particular salt mine were arguments that were basically retrospective. The salt had been there for 300 million years, hence it was geologically stable and so forth. But these facts were all retrospective. To apply them to the future would imply that the conditions were going to be unchanged. Of course, that is not the case, because two miles away people were busy doing solution mining of salt and had bored holes through the site looking for gas. I think there are a number of other options and other places than the Lyons, Kansas, site. Second, chemical separations of the various wastes would cause a problem for a few hundred years, instead of for 300,000 years. Third, structures other than salt mines, such as hard rock formations (in spite of some difficulties), also look attractive, and these things have not been explored. The point is there is so much option space available that I tend to feel optimistic. Also, putting things in what I facetiously call mausolea, which are near-surface storage vaults, is also a good option. I don't like the Antartica proposal because of various difficulties. If you want the amount of heat generation at the bottom of that ice cap to be small compared to the geothermal flow of heat, then you will run out of space for storing wastes soon after the year 2000. Also, if you do generate very much heat, then you can increase the motion of the ice, which also is bad. I tend to prefer options that we know more about.

III

ENVIRONMENTAL
IMPACTS

8

Ecological Impacts
of Energy Production
on Rivers and Lakes*

Robert J. Beyers, Ph.D.

It may be accepted as a fact that there is an increasing world-wide demand for power production. It is estimated that, in the United States alone, electric power production will double approximately every ten years. This geometric growth will result in a rise in total generation from our present production of approximately 3 trillion kilowatt hours (kw-hr) per year to 20 trillion kw-hr per year by the year 2020.[1] It is also a fact that any method of power generation has some deleterious effect upon the environment. The effect depends to a large extent on the source of the energy to be converted into electricity. I would like to devote the first portion of this discussion to some of the nonthermal impacts of power production and the second section to the effects of adding thermally elevated water to freshwater lakes and streams.

NONTHERMAL IMPACTS

Fossil fuels are currently the most common energy source for power production. The use of these fuels has several different ecological implications. Burning these fuels may produce waste products in the form of gases, solids, or both. Three environmentally important gases produced by combustion are carbon dioxide, sulfur dioxide, and water vapor. Water vapor and carbon dioxide are relatively transparent to sunlight but absorb the infrared energy radiating from the earth. Since these gases reradiate some of their absorbed energy back to the planet's surface they tend to warm it. This phenomenon is the well-known "greenhouse" effect.

Sulfur dioxide, under the influence of ultraviolet light, is slowly oxi-

* I would like to thank the staff of the Savannah River Ecology Laboratory for the use of their data, much of it unpublished. I would also like to thank Dr. Laurance Tilly for the use of his unpublished data on eutrophication in Par Pond. Dr. William Lewis critically reviewed the manuscript. Preparation of this manuscript was aided by Contract AT (38–1)–310 between the United States Atomic Energy Commission and the University of Georgia.

dized to sulfur trioxide [2] which combines with water vapors to form sulfuric acid. Carbon dioxide similarly combines with water to form carbonic acid. These two acids in the air attack not only living tissue but also marble structures, as the defaced statues of Europe and the rotten headstones of our own Northeast illustrate.

The solid materials that are produced from the burning of coal and oil are smoke, fly ash, and ash. Smoke and fly ash go up the stack and into the atmosphere. The remaining ash stays in the furnace. Smoke and fly ash in the atmosphere scatter and absorb incoming solar radiation but have relatively little effect on infrared radiation. Thus the net effect is to cool the surface. This effect is opposite from the greenhouse effect of the gases. Obviously, the ultimate combined effect of the materials released to the atmosphere on the heat budget of the earth cannot be predicted unless the ash and gas releasing characteristics of the fuels are known. However, if fossil fuel plants proliferate, there may be potential for climatic changes.

Even the ash remaining in the furnace presents a disposal problem since it has a moderately high and easily leachable plant nutrient content. Open disposal of ash on the landscape could contribute to the eutrophication of our streams and lakes by the transfer of nutrients in runoff from disposal areas.

The mining of fuels, be they coal, oil, natural gas, or uranium, has an impact on the environment. The present controversies about strip mining of coal have provided ample evidence of environmental impact. Bowen [3] has calculated that a nuclear plant will require the movement of 120 million tons of ore over its 30-year life expectancy. The mining of fuels itself is an energy consuming process, as is the transportation of fuel to the power station and the preparation of the fuel for the plant.

Nuclear-fueled steam generating plants are generally assumed to be the type of plant that will provide the bulk of our electrical production in the near future.[4] These plants do not produce large amounts of waste gas and ash, as do the fossil-fueled steam plants, but they share the mining problem. The nuclear power generating stations have unique environmental impacts of their own.

The energy source of a nuclear reactor is the fission of uranium. Most of the actual or potential environmental problems peculiar to nuclear power generating stations are related to fission products. Some of these, such as tritium or radioactive isotopes of the noble gases, may be vented to the atmosphere. In the mining and milling of uranium, radon, another radioactive gas, is produced.

Spent fuel rods from a nuclear reactor must be reprocessed to recover unused uranium or plutonium because the fission products stop the chain reaction before all the uranium fuel is used. It is in this step that the solid fission products may possibly be released to the environment. There is currently great concern over the packaging, shipping, and storage of nuclear wastes that represent a potential environmental hazard of radioactive contamination for many hundreds of years into the future.

ALTERNATIVE ENERGY SOURCES

Geothermal sources have been proposed as a pollution-free source of electrical power.[3] It is true that such geothermal fields as the Geysers in California and the Larderello field in Italy do not produce ash or radioactive wastes. However, there is the potential problem of noxious gases. It is estimated that the amount of sulfur released at the Geysers field is equivalent to that emitted by a fossil-fueled plant of the same size burning low-sulfur oil.[5] Exploration for geothermal fields has not been extensive and the size of this resource is not well known. Excess water is also a problem. At the same field for each kilowatt of power produced, about 2½ quarts of water are used; and it is a "dry" stream field. Bowen [3] states that a hot water field would produce about 10 gal of water for each kilowatt. This water can be highly mineralized. Hammond [5] estimates that a 1,000-Mw geothermal plant utilizing hot water from the Cerro Prieto, Mexico, field would produce salt water containing 12,000 tons of salt per day.

Hydroelectric plants are relatively pollution free, but most of the suitable sites in the United States have already been utilized. Those that remain are enjoying the strong protection of conservationists who wish to preserve a few rivers in this country in the wild and natural state for future generations.

There are three additional possible sources of power—tidal forces, wind, and solar radiation. Few sites are available for the harnessing of tidal forces, and it is not known how the disruption of the normal tidal cycle will affect the rich animal and plant life that normally abounds on shores with large tidal fluctuations. Wind power is too intermittent to be of real value, and the collection of solar energy requires the use of huge quantities of land for collecting mirrors. The plants of this area, deprived of sunlight, cannot grow and produce food.

THERMAL IMPACTS

The present state of our technology requires that all fueled power generating stations (either nuclear- or fossil-fueled) produce electricity through the medium of a steam turbine. The use of the steam turbine necessitates the rejection of a great deal of heat, and this heat is the most important ecological stress resulting from power production. The following account taken largely from Peterson and Schrotke [6] explains the basic process of converting thermal energy to electrical energy.

Rejection of Waste Heat

Steam-electric generating plants operate on the basis of the Rankine cycle, a thermodynamic process in which high pressure, high temperature steam flows through a turbine, transferring energy to the turbine rotor and thus to the generator. In the process of driving the generator the steam expands as it passes through the turbine. The steam leaves at temperatures below 56 C (133 F) and at less than one atmosphere of pressure.

The theoretical efficiency of the conversion of thermal energy to electrical energy depends upon the relationship between intake and an exhaust temperature of the steam. Carnot's law expresses the relationship as follows:

$$\text{Efficiency} = \frac{T_i - T_e}{T_i}$$

where T_i is the intake temperature in degrees absolute and T_e is exhaust temperature in degrees absolute.

In general, with temperatures of about 593 C (1,100 F) and pressures of 3,000 pounds per square inch (psi), modern fossil-fueled units can reach an efficiency of about 38%. Present nuclear generating plants have an efficiency of approximately 32%.

From the turbine exhaust low temperature steam enters the condenser where it is changed to water. The condensing temperature controls the turbine back pressure which, in turn, affects the plant efficiency.

The condenser water is then returned to the boiler (in the case of a fossil-fueled plant) or the heat exchanger (in the case of a nuclear plant) for conversion again into steam. As this cycle repeats, it is necessary continually to remove the heat given up in the condensing process to cooling water circulating through the condenser. This heat is dissipated to the environment from the condenser cooling water by the processes of radiation, conduction, and evaporation. The remainder of this paper is concerned with the biological effects of this waste heat.

General Effects of Temperature on Aquatic Life

There exists a large body of literature on the effects of temperature changes on animals and plants. Mihursky and Kennedy,[7] as a result of their review of the literature, recommend that certain terminology and principles be explained before any discussion of thermal impacts. These are: (1) thermal tolerance, (2) thermal lethality, (3) acclimation, (4) thermal shock, (5) critical thermal maxima, (6) respiratory rate, (7) behavior, and (8) varying response with life history stage.

THERMAL TOLERANCE. Organisms vary in their thermal tolerance. Thomas [8] lists the upper temperature maxima for fresh water fish as ranging from 23 C (73.4 F) to 42 C (107.6 F) and lower minima between 0 C (32 F) and 20 C (68 F). Thus both the length of the zone of thermal tolerance and its absolute placement on the temperature scale varies from species to species.

THERMAL LETHALITY. The standard method of reporting thermal lethality for either high or low temperature extremes is in terms of the LD_{50}'s for varying periods of time.

ACCLIMATION. The thermal LD_{50} of an animal can be greatly modified by the past thermal history of an individual. Temperature acclimation is a change in the thermal level to which an individual is physiologically adjusted. For example, the upper LD_{50} of the green fish *(Girella nigricans)* is 42 C (107.6

F) when acclimated at 37 C (98.6 F), but it is only 30 C (86 F) if acclimated at 12 C (53.6 F).[8] Ability to acclimate is limited, and the maximum upper or lower acclimation point is sometimes called the ultimate incipient lethal level.

THERMAL SHOCK. Lack of time to acclimate to a new temperature level can produce a condition referred to as thermal shock. Fish kills around steam-electric plants immediately after start-up are usually a result of thermal shock.

CRITICAL THERMAL MAXIMUM. A different measure of the effect of temperature change than the LD_{50} is the critical thermal maximum (CTM). The CTM is the temperature at which the locomotory activity of an animal becomes disorganized, and it loses its ability to escape from conditions that will soon cause its death. Extreme temperature may not immediately cause irreversible changes, and recovery may occur if temperature moderates. However, a CTM condition can lead to death from predation by a more active temperature resistant aquatic predator or a nonaquatic one such as a bird. The CTM is thus the ecological upper temperature limit for survival. Like the LD_{50} the CTM can be changed by acclimation. The larva of the dragonfly *(Libellula incesta)* has a CTM of 43.8 C (111 F) when acclimated at 15 C and a CTM of 47.7 C (118 F) when acclimated at 35 C (95 F) (Gentry, personal communication).

RESPIRATORY RATES. Since temperature affects the rate of biochemical reactions, it affects metabolic rates and oxygen consumption in animals. For example, Downing and Merkens[9] found that eight species of fish showed decreased survival at low oxygen tension and high temperature when the temperature was elevated. Weatherly[10] showed that supersaturated water could produce a definite improvement either in time of survival at a fixed lethal temperature or in a lethal temperature reached as a result of heating.

BEHAVIOR. Temperature has an effect on the vertical and horizontal migrations of aquatic organisms.[11] Fishes and other aquatic organisms are known to have temperature preferences [12] and to behave in a manner to achieve these temperature preferenda if free to do so.

LIFE HISTORY STAGE DIFFERENCES. Temperature effects are dependent upon the life history stage of an organism. Effects are modified by age and size of the organism and by season. Various workers have shown thermal requirements for different life process in fish.[13,14,15] Egg survival range is narrower, especially during the hatching process, than it is for other life history stages. Changes in temperature requirements occur with variation in the seasonal environmental temperatures. Range for growth is narrower than that for survival.

THERMALLY AFFECTED AREAS ON THE SAVANNAH RIVER PLANT PAR POND SYSTEM

As many of my examples will be drawn from work done on the Savannah River Plant (SRP), I shall digress and explain the thermal situation there. The SRP is located in Aiken and Barnwell counties of South Carolina, 25 miles

Southeast of Augusta, Georgia.[16] Scattered among the SRP's 300 square miles are three working nuclear reactors and two on stand-by status. These reactors are used for the production of plutonium and tritium and other transuranium isotopes. All of the energy produced is discharged as heat and none is converted to electricity as in a nuclear-steam plant. Cooling water thus leaves the reactor outfall at a much higher temperature than from a power plant.

The effluent from one reactor (P reactor) is discharged into Par Pond. This impoundment was formed in 1957 to 1958 by damming Lower Three Runs Creek. The Pond covers 1,068 hectares (ha), or 2,640 acres, to an average depth of about 6.1 meters (20 feet). The maximum depth near the main or "Cold" dam is about 17 meters (55 feet). A 140-acre portion is separated from the main body by a dam (the "Hot" dam) to form Pond C or the "precooler" pond. There are three major arms or coves. The North, the Middle (also called the "Warm" or "Hot"), and the South (Fig. 20).

Much information about Par Pond has been published.[17-24] The pond has a volume of 6.2×10^7 cubic meters (cu m) and a shoreline development of 4.7. Water color averages about 12.7 Pt-Co units; turbidity, about 1.0 JTU; Secchi transparency, 2.5 m; and epilimnion oxygen, about 8.6 mg/1 during a typical year in the unheated portions of the lake. Par Pond can be classed as a warm monomictic lake because it is stratified from April through October and is nearly homothermal the remainder of the year. The littoral community of Par Pond is unusually well developed for lakes in this vicinity,[17,22] probably because water levels remain relatively stable. Large drawdowns due to water consumption do not occur.

For reactor cooling, water is removed from the tip of the South Arm of Par Pond and then flows underground to a holding basin from which it is pumped with occasional additions of Savannah River water through reactor heat exchangers and back to Pond C (precooler pond) by a system of canals and small impoundments. Pond C connects to Par Pond by means of a culvert through the Hot Dam which introduces warm water several meters below the surface allowing it to mix with cooler water as it moves rapidly to the surface. Most of the water stays in the lake. There is flow over the Cold Dam only during periods of high rainfall. Most of the evaporation is made up by addition of Savannah River water.

Par Pond was originally built to provide cooling water for both P and R reactors. R was placed on stand-by status in 1964, and since then no hot water has entered the North Arm or Pond B, which is a reservoir of 105 ha (260 acres) in the R reactor canal system. The P reactor canal system is still in use. It consists of 6.8 kilometer (km) (4¼ miles) of canals and 5 small impoundments. The total area of these is 92 ha (227 acres) (91.864 ha).

Par Pond is a unique habitat displaying obvious environmental contrasts to the natural aquatic areas in the region. The two most obvious distinctions of Par Pond are high water temperatures, especially in the warm arm, and the extraordinarily large populations of centrarchid fishes, American alligators, and winter waterfowl. These populations may be the result of the absolute restriction on fishing and hunting since the pond was formed.

Figure 20
The Par Pond Reservoir and Canal System

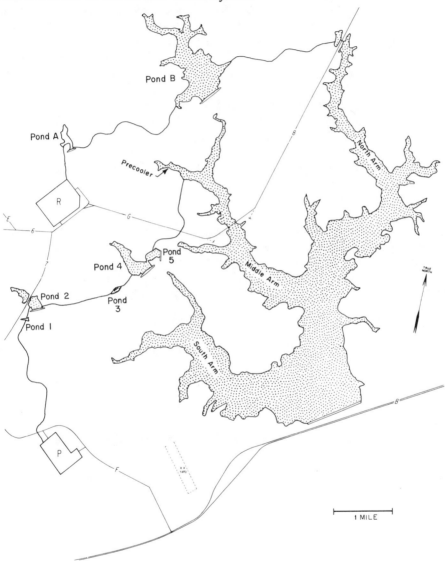

Source: Reference 16.
Note: P reactor is active; R reactor is not. Precooler pond is also called Pond C.

The heated water entering the warm arm maintains temperatures as high as 34 C during the winter months and the temperature never drops below 15 C (59 F). Due to the large size of the reservoir, normal surface temperatures (9 to 14 C in winter and 27 to 37 C in summer) are maintained throughout the year in most of the lake outside of the Middle Arm.[19]

Thermal Streams

The other two reactors presently in use, C reactor and K reactor, currently discharge their effluent into Four Mile and Pen Branch Creeks, respectively. The source of the cooling water is the Savannah River. Four Mile and Pen Branch Creeks flow into the Savannah River Swamp without losing a significant part of their heat load. Also flowing into the Savannah River Swamp are Beaver Dam Creek and Steel Creek. Beaver Dam Creek carries the effluent from a fossil-fuel fired steam-generating station. Steel Creek at one time carried the effluent of two reactors. The discharge of cooling water effluent from one reactor to Steel Creek was discontinued in 1963 when the reactor was switched to cooling with recirculated water from Par Pond. The second reactor discharge ceased in 1968 when the reactor was shut down and placed in stand-by condition.[16] Steel Creek is now an example of a thermal recovery area.

Upper Three Runs Creek deserves mention because it differs from the streams in two respects: its headwaters arise outside the plant site, and it has never received heated discharges of cooling water either from the production reactors or the steam generating plant. Upper Three Runs Creek enters directly into the Savannah River, not into the adjacent swamp area like the other creeks.

The Savannah River Swamp lies in the floodplain of the Savannah River. It is about 10 miles (16 km) long and averages about 1.5 miles (2.41 km) in width. A small embankment or levee has been built up along the north side of the river from sediments deposited during periods of flooding or from dredging operations to keep the river navigable. Next to the levee, the ground slopes downward, is marshy, and contains stands of large cypress trees and other hardwoods. The swamp is bounded on the landward side by the higher ground of the Sunderland Terrace. The Savannah River Swamp may be thought of as a basin receiving reactor effluents, cooling them, and then discharging back to the levee through two small breaks (opposite the mouths of Beaver Dam and Four Mile Creeks) and one major break in the levee opposite the mouth of Steel Creek.

EFFECTS OF THERMAL EFFLUENT ON FISH

Due to their high commercial and sports value, fish have probably been the subject of more thermal studies than any other group of organisms. Good review articles have been written on the subject by Alabaster,[12] Jones,[25] and Thomas.[8]

General Effects on Fish

Fish are poikilotherms and can be affected by high temperatures because they possess no mechanism by which to alter their temperature away from that of the water around them. There are four mechanisms of heat death: coagulation of proteins including enzymes, melting of cellular lipids, changes in cellular permeability, and production of a toxic enzyme.[26] Temperature changes need not be lethal. They can have adverse effects through increasing or decreasing activity [27] and through limiting [28] or changing the timing of reproduction.[29]

Acclimation

Scientists working with the effects of thermal loading on fish have long known the importance of acclimation. The effect of thermal shock on fish can be more harmful than continued exposure to a higher temperature.[30] Two of the best discussions of acclimation are those of Jones [25] and Doudoroff.[31] The latter author, in summarizing the work of Fry and his colleagues,[32,33] concludes that fish that have been acclimated to low temperatures suffered high mortality when briefly exposed to high temperatures but that this mortality could be considerably reduced when the fish had been acclimated at the maximum possible temperature. Doudoroff also points out that, according to Hart,[34] these are seasonal, geographic, and other variations of the thermal tolerance of different species of fish acclimated at the same temperature.

The ability to withstand increased temperatures is acquired by fish at a very fast rate in the temperature range from 26 C to 30 C (78.8 to 86 F).[31] There may be a latent period of one day or longer in which virtually no change takes place in the upper lethal temperature but usually the increased tolerance is achieved in a period of one to three days. Tolerance to high temperatures may persist for considerable periods after return of the fish to the acclimation temperature or even a lower one.[25]

Thermal Death Point

For any particular acclimation temperature, every species of fish has a temperature range within which it can survive indefinitely. This range has an upper limit, the thermal death point, above which the animal cannot live indefinitely but survives for some limited period. Above the thermal death point, the fish is said to be in the zone of resistance; below it, in the zone of tolerance. Within the resistance zone, survival time shortens with a progressive rise in temperature until a point is reached at which the animal is killed instantaneously on transference from water at the acclimation temperature. Above this point is the zone of instantaneous death. If the acclimation temperature is raised the thermal death point also rises, but the rise in the thermal death point is less than the rise in the acclimation temperature. Thus, for every species of fish, a stage is reached where the acclimation temperature meets the thermal death point. This point is called the ultimate upper lethal temperature.[25] Upon start-up of a steam electric facility, fish kills can occur if fish in the cooling water effluent receiving body are suddenly exposed to water above the thermal death point established by the ambient acclimation temperature. If the temperature change is sufficiently slow, the fish can acclimate and no kill need occur. However, if the effluent is above the ultimate upper lethal temperature for the particular fishes involved, a fish kill is inevitable.

Preferred Temperatures

Fish are extremely sensitive to temperature and, when possible, seek out the temperature that is best for their survival. The temperature that fish seek out is termed the preferred temperature. Ferguson [35] and Thomas [8] list the preferred temperatures of many species of fish under field and laboratory conditions. The preferred temperature is approximately proportional to the acclimation temperature. In general the preferred temperature is considerably higher than the acclimation temperature at lower thermal acclimations, up to the final preferred temperature where both coincide. Pitt, Garside, and Hepburn [36] present data that illustrate this phenomenon (Table 8). Ferguson [35] quotes data on seven species of fish from five authors to demonstrate that there is a general positive correlation between acclimation temperature and preferred temperature and that this relationship is characteristic for the species. However, Garside and Tait [37] maintained that the preferred temperatures in rainbow trout were inversely related to acclimation temperature.

Table 8
Temperatures Selected from a
Thermal Gradient by Carp After
Acclimation at Various Temperatures

Acclimation Temperature	Selected Temperature
10°	17°
15°	25°
20°	26°
25°	31°
30°	32°
35°	32°

Source: Data from Reference 36.

Neill, Magnuson, and Chipman [38] used sophisticated electronic equipment that allowed fishes to regulate the temperature in experimental tanks by their spatial movements. Swimming into warmer water caused the temperature of the entire tank to increase. Conversely, swimming into cooler water caused the temperature to decrease. They tested carp, bluegill, largemouth bass, black crappie, rock bass, and yellow perch. All of these fish behaviorly thermoregulated within a span of about two or three degrees Centigrade. Each species chose its own characteristic temperatures and these temperatures were close to the final preferenda reported in the literature.

Effects of Thermal Stress on Fish Growth and Movement

In recent years a number of studies on the effects of thermal stress on the growth, mortality, and movement of fish have appeared in the literature.[23,24,39–42] Most of these studies have been done in the field at the site of some kind of industrial thermal outfall. Marcy,[42] working at the Yankee site on the Connecticut River, found a 100% mortality of entrained fish larvae while Markowski [43] observed no harmful effects of fish passage through a British plant.

Trembley [44] found little evidence that heated waters produced fewer fish or slower growth rates. Almost without exception, the fish taken in heated water in the Delaware River at Martin's Creek were healthy and well fed. In general, they were larger than fish from unheated areas of the river. Trembley attributes this to active feeding throughout the winter months.

Merriman,[45] on the other hand, found that, in spite of a greater availability of food in the discharge canal at the Yankee site, the condition of the brown and white bull heads (*Ictalurus nebulosus* and *I. catus*) was considerably poorer than the condition of the river catfishes living beyond the influence of the thermal discharge. He reasoned that the fishes' higher rate of metabolism in the warmer water, the increased expenditure of energy required to cope with the high flow rate in the canal, and crowding are responsible for this poorer condition.

Benda,[40] working at the site of two generating stations on the White River in Indiana, observed no direct mortality and found fish present in the area immediately below the outfall of the thermal effluent. He found no thermal effect in the length-weight relationship of the fish. The main overall effect of the heated water on the fish populations was the migration of all species of fish from the effluent canal during periods of high temperatures. This was a seasonal effect and with the onset of cool weather, the fish moved back into the abandoned area.

A lot of work has been done with fishes in the thermally altered area of the SRP, particularly the largemouth bass *(Micropterus salmoides)*.[21,23,24,39,46-48] Holland et al.,[48] found that juvenile bluegill *(Lepomis macrochirus)* taken from Par Pond had a higher thermal tolerance than fish from other areas. This fact was true at acclimation temperatures of 25 (77 F), 30 (86 F), and 35 C (95 F). They reported their results in terms of Critical Thermal Maxima rather than LD_{50}. Fish from nonthermal areas had a much higher mortality rate during acclimation at 35 C (95 F) than those from Par Pond (Fig. 20). Genetic selection for thermally tolerant individuals is the most likely explanation of their findings.

Bennett [23] measured the body temperatures of 600 largemouth bass from the Hot Dam and the Cold Dam in Par Pond. Bass captured in the heated environment had significantly higher monthly body temperatures than those from the control area. Body temperatures of bass from the heated area ranged from 12 to 32 C (54 to 90 F). No correlation was found between body condition from the heated environment and body temperature at capture. This finding suggests that the fish either had sufficient food supply to maintain their body condition at higher temperatures or were temporarily emigrating to cooler areas. Gibbons and Bennett [46] reported that the population density of bass is greater in the heated areas of the lake, particularly during the winter. Individual bass exhibit a high mobility in the reservoir, with movements of more than 6 km

(9.7 miles) being of frequent occurrence. The majority of individuals recaptured in the heated areas appears to have remained in the same place. The large winter populations at the Hot Dam are reflected in the data of Gibbons, Hook, and Forney [24] who did comparative angling and underwater observation at the Hot and Cold Dams. Their results are given in Tables 9 and 10. During the study the reactor was shut down for refueling, so that the investigators had a chance to observe the bass population at the Hot Dam during a period of no thermal stress. Their data show that effluent from a nuclear reactor unquestionably influences the activity of largemouth bass occurring in the immediate vicinity during the winter.

Bennett [39] worked with bluegill and black crappie *(Pomoxis nigromaculatus)* in Par Pond. The length-weight relationships determined from the black crappie from the heated and control areas were significantly different. The crappie from the heated environment were heavier per unit length than those from the control areas. There was no difference in the length-weight relationships of the bluegill.

Table 9
Number of Bass Observed Underwater in Par Pond
(at least 240 meters of shoreline were covered by each diver on each run)

Area	Number of Obser- vation Days	Mean Water Temperature[a] Surface	Bottom	Bass Observed/100 Meters of Shoreline Mean	Range
Hot-water dam:					
Heated effluent	4	23.8C	10.8C	47.6	21.3–85.9
Unheated effluent	2	18.0C	12.2C	18.6	8.5–29.0
Cold-water dam	3	10.3C	9.8C	1.3	0.7–3.0

Source: Data from Reference 24.
[a]Recorded about 5 miles from shore.

Table 10
Number of Largemouth Bass Caught Under Three
Environmental Conditions in Par Pond
(at least 60 casts were taken at each station on each sampling day)

Area	Number of Sampling Days	Mean Water Temperature at Surface	Bass/100 Casts Mean	Range
Hot-water dams:				
Heated effluent	11	27.0C	24.7 ± 4.7	7–65
Unheated effluent	6	16.5C	5.7 ± 3.3	1–22
Cold-water dam	9	11.1C	5.8 ± 1.1	2–13

Source: Data from Reference 24.

Parker, Hirshfield, and Gibbons [47] point out that Pond C, an area receiving a high thermal load, contains five species of fish. Pond B, a thermal recovery area, contains eight species of fish, and the South Arm of Par Pond, which has never had any thermal loading, contains 23 species (Fig. 20). The same species of fish might be expected in all three study areas since they were formed from the same stream system and were separated artificially. The fish in Pond C represent those species able to survive under the elevated thermal regime. These same species are present in Pond B with the inclusion of three more species. Since there is no possibility for reinvasion by way of the stream, these three species may be present due to better refuge areas during the period of thermal loading. Or, the shorter time period of heating may have allowed these three species to survive in Pond B, whereas they have been eliminated in the 13-year period during which Pond C has received thermal effluent. Another possible explanation of their presence is through introduction of fish eggs into Pond B by shore birds or some other vector.

EFFECTS OF THERMAL EFFLUENTS ON AQUATIC REPTILES

Turtles

Between July 1967 and September 1969, Gibbons [19] studied populations of the yellow-bellied turtle *(Pseudemys scripta)* in Par Pond and in other bodies of water on the SRP. He found that female *P. scripta* from Par Pond attain larger body sizes than females from other study populations on the SRP. The Par Pond population consequently has a much higher reproductive effort per individual since clutch size increases with an increase in body size. Par Pond females appear to lay as many as three clutches of eggs per year while females from other populations lay only two clutches a year. Therefore, individuals from the Par Pond population have a very high reproductive potential as a result of clutch size and possibly number of clutches when compared with other populations on the SRP.

P. scripta juveniles from Par Pond grow at significantly faster rates than those from Ellenton Bay, another body of water on the SRP. Par Pond turtles are thus younger at sexual maturity. The importance of age at maturity on the reproductive rate of a population has been emphasized by Cole,[49] who pointed out that the earlier the females of any population reach maturity the greater the potential reproductive rate. Gibbons has calculated that, given no mortality and the observed growth and reproductive rates, one pair of Par Pond turtles could produce 10^6 offspring in twenty years, while in the same length of time there would be only several hundred offspring from a pair of Ellenton Bay turtles.

The reasons for the observed size and growth differences between Par Pond turtles and those from other habitats are not completely known. Gibbons feels that it is not a direct result of the hot water but is most probably due to a higher protein diet that is available to the turtles in Par Pond.

Alligators

Brisbin [20] made systematic census counts of the American alligators inhabiting Par Pond. Data collected over a three-year period suggest that each fall, large adult alligators tend to congregate in the Warm Arm. Rather than entering winter dormancy, these alligators apparently remain active in the warm water during the colder months and disperse throughout the lake the following spring to breed. While the arrival of the alligators at the heated area seems to be correlated with both decreasing air temperatures and a decreasing photoperiod, the departure from the heated area begins in middle or late January. This is well before air temperature begins to rise and suggests that photoperiod may be important.

EFFECTS OF THERMAL EFFLUENTS ON BIRDS

Waterfowl

While waterfowl are of great value for both sport and as food, there have been few studies of the impact of heated effluents on these birds. Brisbin [50] made census counts of the waterfowl in a heated (Hot Cove) and nonheated arm (North Cove) of the Par Pond reservoir system. A total of 6,544 birds of ten species was counted. Over 99% of them were counted between the months of October and April (Fig. 21), and this seasonal abundance reflected the fact that most of the waterfowl were migrant winter visitors to the South Carolina area and breed in more northerly latitudes. Over 66% of the birds identified as to species were American Coots *(Fulica americana)*. The heated and unheated areas were separated by approximately 4 km (2.486 miles) of direct overland distance and by approximately 7.8 km (4.847 miles) by watercourse. The Hot Cove was on the average several degrees hotter than the North Cove (Fig. 21).

Although the birds were freely able to move between the hot and cold regimes of the lake, significant differences were observed between the two areas in the numbers and species diversity of the waterfowl. More birds and a greater diversity of birds were found in the unheated area. Dabbling ducks were absent from the heated area and seemed more thermally sensitive than diving ducks. Among the diving ducks, certain species, such as the lesser scaup *(Aytha affinis)*, appeared to exhibit a greater degree of thermal tolerance than other species such as the ring-necked duck *(Aytha collaris)*. Pied-billed grebes *(Podilymbus podiceps)* seemed to show the greatest thermal tolerance, occuring in equal numbers in both heated and unheated areas.

Vegetation is reduced in the Hot Cove of Par Pond.[47] This reduction is undoubtedly an important factor in regulating the thermal responses of at least some of the waterfowl species, which may be dependent on thermally sensitive plant species for food or cover. Some aquatic plants are reduced in number or are completely absent from the Hot Cove. The coot uses the shearing edges on its beak in collecting certain kinds of aquatic vegetation that are unavailable to ducks of either the diving or dabbling groups. Coots were frequently observed feeding on benthic algal-mat growths in the heated study area. The abundance pattern of this species suggests a greater thermal tolerance than that of either the diving or dabbling ducks whose food resources may have been significantly reduced by the heated water.

Figure 21
Total Numbers of Birds and Several Temperatures in
Two Arms of Par Pond Plotted Against Months

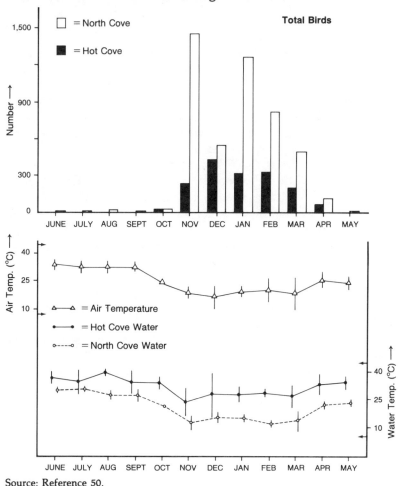

Source: Reference 50.

A marked reduction in the abundance of waterfowl occurred in the North Cove during December (Fig. 21). This reduction occurred after an unusually severe ice and snow storm. It is interesting to note that no such decline in abundance of waterfowl in the Hot Cove occurred during this period. This fact suggests that the warm water habitat may have become unusually attractive to waterfowl by giving them a place of refuge.

It is also important to note that those species and species groups that seemed in this study to be the most sensitive to thermal stress (dabbling ducks and certain species of diving ducks) include some of the more valued species of waterfowl, which are hunted for sport and occasionally used as food by man. Brisbin suggests the possibility that increasing thermal alteration of natural aquatic habitats in the southeastern United States will tend to render such habitats more suitable for less-prized game species, such as the Grebe and Coot, at the expense of the more valued species of dabblers and divers.

Other Birds

In an effort to assess the effects of thermal stress on nonaquatic life, Smith (personal communication) took bird censuses in the summer of 1972 of birds in Steel Creek, Pen Branch Creek, and Upper Three Runs Creek on the SRP. The first creek is a thermal recovery area, the second is currently under thermal stress, and the third is a control area. All these creeks were originally contained cypress swamps but only Upper Three Runs Creek remains untouched. The dominant plant species is cypress *(Taxodium)* and various gums *(Nyssa)*. Epiphytic Spanish moss *(Tilland sia)* abounds in the tree tops. Due to the dense canopy, very little light penetrates to the ground. The low and light frequent flooding of the creek results in a very sparse ground flora.

In Pen Branch and Steel Creek, the heat from reactor effluent has destroyed the original cypress swamp community so that only dead tree trunks, many of which have fallen, are left. These have trapped soil over the years, and a few hardy herbs have begun to grow in the islets thus created. Since 1968, no thermal effluent has been discharged to Steel Creek. Succession has proceeded, and a rich flora is now present that consists mostly of herbaceous ground plants. Although a few willows *(Salix)* and other woody species have begun to invade this swamp, there is no true canopy layer now present.

Bird censuses, begun between 0700 and 0730, were conducted in areas chosen for similar densities of dead or living trees. All study areas were in the deltas of the creeks where they enter the Savannah River Swamp. A transit line was walked for 30 minutes by persons well versed in field identification, and each bird seen or heard was recorded individually. These data were used to calculate a Shannon diversity index for the bird populations in each of the stream beds. This index is made up of two components, species richness and evenness. Species richness is related to the total number of species present, and evenness is related to how the individuals are distributed in species groups.

No significant differences were found between areas in diversity or in species richness. However, the evenness was lowest in Steel Creek, intermediate in Pen Branch, and highest in Upper Three Runs. Thus, the Steel Creek and Pen Branch populations may be responding to alterations of the environment by adjusting the relative abundance of species present, rather than the total number of species.

Thermal stress has greatly altered the habitat in the cypress swamps studied. Many niches have been destroyed, while those that have been created are capable of supporting large populations of a few species. The presence of most of these species in thermally altered cypress swamps is made possible by the structure in the community offered by the dead and fallen trees. These have allowed succession to proceed on a miniature scale, even while thermal stress is present. They provide food and shelter for a few specialized species, notably woodpeckers.

EFFECTS OF THERMAL EFFLUENT ON THE BENTHOS

Stewart [51] summarized the available literature on the effects of thermal stress on fresh-water benthic organisms. Most of the following information is taken from his work. In a study on the effect of warm-water discharges on the Delaware River, Strangenberg and Pawlaczyk [52] found that river-bottom plants and animals decreased in number when the water temperature exceeded 30 C (86 F). The macroinvertebrate biomass was reduced from 1.04 to 0.09 grams per square foot throughout the summer in the areas of maximally heated water, as compared with a control station. A 35 C (95 F) water temperature at the time of sampling was found to be detrimental to many organisms, especially the caddis fly (*Hydropsyche* sp.), many of which were dead. The data suggest that there is a tolerance limit close to 32.2 C (90 F) for a variety of different kinds of benthic animals. Extensive losses in numbers and diversity of organisms accompany further temperature increases (Coutant).[53]

Another classic demonstration on the effects of increasing water temperatures upon the change in the composition of a macroinvertebrate population is presented by Walshe.[54] The thermal index (22-hour LD_{50}) of seven species of midge larvae reflect the probable sequence of preferred temperatures. These seven species and their thermal indices are as follows: *Tanytarsus brunnipes*, 29 C (84.2 F); *Prodiamesa olivacea*, 30 C (86 F); *Anatopynia nebulosa*, 30.4 C (95 F); *C. longistylus*, 35 C (95.9 F) and *Anatopynia varia*, 38 C (101.8 F).

In studies on the shift of the composition of macroinvertebrate populations, Wurtz and Renn [55] showed that no immediate kills resulted from thermal shock of 14 C (25 F). However, persistent exposure to 35 C (95 F) over 24 hours brought about changes in the composition of the macroinvertebrate population.

Studies of particular species of macroinvertebrates have shown that lethal temperatures vary considerably with the type of organism. Noland and Reichel,[56] in studying the fresh-water snail *(Lymnaea stenalis)*, found that cultures died when the water temperature reached 30.5 C (89.6 F). Fresh-water snails *(Viviparus malleatus)* died when held at a temperature of 37.5 C (99.5 F).[57] The fresh-water snail *(Physa gyrina)* has been found to live and reproduce in a waste-water ditch between 28 and 35 C (82.4 to 95 F).[58]

The highest 24-hour median tolerance limit lethal temperatures that could be obtained by raising acclimation temperatures from 10 C (50 F) to 20 C (68 F) were estimated to be 34.6 C (94.2 F) for the sow bug *(Asellus intermedius)* and the scuds *(Gammarus fasciatus)* and 33.2 C (91.8 F) and 29.6 C (85.3 F) for the scud *(Gammarus pseudolimnaeus)*.[59]

The dragonfly larva of the species *Libellula incesta* grow larger in the thermal streams on the Savannah River Plant than in the control stream. At the same time of year the thermal stream larvae were averaging 16.1 ± 0.15 milli-meters (mm) (0.6 ± 0.006 in) while those in the control stream averaged 11.4 ± 0.19 mm (0.5 ± 0.007 in) (Gentry, personal communication). Other studies on thermal effects on aquatic insects include those of Trottier,[60] Lutz,[61] and Lehm-kuhl.[62]

EFFECTS OF THERMAL EFFLUENT ON PLANTS

Macrophytes

Karling [63] concluded that formation of reproductive structures in *Chara fragilis* depended primarily on the length of day and, secondarily, on tempera-ture. Anderson and Lommasson [64] grew *Chara zeylanica* at five different constant temperatures. Growth of the main shoots and lateral branches were recorded separately, for increase in the rhizoidal mass was recorded for each plant at the end of the experiment and notations were made of the presence of reproductive structures. Under the conditions of the experiment the most abundant growth of main shoots and of the rhizoidal system occurred at 24 C (75.2 F). Growth was inhibited at 16 C (61 F). At higher temperatures main shoots ceased to grow. Production of lateral branches increased with an increase of temperature, but at 32 C (90 F) it was limited to small outgrowths. Growth increments were nearly as valid as the number of nodes produced as an index of plant growth. Repro-ductive structures develop on plants growing at all temperatures except 20 C (68 F).

Parker, Hirshfield, and Gibbons [47] studied Par Pond, Pond C and Pond B in the SRP in order to compare the species composition and relative abundance of vascular aquatic plants. Pond C is presently receiving thermal loading, and the South Arm of Par Pond has little elevation of water temperature. Identifica-tion was made of all aquatic plants found in the study areas. The following species were selected for quantitative measurements of abundance: *Typha latifolia* and *T. domingensis, Scirpus cyperinus, Hydrocotyle umbellata, Eleocharis quadragulata* and *Nymphaea ordorata.* The percentage of shoreline occupied by these species was determined in each of the three study areas.

Pond B is intermediate between Par Pond and Pond C in the number of aquatic plants present. All species present in Pond C were also present in Pond B, and all species present in Pond B were also present in Par Pond. In all instances, except for *Scirpus* and *Typha,* relative abundance of the dominant plant species in Pond B was intermediate between Pond C and the South Arm of Par Pond.

Parker, Hirshfield, and Gibbons [47] concluded that the three reservoirs on the Savannah River Plant are distinct in regard to their floral characteristics. The most obvious environmental feature to which these differences can be related is the past or present thermal regime. Several species of vascular aquatic plants have been eliminated. Hence species diversity is reduced. However, relative abundance of certain plant species is consequently enhanced, possibly due to reduced competition from other species. The reduction in relative abundance of most plant species is still noticeable several years after heating has been terminated.

Algae

Cairns, Lanza, and Parker [65] have written a very comprehensive work on the structural and functional changes related to pollution in aquatic communities. The following section on the impact of thermal loading on algae is taken largely from their work.

Algae are exposed to some normal thermal variation in aquatic ecosystems. Optimum temperatures for one cellular function may not be optimum for another. In addition, a temperature optimum for a specific function during brief exposure of a cell may not be identical to that for longer exposure times. Algal cells usually are active metabolically within a narrow range of temperatures (10 to 45 C or 50 to 113 F) known as the biokinetic range. This generalization excludes thermophilic organisms, which tolerate higher temperatures. Populations of blue-green algae existing naturally at temperatures up to 90 C (194 F) exemplify thermophilic types.[66,67] All the known mechanisms of heat death are thought to affect algae,[26] and this direct effect, along with more subtle manifestations of temperature alterations in organisms, influence algal community structure.

Marre [68] has suggested that there are two useful approaches to thermal studies of algae: (1) studies of thermal effect upon species distribution primarily from the ecological viewpoint; and (2) studies of the thermal effect upon the biochemical and biophysical mechanisms of heat tolerance in select species in culture, especially those species which flourish under seemingly adverse thermal stress.

Many thermophilic algae grow in culture at lower temperatures, though in the natural aquatic ecosystem they tend to be suppressed by mesothermal species. For example, blue-greens removed from a hot spring had the capacity for active photosynthesis at temperatures as low as 20 C (68 F).[69] Thermophilic algae seem to have a ubiquitous distribution. Sorokin [70] isolated his high temperature Chlorella from a stream at normal temperature.

Cultured algae sometimes show morphological and physiological alterations when maintained at various temperatures. Cairns and Lanza [71] abruptly exposed populations of *Navicula pelliculosa* and *N. seminulum* cultured at 20 C (68 F) up to 40 C (104 F). Light microscopic examination revealed varying degrees of cellular damage, while ultraviolet microscopic surveys utilizing a fluorescent stain on lipids demonstrated a decrease in cellular fluorescence. Other examples of physiological and morphological changes in algae with temperature can be found in the works of Margalef; [72] Cairns; [30] Wallace; [73] Patrick, Crum, and Coles; [74] and Hopkins.[75]

A recent investigation of the offshore waters of four of Lake Michigan's

22 electric power generating facilities was conducted with reference to the effects of effluents on phytoplankton, zooplankton, and benthos. The phytoplankton consisted mainly of diatoms, along with some of the typically warmer water green and blue-green algae. A slight decrease in numbers of organisms found in power plant outfalls was noted. No other adverse trends appeared in the data.

Trembley [76] studied the effects of condenser discharge water from the Martin's Creek Plant of the Pennsylvania Power and Light Company on river aquatic life. Blue-green algae and certain tolerant green algae increased in abundance with a corresponding loss of less heat tolerant forms. Periphyton were markedly reduced in numbers of species in the heated water.

EFFECTS OF THERMAL EFFLUENT ON THE DECOMPOSERS

There have not been many studies of the impact of energy production on the decomposers. Buck and Rankin [77] did a before-and-after study on the Connecticut River at the Yankee Reactor Site, and Resi [78] has written a short review. Most of the information in this section is taken from their work. Temperature changes in the aquatic environment affect ecological relationships among the microbes. Temperature changes also affect the process of natural purification and the growth and survival of algae, bacteria, and fungi. The microbial content of natural waters is approximately proportional to the amount of organic matter present. Therefore unpolluted waters have lower concentrations of bacteria than waters carrying a high organic load.

The microbiology of natural waters is important because of the possibility of transmission of disease through contamination of water supplies. When a stream is polluted with the fecal material of warm blooded mammals it may possibly contain enteric pathogens. Coliform bacteria are used too as an indicator to measure the potential presence of pathogens from sewage.

The relations of temperature to the growth of bacteria are complex. As with other organisms, some have a wide tolerance and some a narrow one. Microbiologists classify microbes by their temperature requirements for growth. The psycrophiles have growth optima below 20 C (68 F) while the thermophiles will show maximum growth between 55 and 65 C (131 to 149 F). The majority of bacteria are mesophiles and have optimum temperatures between those extremes, usually between 22 and 28 C (70 and 82 F). Pathogenic and enteric bacteria have a narrow optimum range around 37 C (98.6 F).

In the spring of the year the microbiotic cycle is started by autotrophic algae and chlorophyll bearing bacteria which fix carbon into organic matter. The metabolites and decomposition products of these organisms provide nutrients for use by gram-negative bacteria such as *Alcligenes, Aerobacter,* and *Pseudomonas*. After the gram-negative bacilli grow, diatoms or blue-green algae bloom. Which algae dominate depends upon temperature conditions. In cooler waters, the diatoms will do well, and they will be followed by gram-positive heterotrophic bacteria. In warmer situations, the gram-negative bacteria are not displaced, and they grow in conjunction with blue-green algae.[74] The next step in the warm water succession is an actinomycte bloom, and these organisms produce an antibiotic that reduces the gram-negative bacterial population. Gram-positive bacilli follow the actinomycetes. Further details of this cycle may be found in Silvey and Roach.[79]

Organic wastes discharged into natural waters immediately begin to undergo degradation. An increase in temperature within the mesophile range increases the metabolic rate and the division rate of the decomposers. However, this is somewhat counteracted by a decrease in dissolved oxygen at the higher temperature. If dissolved oxygen reaches the zero level, there is a shift in the bacterial populations to facultative anaerobic organisms. These organisms continue the decompositions of organic wastes, but at a slower rate.[80]

In summary, it may be said that increasing the temperature of natural waters may increase the destruction of wastes provided the oxygen level is not diminished too greatly. Theoretically this should lead to an increase in bacterial numbers. However, Buck and Rankin [77] could find no quantitative differences in any of the groups of bacteria they studied before and after the Connecticut Yankee reactor went on line and started its thermal discharge to the Connecticut River.

EFFECTS OF THERMAL EFFLUENT ON COMMUNITY METABOLISM

Opportunities to study effects of temperature elevation on the total community photosynthesis and respiration in the field are difficult to find. Several investigators have looked at this problem by means of the microecosystem or microcosm method. This method consists of taking an assemblage of organisms, sediment, and water from a natural aquatic system and holding them under laboratory conditions.[81,82]

One aspect of community resistance to thermal shock is related to the hypothesis that mature multi-species ecosystems are far more resistant to external perturbations than are less mature or complex systems. [83] This hypothesis is difficult to examine in a large natural ecosystem, but can be conveniently studied in laboratory microecosystems. The results of some studies on this hypothesis are presented here.

Beyers [84,85] investigated the metabolic response of mature, multi-species, benthic microcosms. Nighttime respiration and net photosynthesis were measured at room temperature (23 C or 73 F); then after 24 hours acclimation, at 33 C (91.4 F); and finally, after another 24 hours, at 17 C (62 F). The data from the microcosms were compared with literature data on the effects of temperature on *Daphnia* respiration and on the respiration of a stream sewage community. The respiration of a single species population was more dependent upon temperature than either of the multi-species systems. The balanced, complex laboratory ecosystem was less affected by temperature than the less complex sewage community. The drop in net photosynthesis of the microecosystems at high temperature was due either to an enhancement of respiration during the day or to an inhibition of photosynthesis by temperature. Increased temperature did not stimulate either type of community metabolism.

The microcosm studies appear to show that systems are less likely to be affected by temperature variations than simple ones. Because mature ecosystems are more complex than immature systems, they should have higher resistance to thermal shock. My studies also suggest that the prediction of organism responses to habitat temperature variations from the results of studies of laboratory unspecific cultures may not reflect the actual responses in multispecies situations.

Some investigators have reported data which support my conclusions, but the results of some others have not. Whittaker [86] observed the rates of ^{32}P movement and rates of ecological succession in cool (10 C or 50 F) and warm (25 C or 77 F) microcosms. He found these rates were much less than the two- to three-fold increase expected on the basis of experiments with single species. Copeland and Dorris [87] found that community respiration in ponds containing oil refinery effluent was about the same both summer and winter. Marshall and Tilly [18] conducted studies of net primary productivity in a reservoir receiving reactor cooling water (Par Pond) and found that in the month of December there were 15 stimulations, 7 insignificant differences, and 5 inhibitions of primary productivity by warm water. In June through August, there were 5 inhibitions, 5 insignificant differences and 3 stimulations.

Butler [88] reported that respiration of a pond-type microecosystem exhibited a 20% increase with a 12 C increase in temperature when subjected to high light intensity. With low light, temperature was not limiting to metabolism. Phinney and McIntire [89] report results similar to Butler's for their laboratory stream community. They believe that my data can be explained by nutrient limitation or some other difference between standing and flowing water systems. Thus the response of community metabolism may be complicated by other factors in addition to the comparative complexity of the communities considered.

EUTROPHICATION AND THERMAL LOADING

Eutrophication is a natural aging process occurring in lakes as nutrients increase.[90] It is usually characterized by increased hypolimnetic oxygen deficits, decreased transparency, high rates of sediment deposition, increased nutrient concentration, increased productivity, decreased species diversity, and increased algal bloom with concurrent fish kills. Any process that results in nutrient increase may be expected to result in some of the chemical, physical, and biotic changes associated with eutrophication. Most acceleration of eutrophication associated with the activities of man involve nutrient input to a body of water by agricultural runoff, domestic sewage, or industrial wastes.

Little, if any, attention has been paid to the possible enrichment of lake waters as a result of their use in power plant cooling. Like closed-basin lakes, cooling reservoirs can be expected to accumulate salts through evaporation unless flow-through is relatively large. Increases in dissolved solids may be expected to result in increased productivity and other effects associated with eutrophication.

Tilly (personal communication) has examined Par Pond for evidence of possible eutrophication. Par Pond is surrounded by forest and receives no domestic or industrial waste. Therefore, any of the usual signs of increased eutrophication would indicate that the use of Par Pond water for cooling causes eutrophication by evaporation.

Figure 22 shows the results of Tilly's studies. Primary productivity was about five times greater in 1970 than in 1965. Conductivity, magnesium, sodium, and sulfate appeared to parallel productivity in their increase. Potassium, calcium, chloride, and bicarbonate steadily increased. Total dissolved solids and nonvolatile solids showed a general increase. Reactive silica decreased.

Figure 22
Changes in Conductivity, Net Productivity, and
Nonvolatile Solids in Par Pond from 1965 to 1970

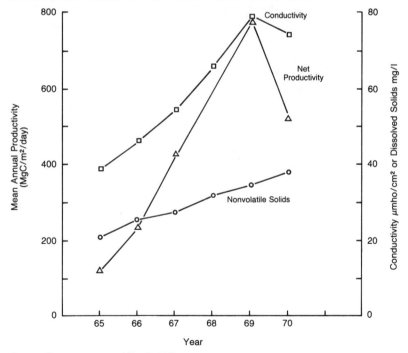

Source: Data courtesy of Dr. L. Tilly.

Most of the waters on the SRP are low in solutes.[91] Par Pond and the Savannah River, while not high in dissolved solids, do appear to be unusually rich in plant nutrients for this area. The river's exceptional solids load may be due to the influence of Piedmont drainage and industrial or domestic pollution.

A comparison of Par Pond and Pond B data suggests that the nutrient increases in Par Pond are related to reactor operations. Pond B received thermal effluent from 1961 to 1964. After 1964, the lake was allowed to equilibrate with its own drainage basin and became independent of the Par Pond system. A comparison of water quality data from 1966 with data from 1971 indicates that concentrations of dissolved ions in Pond B declined on the average more than 20%. These data support the contention that observed increases in nutrients in Par Pond are related to reactor cooling operations rather than to local influences of drainage or microclimate.

The normal use of Par Pond in reactor cooling involves at least two processes that may account for nutrient increase. Evaporation of Par Pond water during cooling would result in an increase in salinity. Additions of Savannah River water (until recently, higher in salinity than Par Pond) would both increase salinity and shift the relative proportions of nutrients in Par Pond water.

Tilly found that while productivity increased the producer biomass remained constant. He could not account for extra organic matter produced. There was no evidence that organic matter is accumulating on the bottom of the lake. A possibility was that the organic matter has been channeled to higher consumers. If this is true, then productivity increases would appear as increased growth of phytoplankton which supports an increased growth of zooplankton. The zooplankton in turn would support an increased growth of forage fish. These fish are the food for the centrarchids, the turtles, and alligators. Turnover of the lower trophic levels increases but standing crops do not. This hypothesis explains the abundance of fishes and the rapid growth rate of turtles in Par Pond.

Because of the very low solute of surface waters on the SRP, eutrophication has not progressed very far in Par Pond. In its early stages, eutrophication is always "good" as it results in high quantities of fish and other top carnivores. In its later stages, it becomes objectionable with foul smelling water, algal blooms, and fish kills. As the age of Par Pond increases, the latter phenomena may possibly be expected. In hard water areas of the country, eutrophication by evaporation may become a real problem if cooling basins are not provided with a large enough drainage area to provide water to replace evaporation and provide for enough flow-through to carry off the solids left behind during evaporation.

CONCLUSION

The ultimate limit on power production is set by the effect it has on the capability of the biosphere to support life. Cole [92] has made some calculations regarding this effect. Quoting various sources, he estimates civilization's energy production to be somewhere around three to five times 10^{19} ergs per second or 25/1,000 of 1% of the total heat radiated by the earth. This heat output has no significant impact on the present average temperature of the earth. Using a conservative 7% per year estimated power increase, he projects that by 2060 man's energy production could raise the average temperature of the earth 1 C (33.8 F). A rise of this magnitude would probably cause significant changes in the boundaries of the major plant communities. By extension of the projection, Cole showed that the earth's temperature will have risen 3 C (37.4 F) within 766 years. The ice caps of Greenland and Anarctica would probably melt under these conditions and the sea level would rise by 100 meters (109 yd). Such an elevation in sea level would drown Florida and inundate most of the world's major cities. The projection predicts that by the year 2949 the mean annual temperature of the earth will have risen to 30 C (86 F), higher than the mean annual temperature anywhere on earth. Such a temperature would, of course, probably render the earth uninhabitable.

Cole's calculations intentionally ignore the fact that fossil and fissionable fuels would probably be long depleted before these drastic effects could be achieved. However, the near inexhaustible availability of deuterium as a fuel for fusion power bring these disastrous environmental effects within the realm of possibility.[93]

It is thus obvious that power demands cannot continue to grow exponentially. The solution to the ecological problems of power generation, like the solution to most other ecological problems, has to be a reduction of the product of population times standard of living. Every rise in the standard of living and every additional person has its ecological price. It appears to me that *Homo sapiens* is left with three choices. He can reduce his standard of living, he can limit his population, or he can take no action. The immense effort being made by the underdeveloped nations of the world seems to demonstrate that our species is unwilling to lower its standard of living. Indeed, man is constantly trying to raise his standard of living and is thereby adding to the burden on the environment. If no action is taken, and the situation continues as predicted, the survival of the species is threatened. Let us hope that the genus *Homo* will be sapient enough to limit his numbers to the carrying capacity of the earth before ecological or social disaster does it for him.

References

1. Parker FL, Krenkel PA: Physical and engineering aspects of thermal pollution: Cleveland, *CRC Press,* 100 pp, 1970.

2. Eriksson E: The yearly circulation of chloride and sulfur in nature; meteorological, geochemical and pedological implications. Part II. *Tellus* **12:** 63–109, 1960.

3. Bowen RG: Electricity from geothermal, nuclear, coal sources. An environmental impact comparison. *Ore Bin* **33:** 197–211, 1971.

4. Levin AA, Birch J, Hillman RE, et al: Thermal discharges: ecological effects. *Environmental Sci Tech* **6:** 244–229, 1972.

5. Hammond AL: Geothermal energy; An emerging major resource. *Science* **177:** 978–980, 1972.

6. Peterson DE, Schrotke PM: Thermal effects of projected power growth. Hanford Engineering Development Laboratory, Richland, WA (HEDL-TME 72–69) 88 pp, 1972.

7. Mihursky JA, Kennedy VS: Water temperature criteria to protect aquatic life. *Trans Am Fish Soc Supp* **96:** 20–32, 1967.

8. Thomas NA: Freshwater Fishes in Temperature and Aquatic Life. *Laboratory Investigations,* Series 6 FWPCA, Cincinnati, 1967.

9. Downing KM, Merkens CJ: Observations on the influence of the new Johnsonville steam plant on fish and plankton populations. *Tenn Game and Fish Comm* pp 85–91. *Spo Fish Abstr* 2(4), 1957.

10. Weatherley AH: Effects of superabundant oxygen on the thermal tolerance of goldfish. *Biol Bull* **139:** 229–238, 1970.

11. Hutchinson GE: A treatise on limnology, vol 2, New York, Wiley and Sons, 1115 pp, 1967.

12. Alabaster JS: The effect of heated effluents on fish. *Int J Air Wat Poll* **7:** 541–563, 1964.

13. McCormick JHK, Hokanson EF, Jones BR: Effects of temperature on growth and survival of young brook trout, *Salvelinus fontinalis. J Fish Res Bd Canada* **29:** 1107–1112, 1972.

14. Bailey JE, Evans DR: The low-temperature threshold for pink salmon eggs in relation to a proposed hydroelectric installation. *Fish Bull* **69:** 587–593, 1971.

15. Brungs WA: Chronic effects of constant elevated temperature on the fathead minnow *(Pimephales promelas Rafinesque). Trans Am Fish Soc* **100:** 659–664, 1971.

16. Langley TM, Marter WL: The Savannah River Plant Site. DP–1323, TID–4500, UC–2, General, Miscellaneous and Progress Reports. National Technical Information Service, Springfield, VA 22151, 175 pp, 1973.

17. Marshall JS, LeRoy JH: Manganese, cobalt and zinc cycles in a South Carolina reservoir. Proc Third Nat Symposium on Radioecology, Oak Ridge, TN, 1973.

18. Marshall JS, Tilly LJ: Temperature effects on phytoplankton productivity in a reactor cooling pond. Proc Third Nat Symposium on Radioecology, Oak Ridge, TN, 1973.

19. Gibbons JW: Reproductive dynamics of a turtle *(Pseudemys scripta)* population in a reservoir receiving heated effluent from a nuclear reactor. *Can J Zool* **48**: 881–885, 1970.

20. Brisbin IL, Jr: A study of seasonal trends in the abundance of American alligators in the vicinity of a source of thermal pollution. *Bull Ecol Soc Amer* **52**: 45–46, 1971.

21. Bennett DH, Gibbons JW: Food of largemouth bass *(Micropterus salmoides)* from a South Carolina Reservoir receiving heated wastes. *Tran Am Fish Soc* **101**: 650–654, 1972.

22. Boyd CE: Chemical analysis of some vascular aquatic plant. *Arch Hydrobiol* **67**: 78–85, 1970.

23. Bennett DH: Preliminary examination of body temperatures of largemouth bass *(Micropterous salmoides)* from an artificially heated reservoir. *Arch Hydrobiol* **68**: 376–381, 1971.

24. Gibbons JW, Hook JT, Forney DL: Winter response of largemouth bass to thermal effluent from a nuclear reactor. *Prog Fish Cult* **34**: 88–90, 1972.

25. Jones JRE: Thermal pollution: the effect of heated effluents. *Fish and River Pollution* Chapt 13: 153–168. Washington, DC, Butterworth and Co, 1964.

26. Heilbrunn LV: Heat death. *Sci Amer* **190**: 70–75, 1954.

27. Moss SA: The responses of young American shad to rapid temperature changes. *Trans Amer Fish Soc* **99**: 381–384, 1970.

28. Edsall TA: The effect of temperature on the rate of development and survival of alewife eggs and larvae. *Trans Amer Fish Soc* **99**: 376–380, 1970.

29. Zawisza J, Backiel T: Some results of fishery biological investigation of heated lakes. *Verh Internat Verein Limnol* **18**: 1190–1197, 1972.

30. Cairns J, Jr: Effects of increased temperatures on aquatic organisms. *Industrial Wastes* **1**: 150–152, 1956.

31. Doudoroff R: Water quality requirements of fishes and effects of toxic substances, in Brown ME (ed), The physiology of fishes. New York, Academic Press Inc, 1957, pp 403–427.

32. Fry FEJ, Hart JS, Walker KF: Lethal temperature relations for a sample of young speckled trout, *Salvelinus fontinalis*. Univ Toronto Studies, Bio Ser 54, *Publ Ont Fish Res Lab* **66**: 1–35, 1946.

33. Fry FEJ: Effects of the environment on animal activity. Univ of Toronto Studies, Bio Ser 54, *Publ Ont Fish Res Lab* **68**: 1–62, 1947.

34. Hart JS: Geographic variations of some physiological and morphological characters in certain fresh-water fish. Univ Toronto Studies, Bio Ser, No. 60, *Publ Ont Fish Res Lab* No 72, 79 pp, 1952.

35. Ferguson RG: The preferred temperature of fish and their midsummer distribution in temperate lakes and streams. *Jour Fish Res Ed Canada* **15**: 607–624, 1958.

36. Pitt TK, Garside ET, Hepburn RL: Temperature selection of the carp *(Cyprinus carpio* Linn.). *Can J Zool* **34**: 555–557, 1956.

114

37. Garside ET, Tait JS: Preferred temperatures of the rainbow trout (*Salmo gairdneri* Richardson) and its unusual relationship to acclimation temperature. *Can J Zool* **36:** 563, 1958.

38. Neill WH, Magnuson JJ, Chipman GD: Behavioral thermoregulation by fishes: a new experimental approach. *Science* **176:** 1443–1445, 1972.

39. Bennett DH: Length-weight relationships and condition factors of fishes from a South Carolina reservoir receiving thermal effluent. *Prog Fish-Cult* **34:** 85–87, 1972.

40. Benda RS: *Effects of thermal effluents upon the growth and distribution of fish in the White River near Petersburg, Indiana,* PhD Dissertation. Indiana State University, 98 pp, 1971.

41. Kendall WA, Jr, Schwartz FJ: Lethal temperature and salinity tolerances of white catfish *(Ictalurus catus)* from the Patuxent River, Maryland. *Chesapeake Sci* **9:** 103, 1968.

42. Marcy BC: Survival of young fish in the discharge canal of a nuclear power plant. *J Fish Res Bd Canada* **28:** 1057–1060, 1971.

43. Markowski S: Faunistic and ecological investigations in Cavandish Dock, Barrow-In-Funness. *J Anim Eco* **31:** 43–51, 1962.

44. Trembley FJ: Effects of cooling water from steam electric power plants on stream biota. pp 334–345 *In* Tarzewell CM (ed) Biological Problems in Water Pollution. *Publ Health Serv Publ* No 99-WP-25, 1965.

45. Merriman D: The calefaction of a river. *Sci Amer* **222:** 42–52, 1970.

46. Gibbons JW, Bennett DH: Abundance and local movement of largemouth bass *(Micropterus salmoides)* in a reservoir receiving heated effluent from a reactor. Proc Third Radioecol Symposium. In press, 1973.

47. Parker ED, Hirshfield MH, Gibbons JW: Ecological comparisons of thermally affected aquatic environments. *J Water Poll Control Fed.* **45:** 726–733, 1973.

48. Holland WE, Smith MH, Gibbons JW, et al: Thermal tolerances of fish from a reservoir receiving effluent from a nuclear reactor. MS, 1973.

49. Cole LC: The population consequences of life history phenomena. *Quart Rev Biol* **29:** 103–137, 1954.

50. Brisbin IL, Jr: Abundance and diversity of waterfowl inhabiting heated and unheated portions of a reactor cooling reservoir, in *Thermal Ecology,* Augusta, Ga, May 3–5, 1973, Gibbons JW, Sharitz RR (eds) *AEC Symposium Series* (Conf 1730505), 1973.

51. Stewart RK: Aquatic plants and benthos. pp 83–96 *In* Mackenthurn KM. Temperature and Aquatic life. *Laboratory Investigations,* Series 6 FWPCA, Cincinnati, 1967.

52. Stangenberg M, Pawlaczyk MZ: The influence of warm water influx from a power station upon the formation of biocenotic communities in a river. Nauk Pol Wr, Wroclaw, No. 40, Inzyn Sanit I: 67–106. *Water Poll Abstr* 35 (3), Abstr No 579, 1962, 1961.

53. Coutant CC: The effect of a heated water effluent upon the macroinvertebrate riffle fauna of the Delaware River. *Penn Acad Sci* **36:** 58–71, 1962.

54. Walshe BM: Oxygen requirements and thermal resistance of chironomid larvae from flowing and still water. *J Exp Bio* **25**: 35, 1948.

55. Wurtz CB, Renn CE: Water temperature and aquatic life. Prepared for Edison Electric Institute Research Project No 49, 99 pp, 1965.

56. Noland LE, Reichel E: Life cycle of *Lymnaea stagnalis* completed at room temperature without access to air. *Nautilus* **57**: 8–13, 1943.

57. Hutchinson L: Analysis of the activity of the freshwater snail, *Viviparus malleatus* (Reeve). *Ecology* **28**: 335–345, 1947.

58. Agersborg HPK: The relation of temperature to continuous reproduction in the pulmonate snail. *Nautilus* **45**: 121–123, 1932.

59. Sprague JB: Resistance of four freshwater crustaceans to lethal high temperature and low oxygen. *J Fish Res Bd Canada* **20**: 387–415, 1963.

60. Trottier R: Effect of temperature on the life-cycle of *Anax junius* (Odonata; Aeshnidae in Canada). *Can Ent* **103**: 1671–1683, 1971.

61. Lutz E: Effects of temperature and photoperiod on larval development in *Lestes eurinus* (Odonata: Lestida). *Ecology* **49**: 637–644, 1968.

62. Lehmkul DM: Change in thermal regime as a cause of reduction of benthic fauna downstream of a reservoir. *J Fish Res Bd Canada* **29**: 1329–1332, 1972.

63. Karling JS: A preliminary account of the influence of light and temperature on growth and reproduction in *Chara fragilis* Bull. *Torrey Bot Club* **51**: 469–488, 1924.

64. Anderson RG, Lommasson RC: Some effects of temperature on the growth of *Chara zeylanica* Wild. *Butler Univ Bot Studies* **13**: 113-120, 1958.

65. Cairns JC Jr, Lanza GR, Parker BC: Pollution related structural and functional changes in aquatic communities with emphasis on freshwater algae and protozoa. *Proc Acad Nat Sci Philadelphia* **124**: 79–127, 1972.

66. Brock TD, Brock ML: The algae of Waimanger Cauldron (New Zealand): Distribution in relation of pH. *J Rhycol* **6**: 371–375, 1971.

67. Wiegert RG, Fraleigh PC: Ecology of Yellowstone thermal effluent systems: Net primary production and species diversity of a successional blue-green algal mat. *Limnol Oceanog* **17**: 215-228, 1972.

68. Marre E: Temperature *In* Lewin RA (ed) Physiology and biochemistry of algae. New York, Academic Press, 1962.

69. Inman OL: Studies on the chlorophylls and photosynthesis of thermal algae from Yellowstone Park, California and Nevada. *J Gen Physiol* **23**: 661-666, 1940.

70. Sorokin C: Calefaction and phytoplankton. *Bioscience* **21**: 1153–1159, 1971.

71. Cairns JC Jr, Lanza GR: The effects of heated waste waters on some microorganisms. Virginia Polytechnic Institute and State University Water Resources Research Center Bull **48**: 101 pp, Blacksburg, VA, 1972.

72. Margalef R: Modifications induced by different temperatures on the cells of *Scenedesmus obiquus* (Chlorophyceae). *Hydrobiologia* **5**: 83–94, 1954.

116

73. Wallace NM: The effect of temperature on the growth of some fresh-water diatoms. *Notulae Naturae,* Acad Nat Sci Philadelphia No. 280, 11 pp, 1955.

74. Patrick R, Crum B, Coles J: Temperature and manganese as determining factors in the presence of diatom or blue-green algal floras in streams. *Proc Nat Acad Sci* **64:** 472–478, 1969.

75. Hopkins JT: A study of the diatoms of the Ouse Estuary, Sussex. L. The movement of the mud-flat diatoms in response to some chemical and physical changes. *J Mar Biol Assoc UK* **43:** 653–666, 1963.

76. Trembley FJ: Research project on effects of condenser discharge water on aquatic life. Progress report 1960 Lehigh University Institute of Research, Bethlehem, PA, *Wat Poll Ab* **34:** 2157, 1960.

77. Buck JD, Rankin JS: Thermal effects on the Connecticut River: Bacteriology. *Poll Control Fed* **44:** 47–64, 1972.

78. Resi LA: Bacteria. *IN* Temperature and Aquatic Life. *Laboratory Investigations,* Series 6 FWPCA, Cincinnati, Ohio, 1967.

79. Silvey JKG, Roach AW: Studies on microbiotic cycles in surface waters. Jour Amer Water Works. *Assoc* **56:** 60–72, 1964.

80. Fair GM, Geyer JC, Morris JC: Water supply and waste-water disposal. New York, John Wiler & Sons, Inc, 1958.

81. Beyers RJ: The microcosm approach to ecology. *Am Biol Teacher* **26:** 491–498, 1964.

82. Cooke GD: Aquatic laboratory microsystems and communities. *in* The Structure and Function of Fresh-Water Microbial Communities. Cairs J, Jr (ed) Research Monograph 3, Virginia Polytechnic Institute and State University, 301 pp, 1971.

83. Cooke GD, Beyers RJ, Odum EP: The case for the multi-species ecological system, with special reference to succession and stability. In Saunder JF (ed) Bioregenerative systems. NASA SP-165: 129–139, 1968.

84. Beyers RJ: Relationship between temperature and the metabolism of experimental ecosystems. *Science* **136:** 980–982, 1962.

85. Beyers RJ: The metabolism of twelve laboratory microecosystems. *Ecol Monogr* **33:** 281–306, 1963.

86. Whittaker RH: Experiments with radio phosphorous tracer in aquarium microcosms. *Ecol Monogr* **31:** 157–188, 1961.

87. Copeland BJ, Dorris TC: Community metabolism in ecosystems receiving oil refinery effluents. *Limnol Oceanogr* **9:** 431–447, 1964.

88. Butler JL: *Interaction of effects by environmental factors on primary productivity in ponds and microecosystems,* PhD dissertation. Oklahoma State University, 1964.

89. Phinney HK, McIntire DD: Effect of temperature on metabolism of periphyton communities developed in laboratory streams. *Limnol Oceanogr* **10:** 341–344, 1965.

90. Sawyer CN: Basic concepts of eutrophication. *J Water Poll Control Fed* **38:** 373–744, 1966.

91. Polisini JM, Boyd CE, Didgeon B: Nutrient limiting factors in an oligotrophic South Carolina pond. *Oikos* **21:** 344–347, 1970.

92. Cole LC: Thermal Pollution. *Bioscience* **19:** 989–992, 1969.

93. Roberts R: Energy Sources and conversion techniques. *Amer Scientist* **61:** 66–75, 1973.

9

Environmental Impacts from Power Plant Sitings and Distribution of Energy

H. J. Young

Despite the fact that today electric energy accounts for only about 10% of our total energy use, measured at the point of use, it seems reasonable to give electricity special attention. At the present time, most of the electricity we use in this country is generated in large central stations. These stations are typically interconnected into regional grids, and the grids are linked one with another. About 5% of our electricity is generated by industrial plants for their own use, and a small fraction is generated by others. The bulk of our supply is generated by large central stations because it is more economic and reliable to do so. My comments are addressed to these major facilities.

As we discuss problems associated with electric power supply we do not want to lose perspective on the reasons that lead most students of the subject to agree that more and more of our energy use will be electric in the future. About a quarter of the energy our country uses today goes to transportation. Almost none of this (except for elevators, a few thousand miles of electric trains, and several hundred thousand golf carts and fork-lift trucks) is electric. We depend on the internal combustion engine for virtually all our individual transportation and most of our mass transportation as well. Of all the energy conversion devices we use, the internal combustion engine is the least efficient. Most people would agree, I think, that the internal combustion engine is presently the most serious contributor to our air pollution problems. It is probable that an increasing portion of our transportation passenger miles—certainly those for mass transportation and increasingly those in other areas—will be electric in the future. Among the reasons for the growth in use of electric energy is that the alternatives are less desirable from an environmental point of view. We should keep this in mind as we review the various impacts that electric generation does have on the environment.

Let me turn to the subject of siting of major electric power facilities. These facilities may be classified as (1) generating stations, (2) transmission lines, and (3) large substations and switching centers. I have been asked to address the environmental impacts of the first two categories. Of course, in addition to environmental considerations, utilities must take into account engineering and physical requirements of the facilities, and economic considerations as well.

Engineering and physical requirements, including system reliability considerations, impose certain relatively inflexible limitations. Hydroelectric plants require water to spin turbines; fossil fuel and nuclear plants need cooling waters for condensers and make-up water for boilers; transmission lines must interconnect loads and sources of supply. Obviously, such factors must be taken into account.

STEAM GENERATING STATIONS

The environmental factors are equally important. Major power facilities cannot help but have some impact; but, in general, they can be considerably more acceptable than many types of industrial facilities and certainly much can be done to reduce their impact. The environmental and engineering work involved is heavily site-oriented and is subject to scrutiny and control by a variety of governmental regulatory bodies. In the case of generating plants, there is always some impact on land and water and, in most cases, on the air. Most of the electric utility industry's generating capacity—about 80%—is made up of steam generating plants that burn coal, gas, or oil. Air and water quality, thermal effects, noise, and appearance are matters of concern with all plants in this category.

From the point of view of potential health effects, it would seem that air pollution is the most serious consideration. Over the years, great improvements have been made in this area, especially in the control of particulate matter. The Clean Air Act of 1970 established a strict time-table under which the federal Environmental Protection Agency (EPA) and the states have been developing standards for control of these and other emissions, notably sulfur oxides and nitrogen oxides. Without entering into a detailed discussion of the Clean Air Act and EPA's actions, it is possible to say that standards set for sulfur emissions at coal burning power plants have had a profound effect on the electric utility industry and, in fact, on the whole fuel supply situation in this country. At the moment, there is no way to meet the sulfur emission standard at coal burning power plants on the kind of continuous, reliable basis necessary to power plant operation without using low-sulfur fuels—either gas, oil, or where it is available, low-sulfur coal.

This does not mean we will never be able to meet the emission standard. Millions, and probably billions, of dollars are being spent worldwide to find a solution. Industries and governments, here and abroad, are working hard on the assumption that a solution *can* be found. There is considerable optimism among technologists in the field that it will eventually be possible to take sulfur out of stack gases after combustion or out of the fuel before combustion, or both. The trouble is that the techniques are not available today.

In stating so categorically our present inability to meet the sulfur emission standard at coal burning plants, except with inherently low-sulfur fuels, I should emphasize the nature of the standard itself. It is, as I have said, an emission standard, regulating discharges at the top of the stack. It is not a health-related standard. As you know, the health-related standards established by the EPA are primarily ambient air standards. It is not necessary for a power plant to meet the emission standard—which, in effect, attempts to put a kind of stopper on each stack—in order to meet ambient air standards.

Use of oil has increased substantially as restriction on coal usage and the lack of availability of gas have grown. The demand for low-sulfur oil is intense, and the capacity of existing refineries does not match it. Other environmental factors related to the use of oil include the potential contamination of ocean waters, disruption of the land by pipelines, and problems surrounding construction and operation of terminal facilities for tankers.

Natural gas presently provides almost one third of the electric energy generated by all fossil fuels, but it has been plagued by a shortage of proved reserves. Despite its desirability as a clean burning fuel, it is increasingly unavailable. Even utilities in the Southwest which have traditionally burned nothing but gas are being forced to other fuels. Gas contains essentially no sulfur, and, in comparison with coal and oil, its combustion creates little particulate matter. All three fuels—coal, gas, and oil—produce nitrogen oxides, but control of these is not viewed as a problem of real magnitude.

Let me summarize this way: utilities, by making use of tall stacks and intermittent control systems and by switching to low-sulfur fuels, are generally able to meet primary ambient air quality standards around power plants. No system is presently available to meet emission standards at power plants except by using low-sulfur fuels, which are in limited supply, but there is considerable optimism that at least one technological alternative will be found by the early 1980's so that the high-sulfur coals that we have in such abundance can be utilized in power plants. Siting of fossil-fuel burning plants must take these standards and this state of technology into consideration, along with the meteorology and topography of locations which meet the engineering, operating, and economic requirements of the power supply system.

HYDROELECTRIC SYSTEMS

Hydroelectric generating plants represent about 17% of the total electric power producing capacity of the country. These plants make direct use of water resources by converting the natural energy of river flow into electric power. Pumped storage hydroelectric systems use water as the medium for the temporary storage of electric energy converted from fossil or nuclear fuels. In addition to pumped storage projects, which require construction of reservoirs at substantial elevations above waterways plus installation of pumping and generating equipment, hydroelectric projects are of three general types:

1. Dams or other structures to create reservoirs that provide the necessary water power to rotate turbines and generators.
2. Diversion structures that divert water from a national waterway to a turbine generator by means of a pipe or canal, sometimes several miles long.
3. Hydroelectric stations which, to be economically feasible, have the ability to store water during periods when their capacity is not required to meet system loads and then use stored water at high rates of discharge for relatively short periods of time to produce large quantities of energy to meet peak loads. Such operating flexibility is essential to the economic justification of this kind of project and involves the ability to leave water in storage as well as to use it at high rates of discharge.

Each type of hydroelectric project has the same basic requirements: adequate water and appropriate geology. The unique environmental factor involved is the physical presence of a structure in a waterway. In the case of a dam, a lake is created and the characteristics of the area are substantially altered. There is, however, no fuel combustion involved and this may be viewed as an advantage from one point of view. On the other hand, hydroelectric projects are generally located at substantially long distances from load centers and may involve construction of lengthy transmission lines. These factors do not help justify the project either economically or environmentally. In any event, the role of hydroelectricity is decreasing in this country, as it is on a world-wide basis.

NUCLEAR POWER GENERATION

The third major category of generating plants is nuclear. On a percentage basis, nuclear power now plays a very small part in our electric power producing capacity—about 3%. However, this percentage is increasing in most parts of the country. During the five-year period of 1973 to 1977, 54 new nuclear power *units* are scheduled to begin operation across the nation. This number illustrates one of the many semantic difficulties involved in talking about electric power production. There may be a number of units at a given power station or site, so to visualize an average of slightly more than ten new nuclear units a year on a nationwide basis over the next five years does not really give us any notion of the number of new sites or plant locations involved, which average about five new sites a year.

It is also somewhat misleading to set nuclear plants apart from other kinds of steam generating stations, as I am doing. In the simplest terms, a nuclear generating plant makes use of the fission process to produce the heat necessary to provide the steam that drives the turbines that generate electricity. Once the heat is provided, there is no essential difference between a nuclear power plant and a fossil-fired plant.

Selecting a site for a nuclear plant involves the same general criteria and consideration as for a fossil-fired plant, with the addition of extensive safety-related factors. Economics dictate that nuclear plants tend to be high capacity, though they may be physically less intrusive than their fossil-fueled counterparts. The reactors in most general use today require the availability of larger quantities of cooling water than do fossil-fired plants of the same capacity, and the thermal discharges involved require special care and handling. Again, the method of treatment—and there is a variety of techniques that may be used—is related to the particular requirements of the site.

From an environmental viewpoint, a nuclear power plant produces little or no air pollution and requires no daily fuel or ash movement. Over the past two decades, one strong impetus to the development of nuclear power has been the view that it represents the long-run solution to the problem of air pollution from thermal power plants. It avoids combustion of fossil fuels and minimizes the volume of fuel required—an advantage both in terms of the amount of land disturbed in mining and storage area needed at the power plant. For example, the 11 tons of coal or 45 barrels of oil needed for one megawatt-day of electric energy, can be replaced by about 3½ ounces of slightly enriched uranium.

Despite its attractions, nuclear power generation is not free of potential environmental impact. Small quantities of radioactive gases, liquids, and solid wastes are produced in a nuclear plant as a result of its operation and these radioactive materials are considerably more toxic per unit weight than are the waste products from combustion of fossil fuels. I hasten to point out, however, that there is a substantial body of experience that indicates that the processes available for handling radioactive wastes are adequate essentially to eliminate any change in the radiation environment of a nuclear power station from that which existed prior to its operation. Nuclear plants have been in operation in this country since the 1950s, and they have been carefully monitored by state and federal agencies, as well as by the plant operators themselves. A recent report by the National Academy of Sciences–National Research Council indicates that nuclear power plant operation has had no effect in the radiation levels around the plants.

By far the majority of the radioactivity associated with nuclear power generation involves fuel recovery processing, which takes place at a central location away from the power plant. The Atomic Energy Commission requires that all such wastes be solidified and transferred to a federal repository for ultimate storage.

To conclude this discussion of environmental impacts of the various alternatives presently available for generation of electric energy, let me refer to a study made about a year ago for the Resources Agency of California by the School of Engineering and Applied Science at the University of California at Los Angeles. This study involved an extensive comparison of the operations of oil-fired and nuclear power plants in an urban setting, with both making use of currently available technology to protect health and safety. The study concluded that:

The public health risk from routine operations of electricity generating plants using nuclear fuel or oil is in the range of the very low hazards to which the public is exposed by uncontrollable events of nature, such as being struck by lightning or bitten by a venomous animal or insect. Interestingly, routine operation of a nuclear plant presents a significantly smaller public health risk than the routine operation of an oil-fired plant, typically by a factor of 10 to 100.

The public health risk due to *accidental* releases from either a nuclear or oil-fired plant are both of the same magnitude, about one hundred thousand times smaller than the risk from *routine* operation of the plants.

TRANSMISSION FACILITIES

Transmission lines are required to move power from generating sources to load centers and to integrate and interconnect electric systems. Obviously, the principal environmental impact of a transmission facility is its physical intrusion on the landscape. Just as obviously, the solution to the problem should be to hide or camouflage the line. In the case of low voltage distribution lines, undergrounding is technically and economically feasible and, particularly in new areas, is carried out increasingly. For high voltage lines, the lines needed to transmit large blocks of power, undergrounding is neither technically or economically feasible over long distances at the present time.

Various techniques are available to reduce the impact of overhead transmission lines. Use of extra-high voltages, for example, requires less land for the same amount of capacity than does use of lower voltage lines. Existing rights of way can be used, and multiple use of rights of way with railroads or other utilities is often possible. Selection of routes can be made with the environment in mind, so that ridges, mountain tops, or skylines in hilly areas can be avoided. Some flexibility exists in locating certain portions of lines but this flexibility is considerably lessened in the vicinity of the terminal stations.

My purpose has been to list the principal environmental impacts of the siting of electric generating stations and transmission lines. All the techniques of generation and transmission and the associated methods of environmental control represent evolutionary advances over the techniques of 20 years ago. It would be foolish to suggest that this evolutionary process will not continue. The technology available to us 20 years from now, or even 10 or 5 years from now, will do much to reduce the relatively slight impacts of currently constructed facilities and hasten the replacement of older, less efficient facilities. In the meantime we will continue to need increasing amounts of electric energy to achieve the overall goals of our society. We need electricity to produce grade A milk and grade A eggs. Large industries use billions of kilowatt-hours a year to run machines needed to provide jobs—and about 10% of the electricity they use powers pollution control facilities.

I have not discussed the complex arrangement of local, state, and federal governmental agencies that regulate the location and operation of electric power facilities, nor have I discussed the need for greater research and development work to provide a greater variety of energy alternatives in the future. These subjects are closely related to mine, but I believe they will be covered by other contributors.

I cannot conclude, however, without this thought: As a society we have become newly conscious of the value of energy. We need to use it wisely and provide it carefully with the best understanding of the environment, economics, and engineering available to us. We need to distribute it without discrimination and plan for its availability in the far distant future as well as for today and tomorrow. The issues involved are not easy, but if we approach them constructively we should find ways to overcome even those problems that seem most insurmountable today.

10

Power Plant Sitings: Views of Environmentalists

William E. Siri, Ph.D.

Whatever else may be said about energy, on one aspect of it everyone agrees: there is an energy "crunch." But the nature of the crunch depends upon who describes it. In the energy industry and government agencies, there is growing apprehension that energy demands may not be met in time; in a concerned and articulate segment of the public, there is growing anxiety that the industry might succeed. On the one hand, the country is geared to an annual increase of 7% in electrical energy consumption; on the other, it faces shortages of readily accessible clean fuels, and the industry is running upstream against a strong flow of public opposition.

Everybody uses electricity, but almost everybody hates power plants. It would seem a paradox that, while the blessings of electricity are so cherished, the purveyors of it are so maligned. It would be a paradox, too, were it not for the ominous environmental consequences of our insatiable appetite for energy.

It would be a dangerously simplistic view of energy problems to assume that the troubles faced by the industry are the result of mindless harassment by wooly minded environmental extremists. The problems are inherent in the nature, or at least in the present practices of energy conversion and uses, which have ravaged land and resources, polluted air and water on vast scales, and now conflict with a new environmental consciousness—anxiety is a better word—held by society. The controversy over energy is not new; it has simply grown exponentially, like that of energy consumption, but with a shorter doubling time. Its stimulus is the recognition, abetted by Apollo space photos, that the earth and its resources are indeed limited, but that population, energy input, and pollution are not, and that a grim end point could lie within the foreseeable future.

ENERGY USE REFORMS

The fundamental objectives of environmentalists, and of many others who have thought about our future on this planet, are simple in principle. The first objective is the need to engender an ethic of energy conservation—rein-forced with rational energy policies, economic incentives, and adequate con-trols—that will lead to an enduring steady state. The second is the need to institute environmental constraints on all forms of energy: on the extraction and transport of fuels; on the conversion, transmission, and uses of energy; and on the disposal of wastes.

Responsible environmental organizations realize that redirection of na-tional policies and institutional machinery and the correction of environmental damage cannot be achieved overnight. They are aware that energy, wisely developed and used, is essential, and that no form of energy is wholly free of environmental liabilities. They are also aware, however, that without challenge and public debate, the necessary reforms in the way we use energy simply will not occur.

In the past few years, hosts of commissions, committees, studies, and panels have spawned an immense volume of analyses and recommendations on the role of energy in our society. As yet this massive cerebral effort has had no perceptible influence in shaping an intelligent national energy policy for the country. It seems clear that all energy sources—fossil fuels, nuclear, hydro, solar, and geothermal—must be coordinated; that more comprehensive environmental safeguards are necessary; that far greater support is needed for research and development of alternative, clean sources and for improved conversion efficien-cies; and, above all, that meaningful measures must be undertaken to conserve energy. Put another way, we need to establish policies, institutional changes, and economic incentives that will lead to an enduring steady state of high quality compatible with our resources and environment, rather than the present course toward maximum entropy.

Yet in the face of dwindling energy resources, a growing dependence on foreign fuels with all the economic and political perils this entails, and our incredibly wasteful use of energy, the substance of current national policy on energy is, "Let us have more of the same and off with the environmental constraints." At best, this merely puts off the impending crisis a few years as we scrape the bottom of the barrel for fossil fuels; at worst, it is a giant step backwards for our future welfare.

Turning to the narrower question of power plant siting, environmental-ists see this as only one facet of the energy problem, but it presents an immediate cause for action. The controversies over siting are often as not contests over land use, aggravated by the growing anxiety about the environmental consequences of our profligate consumption of energy.

National land use planning and adequate economic and statutory con-trols to ensure compliance are considered among key elements in structuring the future role of energy in our society. The contest over land use in this country has already taken on the character of a free-for-all in a Roman Circus, and it can only intensify under the present traditional setting of single-purpose, un-coordinated planning and development in energy, water, transportation, etc., by multitudes of agencies and private interests.

The electric utilities and fuel supplies cannot do the kind of planning that is needed. Understandably, they will not want to embrace planning that impedes their freedom of action any more than do highway departments, or subdividers.

LAND USE PLANNING

Local land use planning generally is ineffectual and uncoordinated and too easily subverted to serve special interests. Nor can national planning be done effectively on a wholly independent state by state basis. The patterns of development in power, water, transportation, and urban development extend beyond state boundaries, and state agencies cannot integrate these elements on a sufficiently large scale.

Nevertheless, states and regional groups of states must be encouraged to play a more productive role in planning, but to be effective they need a strong federal overseer to devise and administer standards governing their efforts and ultimately to coordinate the pieces into a national land use plan. To be effective, such planning must embrace all major uses: power plant siting, transmission lines, transportation, water, agriculture, urban development, recreation and natural reserves, and a multitude of other uses.

Under present procedures, sites for power facilities are selected by the user, too often with little or no regard for other interests, and too often they are disclosed only at the time a permit is sought. The inevitable consequence is a bitter contest with public interest groups over every site. Ideally, future sites for power plants and routing of transmission lines and pipe lines should be designated long in advance of need through the process of forming, under public scrutiny, land use plans. Such plans should be reviewed and updated periodically, but tentative sites should be adopted 20 years in advance of possible use. In effect, and by any of several methods of funding and control, sites conforming with a land use plan and with a national energy policy would be held in inventory until needed. To qualify for use of a site, a utility would be required to file plans for plant construction ten years in advance and seek a construction permit five years in advance of breaking ground.

Final certification of sites and transmission lines, and issuance of construction permits, except for reactors, should be left to regional boards, subject to a superior federal commission. These boards should consist of representatives from those state and regional agencies that are now required by law to review and certify power facilities, including air and water pollution, and fish and game. And they should have as members representatives of the public from consumer and environmental groups.

Land use planning and a comprehensive national energy policy will not in themselves eliminate disputes. A progressively better informed public has already convincingly demonstrated that it is determined to have a voice in deciding how land and resources are used and in what environmental risks and trade-offs it will accept. If the public is to participate in the decision-making process in an orderly, constructive fashion, substantial improvements in the provisions for doing so are needed.

It is essential to provide adequate and timely public hearings at every step in the planning and licensing process. To a large extent this is done, and it is sometimes done conscientiously. But too often the process is inadequate, subverted, or biased, and the findings ignored.

Granted, hearings are often painful, tedious, exasperating, and time-consuming; nevertheless, there is perhaps no better way to sense changing social values, or of developing a comprehensive critique of all the aspects of an impending decision by a public agency.

It is necessary to ensure that public interest groups have standing to participate in licensing proceedings. This should, if it is to be meaningful, include the right to cross-examine witnesses.

Finally, legislation is needed that provides broader ground for appeals and judicial review.

While all energy sources have in common the problem of land use, most of them share additional environmental problems, among which are thermal discharges to water bodies and visual impact.

Water is already a resource in short supply in most parts of the country. Each 1,000-megawatt (Mw) power unit consumes, through evaporative loss in cooling, 15,000 to 25,000 acre feet of water per year. Yet the amount of fresh water available for once-through cooling, wet towers, and cooling ponds is severely limited; of equal importance, thermal loading of rivers, lakes, and estuaries from once-through cooling will progressively be restricted. This may seem to leave coastal sites for water cooling, but again there are severe environmental constraints and such sites could only serve the periphery of the continent. Moreover, it is unlikely that there will ever be public acceptance of power plants beaded along every coast.

This seems to leave diminishing prospects for water cooling and water-related sites and to place greater emphasis on dry cooling towers and development of high conversion efficiencies to reduce water consumption and thermal pollution. Dry tower cooling, while less efficient, has the added advantage of allowing a far greater choice of sites, often closer to load centers and trunk lines.

Among esthetic considerations, greater emphasis should be given to undergrounding transmission lines and plants, particularly nuclear reactors for reasons of safety in anticipation of the liquid-metal fast-breeder reactor. With several hundred thousand miles of high-voltage transmission lines already strung, the country resembles a gigantic package tied by an idiot. Another 400,000 miles of lines projected for the next 30 years will certainly not improve public acceptance of more power lines, no matter how handsomely the tower structures are designed. In the long run, hydrogen may be a better and cheaper means of transmitting energy by the utilization of existing pipe lines.

Each kind of energy source has its own specific environmental problems it may not share with others. Air and water pollution associated with combustion of fossil fuels, especially coal, is familiar to everyone and need not be expanded upon here, beyond noting that strip mining has much to do with controversies over siting of coal-burning power plants. Until the utter destruction of land and pollution of waterways by strip mining is controlled and the land restored, power plants using such fuels will come under increasing public pressure.

NUCLEAR COOLANTS AND WASTE

Most environmentalists are now willing to concede that in normal operation nuclear power plants are clean, although not necessarily environmentally benign when they use once-through cooling. Nevertheless, nuclear power plants have been the target of criticism on grounds of their potential for accidental release of radionuclides.

It has justifiably been said over the years that no other hazard has ever been studied as thoroughly or is as well understood as are the effects of ionizing radiations and the behavior of radionuclides in biosystems. While our understanding of the biological effects of radiations may be adequate to set environmental levels that should not be exceeded, the questions asked by environmentalists are directed to the likelihood of accidental releases of radionuclides and more particularly, catastrophic accidents resulting from miscalculation, design failure, faulty operation, and mismanagement. In the rush to develop nuclear energy, have important aspects of safety been given less than the necessary attention? Many experts in the field say yes. The Atomic Energy Commission (AEC) itself has listed more than 100 unsettled safety questions, 44 of which are regarded as urgent key problem areas that still remain to be explored. Yet, about 100 large light-water reactors are under construction and on the drawing board for the seventies.

The controversy over the emergency core cooling system (ECCS) is still fresh in everybody's mind and still unresolved. In spite of assurances from the industry that each unit in an ECCS is conservatively designed, bench tested, and reliable, there appears reason to believe that under certain conditions the assembled system will not work fast enough or well enough in large reactors to forestall disaster in the event of sudden loss of coolant.

At this point in time, with light-water reactors growing rapidly in size and number, and liquid-metal fast-breeders only a decade away, no one seems able to give even an order of magnitude of the risk of major accident. Although $53 million is now budgeted for reactor safety research, its adequacy has been questioned because of the ten-year backlog in unfinished safety research. Moreover, the management of the program has been vigorously criticized even within government circles on the grounds that the safety research funds funnel through the Division of Reactor Development and Technology, whose main thrust, understandably, is reactor promotion. At best, it will take some years before answers to some crucial reactor safety questions will be at hand. It should be added, however, that the Atomic Energy Commission has proposed reducing the power level of large reactors until the ECCS question is settled, which should reduce to negligible levels the risk of accidents that could result in the release of radionuclides.

In the second area unique to nuclear power plants, environmentalists are not alone in their anxieties about permanent disposal of high level wastes. This concern is shared by the utilities and many an expert in the field. The regretable salt-mine affair at Lyons, Kansas, simply highlighted both the technical and management problems of disposal. In that instance, it was a poor choice of site, the disposal method was insufficiently researched, and the project was ill managed, at least in its relations with the public and the state of Kansas. But, given the first two faults, the third was probably inevitable.

The question arose and still lingers as to the risk that a decision maker will succeed in making a nonretrievable burial of trillions of curies of fission products that later proves to have been little better than simply flushing it down the drain. The risk of having such decisions implemented, it is argued, can be reduced if significant decisions are first advanced as proposals and subjected to public scrutiny. It is, after all, the public that must bear the risk.

Fortunately, for the near term at least, the problem of high level waste disposal was sensibly resolved by the AEC. The wastes are to be securely stored as inert solids in retrievable form at federal repositories until we are more confident about the reliability of permanent disposal methods.

RADIATION EFFECTS

Radioactive emissions from nuclear power plants have not greatly troubled environmentalists for the past year. The bitter quarrel that raged for some three years was largely dissipated by the AEC's lowering of the allowable design emission levels below even the levels proposed by the severest critics. In one sense this demonstrated what can be achieved with a conscientious effort by the industry and the AEC. In another sense, it transferred the burden of the problem to the fuel reprocessing centers and disposal sites. Until comparable emission limits, now being formulated by the AEC, are applied to reprocessing plants, the overall problem of releases into the general environment is not fully resolved. There then remains only the perplexing question, perhaps now academic, that if the industry can live with such low emission levels, why not lower the radiation dose limits for the general public? A maximum average of 170 milliroentgen equivalents man (mrem/year) for nonmedical exposure seems inconsistent both with what is now practical for nuclear power development and with the basic philosophy of the National Council on Radiation Protection (NCRP), namely that exposure should be kept "as low as practicable." If the NCRP adheres to its basic tenets of no-threshold for deleterious radiation effects and that maximum permissible dose must be based on a pragmatic balancing of benefits and risks, then there would now seem some justification for lowering the general population exposure limits.

In spite of—or perhaps because of—the intense polarization between a growing segment of the public and the energy industry, significant progress has been made toward accommodation of energy facilities with emerging social goals. Some meaningful legislation controlling pollution and siting of facilities has been enacted; a national energy policy is in the primitive stage of formation; and land use planning is struggling to assert itself and may succeed in time to avert irreparable damage to the land.

It is too much to expect that everyone will always work harmoniously together, and perhaps they should not. A reasonable level of controversy keeps everyone alert and motivated to solve problems. We may even muddle through before we run out of resources, land, and patience, or choke on our own debris.

11

Other Ecological Impacts

Frank L. Parker, Ph.D.

In this context we can take "other ecological impacts" to mean impacts due to gaseous and solid waste releases from energy production. To make this more meaningful, we need to indicate source terms of the releases and put them on a comparative basis and then consider their effects. In this instance we shall also indicate only those source terms from the production of energy and not from the total fuel cycle—whether fossil fuel, nuclear, or hydro—and only from electrical power production and not from the other major energy uses, transportation, heating, and process use. It is hard to ignore completely these uses, but if one gets into transportation problems, for example, with their particular effluents from automobiles, trucks and airplanes, the discussion becomes so broad as to be meaningless in the time that we have available to us. Therefore, I shall restrict my paper to the production of effluents at the electrical power plant site itself.

I make this restriction quite reluctantly since I have lived in Appalachia for close to 20 years and the signs of the winning of the coal are all too evident about us—the stripped mountains, the rubble and the ruin produced by strip mining on the lovely mountains and hills, the acidification and siltation of the rivers and streams, the subsidence of the land above the deep mines, the slag piles fouling the landscape and the air, the crippled and maimed from coal mine accidents, the black lung victims, and, possibly even more poignant, the deserted company towns and their forlorn inhabitants. A few numbers about these effects, however, might be appropriate. Contrary to popular belief, the major problem is not yet in strip mining but in deep mining. Appalachia produces about 70% of the nation's coal. Sixty percent of the nation's bituminous fuel is from underground mines. The result is that 158,000 acres of urban land has undergone noticeable subsidence. Eleven thousand miles of stream and 15,000 acres of impounded waters receive each year more than 4×10^6 tons of sulfuric acid (75% due to deep mines). In addition, in 1969 there were over 110 underground fires and over 460 refuse bank fires.[1]

However, these forms of pollution are localized in a region where few people visit and have comparatively little effect upon the rest of the country.

What happens at power plants, though, is of much greater interest since they are ubiquitous and therefore release their effluents over a much wider landscape and atmosphere.

POWER PLANT EFFLUENTS AND RESIDUES

Let us now look at the effluents from a standardized nuclear power plant and then from a standardized fossil fueled power plant, all under *normal* operating conditions. For pressurized water reactors (PWR), a site will be assumed to contain two base load plants rated at 2,600 Mw (t) (870 Mw (e)) and for boiling water reactors (BWR), a site will be assumed to contain two base load plants rated at 3,300 Mw (t) (1,100 Mw (e)). The radioactive releases from each site with no treatment are shown in Tables 11 and 12.[2] In order to meet the proposed guidelines of 5 milliroentgen equivalents man (mrem) per year at the perimeter for liquid and gaseous releases each, a variety of treatment schemes are suggested that include, for the PWR system, 60-day decay storage in tanks or on charcoal beds, HEPA (high efficiency) filters, recombiners of the radiolytic hydrogen and oxygen, clean steam for gland seal, cryogenic distillation for removal of noble gases, selective absorption for removal of noble gases, cover gas recycle for selective removal of noble gases, and the storage of 99.9% of ^{85}Kr for 30 years. The releases of gases will be reduced down to 2.2 X 10^3 curies of noble gases and 0.06 curies of ^{131}I (10^5 maximum permissible occupational body burdens in the thyroid) annually at mills per kw-hr cost of 0 (no treatment) to 0.20 (operations and maintenance costs assumed proportional to capital costs). Treatment schemes for BWR systems include 100-meter stacks, recombiner, 300-minute decay, HEPA filter, 60-day decay of Xe and 4.5-day decay of Kr on ambient or 0 F charcoal beds, and cyrogenic distillation or selective removal of noble gases will reduce noble gases to 5.1 X 10^3 curies and ^{131}I to 0.11 curies per year (1.5 X 10^6 body burdens in the thyroid) at a cost of 0.022 mill/kilowatt hour (kw-hr) to 0.18/kw-hr.

In addition, waste heat must be discharged to the atmosphere or to the hydrosphere depending upon the use of cooling towers. If cooling towers are used then evaporated water and drift will be discharged to the atmosphere as well as blowdown to the hydrosphere. At 100% load and 100% utilization and no cooling towers, the PWR units would discharge directly to the atmosphere 7.8 X 10^{12} BTU/yr, and the BWRs would discharge 1 X 10^{13} BTU/yr. It is recognized that the total quantity of heat produced by combustion must eventually be discharged to the atmosphere, the ultimate sink. If cooling towers are used then the heat is discharged locally, 1 X 10^{14} BTU/yr for PWR units and 1.3 X 10^{14} BTU/yr for BWR units. If all of this heat were discharged directly to Lake Michigan, uniformly mixed and retained in the lake waters, and there were no other heat sources or sinks, the BWR discharges would raise the temperature 0.012 F. If, however, the heat were added to the Chicago River at its mandated minimum flow of 3,200 cubic feet per second (cfs), then the temperature would be raised 26 F and 34 F by the PWR units and the BWR units

Table 11
Source Term for PWR – Calculated Annual Release of Radioactive Materials in Gaseous Effluents

(for two reactors)

Nuclide	Half-Life	Primary System		Secondary System			Building Ventilation			Total (Ci/yr)
		Shutdown Degasification (Ci/yr)	Shim Bleed Stripping (Ci/yr)	Blowdown Vent (Ci/yr)	Air Ejector Exhaust (Ci/yr)	Gland Seal Exhaust (Ci/yr)	Containment Purge (Ci/yr)	Auxiliary Building (Ci/yr)	Turbine Building (Ci/yr)	
^{83m}Kr	1.86 h	4.5×10	3.2×10^2	a	3.0	a	a	3.0	a	3.7×10^2
^{85m}Kr	4.4 h	2.4×10^2	1.7×10^3	a	1.6×10	a	a	1.6×10	a	2.0×10^3
^{85}Kr	10.74 y	1.9×10^2	1.2×10^3	a	1.1×10	a	2.2×10	1.1×10	a	1.4×10^3
^{87}Kr	76 m	1.3×10^2	9.2×10^2	a	8.9	a	a	8.9	a	1.1×10^3
^{88}Kr	2.79 h	4.2×10^2	3.0×10^3	a	2.8×10	a	1.0×10^{-1}	2.8×10	a	3.5×10^3
^{89}Kr	3.18 m	7.3	4.5×10	a	6.7×10^{-1}	a	a	6.7×10^{-1}	a	5.3×10
^{131m}Xe	11.96 d	2.0×10^2	1.4×10^3	a	1.3×10	a	4.8	1.3×10	a	1.6×10^3
^{133m}Xe	2.26 d	4.5×10^2	3.2×10^3	a	3.0×10	a	2.1	3.0×10	a	3.7×10^3
^{133}Xe	5.27 d	3.5×10^4	2.4×10^5	a	2.3×10^3	2.3	3.8×10^2	2.3×10^3	5.3×10^{-1}	2.8×10^5
^{135m}Xe	15.7 m	2.6×10	1.8×10^2	a	2.0	a	a	2.0	a	2.1×10^2
^{135}Xe	9.16 h	7.0×10^2	5.0×10^3	a	4.8×10	a	5.8×10^{-1}	4.8×10	a	5.8×10^3
^{137}Xe	3.82 m	1.6×10	9.9×10^1	a	1.4	a	a	1.4	a	1.2×10^2
^{138}Xe	14.2 m	9.1×10	6.3×10^2	a	6.6	a	a	6.6	a	7.4×10^2
TOTAL NOBLE GAS		3.8×10^4	2.6×10^5	a	2.4×10^3	2.3	4.1×10^2	2.5×10^3	5.3×10^{-1}	3.0×10^5
^{131}I	8.06 d	5.5×10^{-3}	3.9×10^{-2}	1.4	3.4×10^{-1}	7.0×10^{-4}	9.8×10^{-1}	1.9×10^{-1}	1.5×10^{-1}	3.1
^{133}I	20.8 h	6.7×10^{-3}	4.8×10^{-2}	6.2×10^{-1}	1.5×10^{-1}	2.9×10^{-4}	1.3×10^{-1}	2.3×10^{-1}	6.0×10^{-2}	1.2

^{a}Xe or Kr release rate less than 10^{-1} Ci/yr or 1 release rate less than 10^{-4} Ci/yr.

Table 12
Source Term for BWR—Calculated Annual Release of Radioactive Materials in Gaseous Effluents

| Nuclide | Half-Life | Primary System | | Building Ventilation | | | Total (Ci/yr) |
		Air Ejector Effluent (Ci/yr)	Gland Seal Effluent (Ci/yr)	Reactor Building (Ci/yr)	Radwaste Building (Ci/yr)	Turbine Building (Ci/yr)	
^{83m}Kr	1.86 h	1.4×10^5	1.7×10^2	a	a	2.7×10^1	1.4×10^5
^{85m}Kr	4.4 h	2.6×10^5	2.8×10^2	a	a	4.5×10^1	2.6×10^5
^{85}Kr	10.74 y	1.4×10^3	1.4	a	a	2.3×10^{-1}	1.4×10^3
^{87}Kr	76 m	6.4×10^5	8.3×10^2	a	a	1.4×10^2	6.4×10^5
^{88}Kr	2.79 h	8.0×10^5	9.0×10^2	a	a	1.4×10^2	8.0×10^5
^{89}Kr	3.18 m	5.3×10^3	2.4×10^3	a	a	5.8×10^2	8.3×10^3
^{131m}Xe	11.96 d	1.3×10^2	1.3	a	a	2.0×10^{-1}	1.3×10^2
^{133m}Xe	2.26 d	1.8×10^4	1.8×10^1	a	a	2.8	1.8×10^4
^{133}Xe	5.27 d	4.9×10^5	5.0×10^2	a	a	7.9×10^1	4.9×10^5
^{135m}Xe	15.7 m	4.0×10^5	1.4×10^3	a	a	2.4×10^2	4.0×10^5
^{135}Xe	9.16 h	1.4×10^6	1.4×10^3	a	a	2.3×10^2	1.4×10^6
^{137}Xe	3.82 m	2.7×10^4	4.3×10^3	a	a	9.8×10^2	3.2×10^4
^{138}Xe	14.2 m	1.4×10^6	4.3×10^3	a	a	7.5×10^2	1.4×10^6
TOTAL NOBLE GAS		5.6×10^6	1.7×10^4			3.2×10^3	5.6×10^6
^{131}I	8.06 d	3.4×10^1	7.5×10^{-3}	2.5×10^{-2}	1.0×10^{-3}	1.1	3.5×10^1
^{133}I	20.8 h	1.8×10^2	3.5×10^{-2}	7.5×10^{-2}	5.0×10^{-3}	5.6	1.9×10^2

a Xe or Kr release less than 10^{-1} Ci/yr or I release rate less than 10^{-4} Ci/yr.

discharges, respectively. The evaporation losses for a range (degrees water is cooled from the inlet to the outlet of the tower) of 25 F are 50 cfs for BWRs and 40 cfs for PWRs. This is equivalent to the water requirements for a population of 320,000 and 254,000, respectively. The drift at 0.03% of circulating water in cooling towers is equal to 0.8 cfs and 0.65 cfs for BWRs and PWRs, respectively, or equivalent to populations of 5,100 and 4,100, respectively. Whereas the evaporation is pure water, the drift contains all the chemical additives that are in the cooling tower waters.

The equivalent source terms for fossil fueled plants are the chemical combustion products and the natural radioactivity contained in the fuels. For the same size plants as the BWR, 1,100 Mw$_e$, the following combustion products in tons are released annually to the atmosphere: particulates, 5,200; sulfur oxides, 274,000; carbon monoxide, 3,600; hydrocarbons, 110; nitrous oxides, 1,988,000; aldehydes, 18; and carbon dioxide, 19,900,000 for a cyclone burner plant utilizing electrostatic precipitators with an efficiency of 97% and utilizing a fuel with 10% ash content.[3] The plant is again assumed to be on line at full load 100% of the time. In addition, associated with the fly ash, the plant releases annually to the atmosphere the following radioactive material in millicuries: ^{226}Ra, 5.85; ^{228}Ra, 4.8; ^{228}Th, 3.30; ^{232}Th, 6.83.[4] This is equivalent to the following population having maximum permissible occupational body burdens in the critical organ: ^{226}Ra, 58,500; ^{228}Ra, 30,000; ^{228}Th, 193,000; and ^{232}Th, 170,500. If it is individual members of the public who are exposed then the numbers would be increased by a factor of 10.

The waste heat problem is not eliminated by switching from nuclear to fossil fuel but is somewhat reduced. The temperature rise in the Chicago River would be 19 F. The loss by evaporation would be 33 cfs, which would supply water to a population of 213,000.[5] The drift losses would be 0.5 cfs and would supply water to 3,400 people.

The residues from nuclear-fueled and fossil-fueled plants may also have ecological consequences. The quantities stored on site and at burial grounds are detailed below. For the fossil-fueled plant 4.2 X 10^5 tons per year of ash must be stored, usually on site. For the nuclear-fueled plant using a LWR of 1,000 Mw$_e$ of the Diablo Canyon type zircaloy clad UO$_2$, 3.3% enriched in ^{235}U and irradiated for 33,000 Mwd/Mt at a specific power of 30 Mw/Mt, the following quantities of isotopes are stored at one year after processing.[6] Processing occurs at 90 days after release from the reactor and after approximately 3 years in the reactor. Significant fission products are 1.5 X 10^8 curies, including 2.7 X 10^4 curies of tritium (^{3}H), 7 X 10^5 curies of ^{85}Kr, 5.1 x 10^6 curies of ^{90}Sr, and 7.1 X 10^6 curies of ^{137}Cs.

Important actinide isotopes are 8.4 X 10^6 curies including 2.2 X 10^4 curies of ^{239}Pu, 2 X 10^4 curies of ^{241}Am and 1.2 X 10^3 curies of ^{243}Am. Important activation product isotopes are 6.7 X 10^5 curies including 3.8 X 10^4 curies of ^{60}Co and 3.8 X 10^4 curies of ^{63}Ni. These would all be stored in 24,000 gal of waste or, if solidified, in 240 cu ft of solids.

These are the major inputs to the environment from both fossil-fueled and nuclear power plants. We shall now examine the ecological impact of these inputs other than on rivers and lakes. First we shall look at the inputs that are common to both fossil-fueled and nuclear power plants, heat and moisture.

HEAT AND MOISTURE POLLUTION

Among the first problems to be answered is the question of major climatic changes due to waste heat rejection to the atmosphere. It has been shown that the amount of heat rejected from our major cities is a not negligible fraction (3%) of the solar heat reaching the earth's surface for that region. In some instances it is already equal to the solar heat at the earth's surface. At present over the entire earth's surface the yearly production of man-made energy is about 1/2,500 of the radiation balance of the earth's surface. It could equal the surface radiation balance if compounded annually at 10% for 100 years. Its present growth rate is 4% per year. Therefore, even if we alleviate local thermal pollution problems now, the global problem will be upon us in a few decades. In the meantime the following general conclusions hold.[7]

(1) It does appear to be within man's engineering capacity to influence the loss and gain of heat in the atmosphere on a scale that can influence patterns of thermal forcing of atmospheric circulation.

(2) The inadvertent influences of man's activity may eventually lead to catastrophic influences on global climate unless ways can be developed to compensate for undesired effects. Whether the time remaining for bringing this problem under control is a few decades or a century is still an open question.

(3) The diversity of thermal processes that can be influenced in the atmosphere, and between the atmosphere and ocean, offers promise that, if global climate is adequately understood, it can be influenced for the purpose of either maximizing climatic resources or avoiding unwanted changes.

The consequences of such energy releases upon the climate are not yet well understood. Energy production of various man-made and natural events is detailed in Table 13.[8] Small-scale effects (i.e., less than 1 kw) are primarily cooling tower plumes, fogs, humidity, and drizzle.

Studies from February through July at the Keystone Plant near Indiana, Pennsylvania, with four 325-ft hyperbolic towers and two 800-ft chimney stacks show that over 30% of the time the plumes evaporated into invisibility, with most (87.5%) evaporating within 5 tower lengths. In about 15% of the time the plume was absorbed in the overcast, usually within 15 tower lengths. In only 2% of the cases did the plumes lead to cloud building.[9] In addition, the mixture of the plumes from the cooling towers and the chimney stacks did lead to the formation of dilute sulfuric acid. However, the Central Electricity Generating Board in England has concluded that the growth rate of water droplets due to SO_2 is so slow that acid drops seldom reach the ground.[8]

In the mesocale, from 1 km to 50 km, the generation of heat by a 1,000-Mw power station is comparable to that generated by mesocale atmospheric phenomena. Therefore, "it is possible that heat and moisture pollution presently are of sufficient magnitude to affect the atmosphere significantly." [10] When the tower plume reaches the cross sectional area of a thunderstorm, its energy flux is 10% of that of the thunderstorm. For effects extending over 50 km, synoptic systems, it is not known how the added heat and moisture will affect atmospheric conditions.

Table 13
Energy Production per Unit Area of Natural and Artificial Processes at Various Scales

Area, m^2	Natural Production, W/m^2		Artificial Production, W/m^2	
	Event	Rate	Type of Use	Rate
5×10^{14}	Dissipation of kinetic energy	5	Man's ultimate energy production	0.8
	Solar-energy absorption by atmosphere	25		
	Solar flux at top of atmosphere	350		
10^{12}	Cyclone latent heat release (1 cm rain per day)	200	Northeastern United States ultimate production (10^8 people, 20 kw each)	2.0
	Cyclone kinetic energy production	30		
10^8	Thunderstorm		Suburban area (400 persons	
	Kinetic energy production	100	per km^2, 10 kw per capita)	4
	Latent heat release (1 cm rain per 30 min)	5000	Super energy center or city	1000
	Evaporation from lake	100	Agroindustrial complex	100
10^4	Tornado kinetic energy production	10^4	Cooling pond (1000 kw per 2 acres)	130
			Cooling tower (10^6 kw per $10^4 m^2$)	10^5

It has, however, already been shown that cities do have measurable effects on their climate as shown in Table 14.[11] Landsberg noted "that the influences of the city on precipitation are not easily unraveled. We can say with reasonable confidence, however, that most of them tend to increase precipitation."

Czapski has suggested that the climatic effects "observed" near cities may be due more to the effect of the added heat than the condensation and freezing nuclei to which they are usually attributed.[12] Czapski foresees severe consequences of large latent heat and thermal emissions: (1) rainfall will be increased downwind for a considerable distance; (2) cumulus clouds will prevail most of the time downwind from a large power plant; (3) severe thunderstorms and even tornadoes can be caused in very unstable weather by dry and clear heat.

Studies of the Zion Nuclear Power Station indicate that, in conjunction with macroscale storm systems, annual snowfall could be increased 1 to 2 inches over a semicircle 2 miles in radius.[13] Localized ground fog does occur around many cooling towers when the cooling air water vapor exceeds the capacity of the ambient air for water vapor. Based on the theory of plume rise from isolated stacks and the theory of cumulus cloud growth, it is possible to predict plume rise for either uncondensed or completely condensed plumes, but cloud depth and maximum water content cannot be estimated easily.

Table 14
Climatic Changes Produced by Cities

Element	Comparison with Rural Environs
Contaminants:	
dust particles	10 times more
sulfur dioxide	5 times more
carbon dioxide	10 times more
carbon monoxide	25 times more
Radiation:	
total on horizontal surface	15 to 20% less
ultraviolet, winter	30% less
ultraviolet, summer	5% less
Cloudiness:	
clouds	5 to 10% more
fog, winter	100% more
fog, summer	30% more
Precipitation:	
amounts	5 to 10% more
days with 0.2 in.	10% more
Temperature:	
annual mean	1 to 1.5 F more
winter minima	2 to 3 F more
Relative Humidity:	
annual mean	6% less
winter	2% less
summer	8% less
Wind Speed:	
annual mean	20 to 30% less
extreme gusts	10 to 20% less
calms	5 to 20% less

It is obvious that mechanical draft towers discharge their heat at lower elevations and with higher velocities that cause greater entrainment of the ambient air. Consequently, the mechanical draft towers are far more likely to cause fog, and icing, than are natural draft towers. Proper design and location can in most instances alleviate these problems. The probability of fogging is shown in Table 15.[14] Though many of the models do predict ground fog and icing, reports based upon long European experience indicate that the likelihood is not great, particularly for natural draft towers. The shadowing effect of the tower plume is considered the most serious environmental impact of natural draft towers by Swiss investigators.[15]

There are possible synergistic effects of cooling tower plumes and radioactive and fossil-fueled plumes. Water vapor and radioactive materials combine to fall out more quickly on local vegetation and enter the food chain more rapidly, which would be of consequence for short lived isotopes such as ^{131}I.

The intimate mixture of water vapor and sulfur and nitrous oxides could result in their quicker fallout, as well as in acidic rains and mists.

The drift from cooling towers would contain chromates, phosphates and other exotic chemicals used to reduce corrosion and scaling and to prevent the growth of organisms in the system as well as to prevent general fouling. If saline water is used for cooling, then the drift would be two to four times more concentrated than the initial feed water itself. As this material falls upon the local landscape and vegetation, it could seriously reduce the productivity of these lands, as well as present a health hazard to those ingesting crops grown in this area.

Table 15
Probability of Surface Fogging

Type of Cooling System	Descriptive Probability of Obstructing Visibility
Tall, natural-draft towers standing alone, fully equipped with drift eliminators.	Extremely low, virtually zero.
Tall, natural-draft towers alone but without drift eliminators.	Low, but likely to occur with high humidity and stagnation.
Tall, natural-draft towers close to fossil-fuel smokestacks emitting acid-producing stack gases.	Low to substantial, depending on prevalence of wind direction and spacing of stack and tower(s).
Mechanical-draft towers emitting at low level.	Substantial, but highly variable, depending upon wind and orientation or grouping of units.
Slack water, ponds, and spray ponds.	Low to substantial, depending upon the stagnation of the atmosphere and confinement of humidified air.

Large, high speed, rotating machinery and enormous quantities of air moving through restricted spaces and free falling water splashing on the tower fill and into the collecting basin causes noise. Consequently, around mechanically induced draft cooling towers, there are going to be high sound levels, 80 to 100 decibels (dB). Because of the lack of the rotating machinery, the noise level at natural draft towers is reduced to 80 to 85 dB.

The aesthetic aspects of cooling towers are more difficult to estimate. Some find natural draft towers 500 feet tall and 300 feet wide to be objectionable. Others object to mechanical draft towers 1,600 feet long, 60 feet wide and 60 feet tall.

The release of radioactive materials from nuclear reactors operating under the suggested guidelines and fossil-fueled (coal) plants is not dissimilar. Their impact, however, is primarily to health, which will be treated by other contributors to this Conference.

Common to both fossil-fueled and nuclear power plants is the storage of their residues. We cannot ignore the effects of the failure of ashponds. The collapse of these ponds and the flowage of slag piles have resulted in a number of human deaths. The collapse of one such pond and its subsequent release into the Clinch River in Virginia and Tennessee wiped out the entire aquatic population of that river for 100 miles. It was two years before the river was back to its previous condition.

PARTICULATE MATTER AND CARBON DIOXIDE

Possibly the most widely discussed environmental impacts from power generation are due solely to fossil fuel combustion, the increase of particulates and carbon dioxide in the atmosphere. Carbon dioxide permits the short wave solar radiation to reach the earth but partially blocks the long wave radiation reflected from the earth from returning to the stratosphere. This is sometimes called the "greenhouse" effect and would result in an increase in the earth's surface temperature. The increase in temperature could cause additional interactions between clouds and the water vapor in the atmosphere and cause slightly lower temperatures. The ambient concentration of CO_2 is 323 parts per million (ppm) and is expected to reach 375 ppm by the year 2000 with a resulting global temperature increase of about 1 F. In the century 1850 to 1950, fossil fuel burning produced an amount of CO_2 equal to 10% of the amount estimated to be in the atmosphere in 1950.[17] It is estimated that by 1970 this had increased to 16.2% of the 1950 natural concentration. There is, however, a great deal of uncertainty in the forecast because of lack of sufficient knowledge about CO_2 sinks, the atmospheric oceanic CO_2 exchange, and the photosynthetic processes.

Particulate matter in the atmosphere scatters and absorbs both short wave solar radiation and long wave terrestrial radiation and also acts as condensation nuclei. Sulfur dioxide, nitrous oxides and hydrocarbons are all gaseous precursors to particulates. The net effect would appear to be a cooling of the earth's surface temperature. Man's contribution to the particulate matter smaller than 20 microns radius in the atmosphere ranges from 5% to as much as 45% of the total.[16]

The temperature at the earth's surface had risen slowly from 1880 (first good data) till about 1945 (0.008 C/yr) and has dropped more rapidly than that since 1945,[16] despite drastically increased fossil fuel consumption.

The health effects of the chemical emissions of fossil-fueled plants will be described by other contributors so I shall limit my remarks here to other effects that include reduction in crop growth, increased corrosion, increased soiling, lowered property values, reduced visibility and clarity, and important aesthetic considerations. Estimates of the costs of these effects by 1977 in the United States (in 1970 dollars) for stationary source fuel combustion are (in millions of dollars) residential property, $4,240; materials and vegetation, $3,-650.[18] These estimates are extremely speculative but are the best available. Steam electric power plants contributed by weight 44% of the particulates, 65%

of the sulfur oxides, and 56% of the nitrous oxides from stationary fuel combustion sources.[18]

We have shown therefore that environmental impacts other than health and in rivers and lakes can be severe from both fossil-fueled and nuclear power plants. However, except for the thermal discharges, which are relatively more severe for nuclear plants, under normal operating conditions fossil-fueled plants cause far more ecological impact.

References

1. Garvey G: *Energy, Ecology, Economy.* New York City, WW Norton and Company, 1972.

2. Blanco RE, et al: *Radiological Impact Study-Part I. Cost of Radioactive Waste Treatment at Nuclear Power Plants,* Oak Ridge National Laboratory, Oak Ridge, TN, May 1972.

3. *Compilation of Air Pollution Emission Factors* (Revised). Environmental Protection Agency, Washington, DC, February 1972.

4. Martin JE, Harvard ED, Oakley DT: Radiation Doses from Fossil-Fuel and Nuclear Power Plants *in* Power Generation and Environmental Change, Berkowitz DA, Squires AM (eds), Massachusetts Institute of Technology Press, Cambridge, MA, 1971.

5. Parker FL: *Thermal Effects of Heated Water Releases from Power Plants.* Ambiente, October 1972.

6. *Siting of Fuel Reprocessing Plants and Waste Management Facilities.* ORNL-4451, Oak Ridge National Laboratory, July 1970.

7. Fletcher JO: Managing Climatic Resources. Rand Corporation, Santa Monica, CA, 1969.

8. Hanna SR, Steven R, Swisher SD: Meterological Considerations of the Heat and Moisture Produced by Man. *Nuclear Safety,* March-April, 1971.

9. Bierman GF, et al: Characteristics, Classification, and Evidence of Plumes from Large Natural Draft Cooling Towers. *Proc Amer Power Conf,* Chicago, 1971.

10. Hanna SR, Swisher SD: Meteorological Considerations of Heat and Moisture Produced by Man. *Nuclear Safety* **12(2):** 114–122, 1971.

11. Landsberg HE: City Air—Better or Worse. Public Health Service, Cincinnati, 1961.

12. Czapski UH: Possible Effects of Thermal Discharges to the Atmosphere, Proc Fifth Ann Environmental Health Research Symposium—Thermal Discharges, New York State Department of Health, Albany, NY 1968.

13. Huff FA: Effect of Cooling Tower Effluents on Atmospheric Conditions in Northern Illinois. Illinois State Water Survey Circular 100, Urbana, Illinois, 1971.

14. Decker FW: Probabilities of Cooling System Fogging in Cooling Towers. American Institute of Chemical Engineers, Houston, 1972.

15. Bogh P, et al: A New Method of Assessing the Environmental Influence of Cooling Towers as First Applied to the Kaiser Angst and Liebstadt Nuclear Plants. Report at Nuclear Meeting, Basel, Sept 25, 1972.

16. Inadvertent Climate Modification. Massachusetts Institute of Technology Press, Cambridge, MA, 1971.

17. Man's Impact on the Global Environment. Massachusetts Institute of Technology Press, Cambridge, MA, 1970.

18. Environmental Protection Agency: The Economics of Clear Air. Senate Document No 92–67, Washington, DC, March 1972.

Discussion

Q: Dr. Beyers, have you found any concentrations of radioactive wastes in the biochain in your work in Savannah Creek?

Dr. Beyers: There is some radioactivity in Par Pond but it is the result of a release from a reactor basin about 20 years ago and the radioactivity in the biota has been going down over a long period of time.

Q: Has there been an increase in concentration of radioactive materials in the organisms?

Dr. Beyers: No. Actually what we find is a biological demagnification rather than biological magnification.

Dr. Rose: In this discussion on the salt mine business, I would just like to agree with my colleague, Dr. Parker, that the use of the Kansas salt mine for an experiment was perfectly reasonable. It was indeed the decision to go ahead and make a repository that got everybody into trouble.

Dr. Forrest E. Rieke: I had a chance to visit the mine in Braunschweig last December. It seemed pretty convincing to all the U.S. people who were there that it was a pretty good operation. Professor Borchert there said that there were salt mines scattered around the edges of the United States that might be much more satisfactory than Lyons. You might care to comment on that. Actually, they gave us the impression that the handling of the fuel, at least in Germany, was going to be resolved in that manner.

Dr. Parker: Professor Borchert and his colleagues visited the Kansas mine during the early days and, as a matter of fact, some of their original work was done there.

Q: I would like to ask Dr. Beyers to elaborate a little in regard to his closing remarks about the eutrophication of the actual pond or lake.

Dr. Beyers: Well, essentially what is happening is that the evaporated water in the lake is not being replaced by natural runoff; it is being replaced by Savannah River water, which has a finite salt content. Thus you are evaporating off pure water, leaving the salts behind, and then putting in relatively salty water. Consequently the entire suite of dissolved materials is increasing as indeed the slide showed. This is exactly the same net effect as if you had agricultural runoff, sewage, or domestic wastes entering the lake.

Dr. White: It is very important in looking at any source of power that the total environmental effects of each source be evaluated. For example, people living in a region of strip or open-pit uranium or coal mines are principally concerned about the local environmental effects of the mining. The coal and/or the uranium are then generally transported elsewhere for processing and possibly to a third area for developing electricity; each operation is accompanied by a specific set of environmental consequences. The important aspect, of course, is the *total* impact of *all* of the different effects on the environment. Utilization of geothermal energy, which happens to be one of my major interests, also has environmental consequences, but most of the effects are likely to be concentrated in one area. For a fair comparison of different energy sources, the total effects must be looked at.

IV

ENERGY PRODUCTION AND HUMAN HEALTH

12

Health Hazards from Power Plant Emissions

John R. Goldsmith, M.D.

Power plants are absolutely essential if thermal stress in urban cities of the United States is to be avoided. The health implications of inadequate household heating could be studied in the slum buildings whose power plants or heating systems have failed because of neglected maintenance. In addition, a number of studies have shown how much excess mortality occurs during heat waves and cold spells. Power plants in modern urban areas provide for heating and for air conditioning. However, the extent to which power generation is needed for the latter purpose and, to some extent, for the former is capable of being modified by building layout and design. The amounts of energy that now appear to be objects of planning may thus exceed the amounts that are necessary. Some of these possibilities have been reviewed in a recent RAND report.[1]

Given that power generation is necessary, it becomes a complex question as to where to generate it, with which fuels, with what size plants, with what allocation of costs, and with what degree of control over emissions. A large number of these questions must be answered without benefit of information concerning health. (Possibly all of the questions will be answered without benefit of information concerning health.) Health consequences could be grave, and can be avoided, since there exists a substantial body of useful information concerning the health implications of power plant emissions. This body of information has been collected in the air quality criteria reports of the Environmental Protection Agency,[2] in the report of the Royal College of Physicians of London[3] on Air Pollution and Health, in a symposium report from the State Commission for Technology of Czechoslovakia,[4] and in reports of the World Health Organization,[5] particularly the Technical Report Series #506, Air Quality Criteria and Guides for Urban Air Pollutants. A less formal source of valuable information from the World Health Organization is found in the recent report "Health Hazards in the Human Environment."[6] A recent International Symposium in Poland on Ecology of Chronic Non-Specific Respiratory Disease[7] reported on studies from 15 countries.

Representation of the noxiousness of power plant emissions that use fossil fuel has been, in some cases (unintentionally, perhaps), misleading. The need for an objective evaluation of the relative health risks of different types of fueling and location of power plants is urgent if (a) our society is not to dissipate a great deal of its resources, (b) our scientific community is not to dissipate a great deal of its credibility, and (c) our populations are not to be subjected to easily avoided health risks.

An analogous situation occurred when the health hazards of community air pollution tended to be greatly overstated by people whose major concern was to exonerate cigarette smoking in producing such effects as increases in lung cancer, chronic bronchitis, and heart disease. Fortunately, we have surmounted that pattern of misrepresentation and the hazards of cigarette smoking are now well established and generally widely accepted.

Appropriate comparisons among health implications of various power plant operating characteristics must be based on the selection, reporting, and representation of evidence by credible reporters. There are two major sorts of evidence, one of them due to experimental exposures and the other due to the epidemiologic study of human population. The former studies generally do not include long-term exposures of human subjects and, therefore, relate very little to the long-term illnesses that might be the consequences of pollution exposure. The epidemiologic studies generally include such a large number of coexisting and fluctuating variables that separating the effects of single pollutants is difficult and often uncertain.

Thus, the experimental studies in the laboratory may produce specific but unrealistic data for interpretations of human health effects. The epidemiologic studies tend to produce nonspecific but realistic data. Inferences soundly based on both sorts of data are needed for policy decisions.

A prototype mechanism for the credible evaluation of such problems exists in the Air Conservation Commission(s), the original one being a creation of the Committee on Science and the Promotion of Human Welfare of the American Association for the Advancement of Science [8] and the more recent, an organization supported by the National Tuberculosis and Respiratory Disease Association, now called the American Lung Association. Among such groups can be found scientists whose feelings and concerns closely reflect the judgement of the informed scientific and lay communities, and, while knowledgeable in areas of special relevance, they are not necessarily identified with governmental programs on the one hand or with major industrial organizations on the other.

The remainder of this paper will concern itself with what is known, what is suspected, and what is useful about the information concerning the pollutants, sulfur oxides, black suspended particulate matter (soot), nitrogen oxides, carbon monoxide, hydrocarbons, and other particulate matter.

SULFUR OXIDES AND BLACK SUSPENDED MATTER

The most convincing case for long-term effects of air pollution, as well as for the effect of air pollution on mortality of persons chronically ill, has been based on the experience of the populations of London during the 1952 air pollution disaster and subsequent data collected and published for previous and subsequent years. Such data have been reviewed by the Royal College of Physicians [3] and the World Health Organization [5,6] and have made a convincing case for the increase in mortality due to the combined increase of sulfur dioxide and smoke, for example, in December 1952. A convincing case also exists for an increased frequency and aggravation of chronic bronchitis among exposed populations.[7] Table 16 shows the proportional increase and mortality from various causes of death following the London smog episode of 1952, and Figure 23 shows the relationship of smoke and SO_2 to number of deaths per day. However, most of this pollution was associated with inefficient coal-fired home heating, not power plants. Subsequently, analysis by Lawther [9] yielded some numbers above which the expectation of increased mortality might be likely to occur.

Later, Lawther,[10] using diary methods, showed that there is an increase in the likelihood of chronic bronchitis being worse at times when there is an increase in *both* sulfur oxides and suspended particulate matter. It has also been shown that the residents of places with high levels of sulfur oxides and particulate matter have a higher mortality due to chronic bronchitis than do the residents of places with relatively lower pollution. In addition to that, there are higher rates of morbidity in such groups, as is shown in Figure 24.

The prevalence of bronchitis in children in Great Britain, where cigarette smoking is thought not to be a significant factor, is related to the residence in locations with high levels of air pollution (Fig. 25). There is also a social class differential among children, with low rates in those children from professional and managerial families to highest rates in those children of semiskilled and unskilled workers.[32]

Among the studies reported in other countries are those documenting an increase in respiratory symptoms and impairment of lung function in children in Kawasaki reported by Toyama [11] and the increased frequency of asthma and of aggravated bronchitis in Yokkaichi by Yoshida et al.[12] Zapletal et al [13] have reported alterations of pulmonary function in Czech children living in areas polluted by power plant emissions.

The amount of energy produced in power plants in Japan and Great Britain has continued to go up while the pollution levels have diminished in Great Britain rather strikingly over the interval from 1958 to 1968. Associated with this decrease has been a lesser mortality during the London "episode" in 1962 when sulfur dioxide concentrations were as high as in 1952, but suspended particulate matter was a great deal less. According to a panel study by Fletcher et al,[14] there appears to be a decrease in the amount of sputum produced by individuals with chronic bronchitis. With the decrease in suspended particulate matter, there seems to have been a substantial improvement in the respiratory morbidity and mortality effects of this type of pollution, notwithstanding that there was, over this period of time, little change in the concentrations of sulfur dioxide.

Table 16
Mortality Increase in the London Smog of 1952

Cause	Seasonal Norm	No. of Deaths in the Week After Smog	Relative Increase
Bronchitis	75	704	9.4
Coronary disease	122	281	2.3
Myocardial degeneration	84	244	2.9
Pneumonia	37	168	4.5
Vascular lesions of CNS	98	128	1.3
Respiratory tuberculosis	17	77	4.5
Cancer of lung	36	69	1.9
Other respiratory diseases	8	52	6.5
Other causes	410	761	1.9
All causes	887	2,484	2.8

Source: Reference 3.

Figure 23
Death and Pollution Levels in the London Fog of December 1952

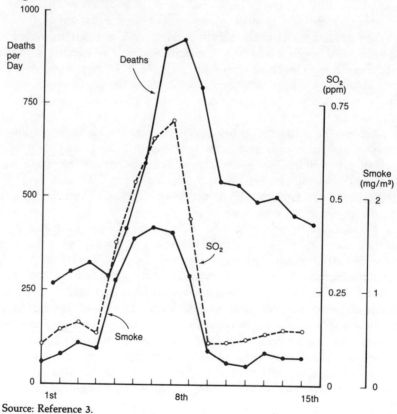

Source: Reference 3.

Figure 24
Bronchitis in Relation to Smoking and Air Pollution

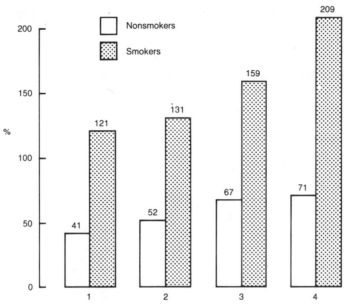

Source: Lambert and Reid, Reference 3.

These findings lead to the following interpretations: first, that sulfur oxide and particulate matter, together, can increase the death rate due to chronic disease and can aggravate these diseases; second, that they can be a causal factor in the occurrence of chronic bronchitis in children and in adults.[15] The evidence favors the particulate matter rather than the sulfur compounds as the chief culprit.

The questions which this analysis raises have to do with how low a concentration one can be exposed to before there no longer can be found some contributory role of either of the pollutants. This question cannot now be answered definitively. The World Health Organization analysis [5] comes close to an acceptable answer when it suggests that a long-term goal would be 98% of observations below 200 micrograms per cubic meter (μg/cu m) of sulfur oxide and an annual mean of less than 60 μg/cu m, along with an annual mean of suspended particulate matter below 40 μg and 98% of observations below 120 μg. (Note that these numbers refer to measurement methods used in Great Britain and are not necessarily equal to those used in the United States.)

While sulfur oxide and soot pollution have been present in many parts of the United States and, no doubt, have had some effects on health, the procedures for measuring that effect are not as well established as in Great Britain. For example, Lave and Seskin [16] have reported on the statistical association of

156

a number of factors with mortality among standard metropolitan statistical areas in the United States (including the proportion of the population over 65, the proportion that are nonwhite, the proportion in different occupations, etc.). Unfortunately, the mortality data have not been age-adjusted. Some of the computations have been carried out for mortality in infants, which, of course, is age-specific. Climatologic and household heating variables appear to account for much of the variation, which, on first examination, appeared to be related to pollution. These analyses, therefore, do not permit a conclusion as to whether excess chronic disease mortality has been caused in American urban areas by pollutants.

Figure 25
Incidence of Bronchitis in Children at Different
Local Levels of Air Pollution

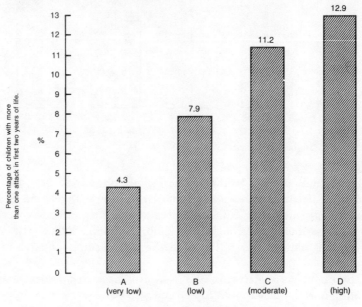

Source: Data in Table VI, Reference 31.

Similarly, variations of morbidity in time have been reported by Spicer[17] and by the series of papers by McCarroll et al;[18] these variations reflect both meteorologic and pollution variables, but the separation of one from the other has not been easily accomplished. A series of studies (CHESS) by the Environmental Protection Agency has used population samples in different locations, and the results are not yet completely available. They indicate some association between sulfates and respiratory symptoms, but in the large series of studies that have been reported to date, the highest frequency of respiratory morbidity in both adults and children has been in a community that appears to have intermediate levels of air pollution.

Carnow et al [19] have reported associations of SO_2 with respiratory morbidity in Chicago. Particulate pollution may have also played a role. On the other hand, the studies of Schimmel and Greenberg [20] on excess mortality in New York City for 1963 to 1968 define a contribution of air pollution to variability of daily mortality.

The data from England do not necessarily apply in the United States. A further source of uncertainty has to do with the relationship of the experience in Great Britain, where pollution has come mostly from household heating and, therefore, from low chimneys, to what would be relevant to power plant stacks and the relatively greater emission height. Possibly the experience in New York City reflects an elevated emission of pollutants.

In any event, there is no doubt that air pollution can be a factor in increasing mortality and in increasing respiratory morbidity, and that the combination of sulfur oxides and particulate matter is capable of producing such an effect. Furthermore, from the World Health Organization reports and analyses, we have a value for the joint level of these two pollutants below which such effects are not likely to occur.

Concentrations of pollutants that can cause these do not need to occur in the vicinity of well-designed and well-operated fossil fuel power plants in the United States. However, that depends a good deal on the technology applied and the location of populations in the vicinity of such plants. It must be stressed that the ability to detect an increase in mortality requires that a population exposed be on the order of magnitude of a million [21] or so. Even if, in smaller populations, effects that might make occasional contributions to mortality or incremental contributions to morbidity occur, it is unlikely that such effects will be detected. There are, therefore, relatively few circumstances in which the relationship of power plant emission and populations exposed could be close enough so that subtle effects on mortality could be detected.

The experimental studies in humans do not necessarily explain the epidemiologic data in man. In this sense, the concentrations that are able to produce detectable effects on airway resistance, or those that are capable of aggravating respiratory symptoms in the laboratory, appear to be higher than the levels that occur during community air pollution episodes. The most likely explanation is that the sulfur dioxide alone is not acting, but that the sulfur dioxide is oxidized to an acid aerosol and that it is an acid aerosol that is the culprit in community exposures. Work on acid aerosol exposures of human subjects (for example, Amdur [22] and Corn [23]) tends to support this hypothesis, but this work does not tell us at what level sensitive groups in the population are affected, since most of the experiments are done with relatively healthy adults.

In addition, there are no experimental data in children, and there should not be. It would be ethically contraindicated. Epidemiologic studies in children have been scant, and studies in this country have not been decisive in the results with respect to sulfur oxides and particulate matter.

CARBON MONOXIDE

Carbon monoxide is a pollutant of great consequence in motor vehicle exhaust, but it is unlikely that carbon monoxide from power plants would make an important contribution to community pollution where the power plant was properly operated. However, for purposes of discussion and reference, it is useful to point out that the carbon monoxide exposures can be shown to have an effect that is related to the resulting carboxyhemoglobin in blood.[24] The carboxyhemoglobin in blood is readily estimated from expired air analysis,[25] so, if a question of the exposure of the human population to carbon monoxide arises, there are simple procedures for discovering the true state of affairs.

NITROGEN OXIDES

In the Los Angeles Basin, thermal power plants, located along the sea coast (upwind of the metropolitan area under usual meteorological regimes), make an important contribution to the oxides of nitrogen that participate in photochemical smog reactions. The photochemical reactions require hydrocarbon vapors, oxides of nitrogen, and sunlight. The resulting effects include eye and respiratory irritation, production of ozone in the atmosphere, interference with visibility, and characteristic forms of vegetation damage. The initial strategy for controlling photochemical oxidant has been directed to controlling motor vehicular hydrocarbon emissions. But this strategy has not succeeded in Los Angeles, and it is now necessary to control also for emissions of oxides of nitrogen. Without controls, about one third of the oxides of nitrogen emitted into the Los Angeles Basin (305 tons per day, 1970 data) has been estimated to be emitted from thermal power plants,[26] and, since most of these plants are located along the sea coast, the effect is sufficient to require consideration and controls from a public health point of view. The internal combustion engine contributes most of the remainder (565 tons per day, 1970 data).

The health effects of oxides of nitrogen [27] are less well defined than those of combined sulfur oxides and particulate matter or than those due to carbon monoxide. This is partly because there is an active shift in the state of the oxides of nitrogen primarily involving nitric oxide (NO) and nitrogen dioxide (NO_2). Of these two oxides, NO is primarily emitted from processes of high temperature and pressure combustion. It is oxidized to NO_2 more rapidly in the presence of hydrocarbon vapors than it would be otherwise, and the health effects of nitrogen dioxide are several times more severe than those due to nitric oxide. In experimental animals, continuous nitrogen dioxide (NO_2) exposures can lead to alterations in the cells lining the terminal respiratory bronchioles.[28] In concentrations of several parts per million, NO_2 can lead to a condition in experimental animals that resembles pulmonary emphysema in man.[29]

Whether or not in other communities this problem occurs to the same extent as in Los Angeles is not clear. Certainly the severity of photochemical oxidant pollution is nowhere as prevalent and severe as in Los Angeles. Control systems have been designed and are being implemented to reduce the oxides of nitrogen emissions in the Los Angeles Basin. By 1970, power plant emission controls had cut the emissions to 100 tons per day, a decrease of one-third, and current amounts are thought to be less.

HYDROCARBONS

There is virtually no evidence that any of the types of hydrocarbons usually emitted from modern power plants are of long-term consequence to human health. The use of coal in power generation permits the emission of somewhat more complex groups of hydrocarbons than does fuel oil which, in turn, is likely to have a greater variety than natural gas. However, assuming efficient combustion, minimization of smoke, and a reasonable effort to keep sulfur oxides from reaching undesirable ground level concentrations, it is unlikely that hydrocarbon emissions will be a matter of much consequence.

PARTICULATES OTHER THAN SOOT

The experience in Great Briatin with suspended black particulate matter, which was quantitatively referred to in the section on sulfur oxides and particulate matter, does not necessarily include some of the other substances that can be of importance. For example, the experience with low quality coal in highly mineralized areas in Czechoslovakia will permit the emission of arsenic and possibly beryllium in some significant quantities.[4] Furthermore, certain fuel oils contain substantial amounts of vanadium, and their consumption in power plants would necessarily cause vanadium to be emitted. In addition, some plants are considering the addition of a manganese [30] compound to impair the visibility of smoke. Under these conditions, the manganese compounds would also be emitted, presumably in particulate form. For any given location, power plant siting, design, and impact analysis should treat them as explicitly as possible.

DISCUSSION

In addition to the chemicals and the particulate matter emitted from power plants, their appearance on the skyline of the vicinity of a residential area creates a type of "visual" pollution. There is also a problem associated with waste heat dissipation for plants of most sorts. However, these effects should not be considered as health problems. Occasional power plants, particularly those using fuel oil or coal, may have an odorous emission, especially if the fuel is high in sulfur and the stack is low. This problem is covered in a general way by the existing policies with respect to emissions of sulfur oxides and the fuel content of sulfur and will not be discussed further.

In general, therefore, it is not likely that well-designed modern power plants, appropriately located and operated with respect to the potential dispersal of pollutants, will produce any serious health effects. The guidelines for analysis of such problems are best found in the work on air quality criteria and standards. In each case, decisions should be made based on the populations at risk, the type of fuel likely to be used, the location of the plant and prevailing meteorology and topography, and the question of the extent to which existing knowledge concerning emission controls is being applied.

Based on present technology and information, power generation from fossil fuels can, at some cost, be carried out without any appreciable health hazard in the United States. Any representation to the contrary is misleading. The costs of complete health protection from power plant emissions may be more than society wishes to pay. However, it is time for the medical profession to engage, as a full partner, in the discussion of the costs of environmental health protection and their allocation.

References

1. Doctor RD, Anderson KP, Berman MB, et al: California's electricity quandary, summary: III Slowing the growth rate. Prepared for the California Assembly Committee on Planning and Land Use, RAND Corp, October 13, 1972 (multilith) R-1116-NSF/CSA.

2. Environmental Protection Agency (DHEW) US Government Printing Office. Air quality criteria for photochemical oxidants AP-62, Air quality criteria for carbon monoxide AP-63, Air quality criteria for hydrocarbons AP-64, Air quality criteria for sulfur oxides AP-50, Air quality criteria for particulates AP-49, Air quality criteria for nitrogen oxides AP-84.

3. Royal College of Physicians (London): Air pollution and health. Pitman, 1970, 80 pp.

4. (Czechoslovakia) State Commission for Technology: International Symposium on the Control and utilization of sulphur dioxide and fly-ash from the flue gases of large thermal power plants. Liblice 1965, Duchoslave J, (ed). Statni komise pro techniku, Praha, 1966.

5. World Health Organization, Technical Report Series #506: Air quality criteria and guides for urban air pollutants. Report of a WHO Expert Committee, Geneva 1972.

6. World Health Organization: Health hazards of the human environment. Geneva, 1972, 372 pp.

7. Brzezinski Z, Kopczynski J, Sawicki F, (eds): Ecology of Chronic non-specific respiratory diseases—an international symposium. Sept 7–8, 1971, Warsaw, Poland. Warsaw 1972 Panstwowy Zakad, Wydawnictw Lekarskich.

8. American Association for the Advancement of Science: Air conservation. Monograph #80, AAAS, Washington, DC, 1965.

9. Lawther PJ: *J Inst Fuel* **346**:341, 1963.

10. Lawther PJ: Proc Roy Soc Med **51**:262, 1958.

11. Toyama T: *Arch Environ Health* **8**:1953, 1964.

12. Yoshida K, Oshima H, Imai M: Air pollution and asthma in Yokkaichi. *Arch Environ Health* **13**:763, 1966.

13. Zapletal A, Jech J, Paul T, et al: Pulmonary function studies in children living in an air polluted area. *Am Rev Resp Disease* **107**:400–409, 1973.

14. Fletcher CM: Recent clinical and epidemiological studies of chronic bronchitis. *Scand J Resp Dis* **48**:285–293, 1967.

15. Holland WW, Halil T, Bennett AE, et al: *BMJ* **2**:205–208, 1969.

16. Lave LB, Seskin EB: Air pollution, climate, and home heating: Their effects on US mortality rates. *Am J Public Health* **62**:909–916, 1972.

17. Spicer WS, Storey PB, Morgan WKC, et al: *Am Rev Resp Diseases* **86**:705, 1962.

18. McCarroll JR, Cassell EJ, Ingram W, et al: Health and the urban

environment, air pollution and family illness, I. design for study. *Arch Environ Health* **10:**357, 1965.

19. Carnow BW, Senior RM, Karsh R: The role of air pollution on chronic obstructive pulmonary disease. *JAMA* **214:**894–899, 1970.

20. Schimmel H, Greenburg L: A study of the relation of pollution to mortality: New York City 1963–1968. *J Air Pollut Control Assoc* **22:**607–616, 1972.

21. Lawther P, Martin AE, Wilkins ET: Epidemiology of air pollution. WHO Public Health Paper #15, Geneva, 1962.

22. Amdur MO: Aerosols formed by the oxidation of sulfur dioxide. *Arch Environ Health* **23:**459, 1971.

23. Corn M: Measurement of air pollution dosage to human receptors in the community. *Environ Res* **3:**218–233, 1970.

24. Forbes WH: Carbon monoxide uptake via the lungs. *Ann NY Acad Sciences* **174:**72–75, 1970.

25. Goldsmith JR: Contribution of motor vehicle exhaust, industry and cigarette smoking to community carbon monoxide exposures. *Ann NY Acad Sciences* **174:**122–134, 1970.

26. Air Pollution Control District, County of Los Angeles; Profile of air pollution control 1971 Los Angeles, 1972.

27. Goldstein E: Evaluation of the role of nitrogen dioxide in the development of respiratory diseases in man. *Calif Med* **115:**21–27, 1971.

28. Parkinson DR, Stephens RJ: Morphological surface changes in the terminal bronchiolar region of NO_2-exposed rat lung. *Environ Res* **6:**37–51, 1973.

29. Goldsmith JR: Prevention of chronic lung disease. *Postgrad Med* **51:** 93–99, 1972.

30. Los Angeles Department of Water and Power; Letter to California State Department of Public Health.

31. Douglas JWB, Waller RE: Air pollution and respiratory infection in children. *Brit J Prev & Soc Med* **20:**1–8, 1966.

32. Colley JRT, Reid DD: Urban and social origins of childhood bronchitis in England and Wales. *Brit Med J* **2(5703):**213–217, 1970.

13

Health Hazards from Radioactive Emissions

Merril Eisenbud, Sc.D.

About 700 reactors have been constructed and operated throughout the world since the first was operated briefly in Chicago in December 1942. Among these are more than 100 power reactors on vessels of the U.S. Navy, and 29 privately owned nuclear power plants that have operated in the United States. At the end of 1972, 160 nuclear power plants were in operation or had been ordered from manufacturers. (The location of each of these plants is shown in Figure 26.)

The so-called light-water reactors are by far the most prevalent type and are likely to be predominant well into the 1970s. This class of reactors includes two types, the boiling-water reactors (BWR) and the pressurized water reactors (PWR). The fuel in both is usually slightly enriched uranium in the form of sintered uranium oxide pellets contained in stainless steel or zircalloy tubes. Water is used for both coolant and moderator. The high-temperature gas reactor (HTGR) has just begun to emerge as a second class of commercial power reactors. Looking into the future, the first of the liquid-metal fast-breeders (LMFBR) is now being designed and is scheduled for operation in the early 1980s.

SOURCES OF PUBLIC EXPOSURE TO RADIATIONS FROM POWER REACTORS

During normal reactor operation, traces of radioactive substances are released to the environment in both liquid and gaseous forms.

The water used to cool and moderate the reactor accumulates traces of corrosion products and other impurities, which become radioactive in passing through the reactor core. These radioactive substances are called activation products and are mainly nuclides of chromium, cobalt, manganese, iron, and other metals. Most of the fission products produced within the reactor core are retained in the uranium oxide fuel, but certain of the more labile elements such as cesium, the halogens, the noble gases, and tritium tend to diffuse from the fuel to the coolant in small amounts.[1]

Most of the liquid waste is generated in the course of maintenance or

163

Figure 26
Nuclear Power Reactors in the United States

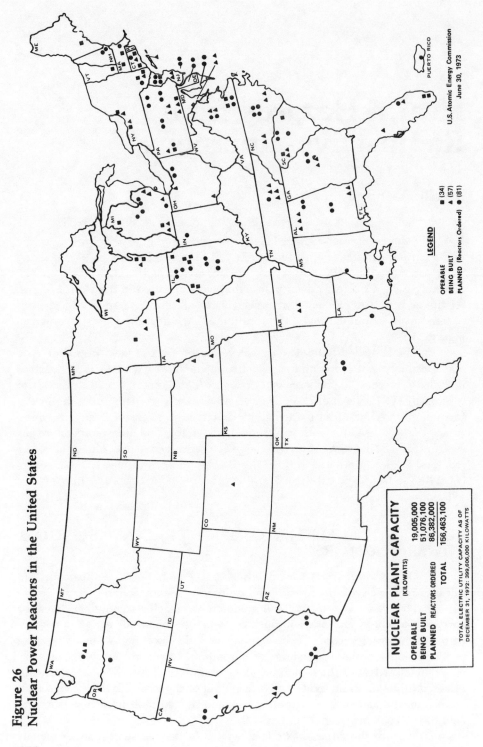

NUCLEAR PLANT CAPACITY
(KILOWATTS)

OPERABLE   19,005,000
BEING BUILT   51,076,100
PLANNED REACTORS ORDERED   86,382,000
              TOTAL   156,463,100

TOTAL ELECTRIC UTILITY CAPACITY AS OF
DECEMBER 31, 1972: 399,606,000 KILOWATTS

LEGEND

OPERABLE   ■ (34)
BEING BUILT   ▲ (57)
PLANNED (Reactors Ordered) ● (81)

U.S. Atomic Energy Commission
June 30, 1973

164

refueling operations. When the reactor system is serviced or when quantities of contaminated coolant must be prepared for disposal, the waste water is first passed through a gas stripper, after which the liquid can be decontaminated by filtration, cation-anion exchange, or evaporation. The latter processes result in concentration of most of the radioactive substances as sludges or solids which can be placed in drums, mixed with concrete, and shipped to approved radioactive storage sites. The radioactive gases can be stored in tanks to permit the shorter lived nuclides to decay, following which the longer lived gases can be released to the atmosphere at a controlled rate.

Most power reactors are located on bodies of water to facilitate dissipation of heat from the condensers. Since the condenser coolant flow is apt to be several hundred thousand gallons per minute, this stream offers a convenient method of diluting the low-level liquid wastes to the concentrations permitted by the AEC license. It is important to emphasize that the liquid wastes produced by reactors are only mildly radioactive. They are discharged to the environment at concentrations that are generally regarded as safe for continuous human consumption. More will be said later about the standards by which the amounts of the various nuclides that can be discharged to the environment are regulated. However, at this point it should be emphasized that the opportunities for accidental release of massive quantities of stored radioactive wastes do not exist in the normal routine of reactor operation.

The relative composition of radionuclides in the liquid waste discharge from a typical light-water reactor is shown in Table 17. The amounts of the various nuclides in this table are shown relative to cesium-137, which is taken as unity.

The quantities of radioactive gases released from a reactor vary greatly depending on whether it is a pressurized-water or boiling-water reactor. The gaseous releases from the PWR are so insignificant as to be relatively less than the atmospheric discharges from fossil-fuel plants. The burning of coal or oil releases several radionuclides to the atmosphere, including radium-226, radium-228, uranium, thorium, and potassium-40.[2,3] These are, of course, released in very small quantities, and there has been no suggestion that they represent a public health hazard; but the radioactive gaseous releases from nuclear reactors under normal operating conditions have been shown to be even less than those from fossil-fuel plants.

In the boiling-water reactor, the steam passes directly from the reactor to the turbine and carries with it copious amounts of relatively short-lived noble gases as well as traces of other volatile fission products. In most of the boiling-water reactors built to the present time, the radioactive gases carried by the steam through the turbine are stored for 30 minutes to allow the short-lived nuclides to decay, after which the gases are passed through filters before being released to a stack. The composition of the radioactive mixture discharged from such a typical boiling-water reactor is shown in Table 18. It is possible to provide for considerably longer hold-up of the gases from a BWR, thereby considerably reducing the rates of release. It is likely that all future BWRs will be so equipped, in which case the emissions will be more comparable to those of a PWR.

Table 17
The Annual Average Radionuclide Composition Relative to the Concentration of ^{137}Cs from a Typical Pressurized Water Reactor

Nuclide	Relative Concentration
Hydrogen-3	5.3×10^2
Chromium-51	$< 1.7 \times 10^{-2}$
Manganese-54	2.8×10^{-1}
Iron-55	8.1×10^{-2}
Iron-59	$< 2.4 \times 10^{-3}$
Cobalt-58	2.1×10^{-2}
Cobalt-60	1.1×10^{-1}
Zinc-65	$< 3.1 \times 10^{-3}$
Strontium-90	6.6×10^{-4}
Yttrium-91	2.6×10^{-3}
Zirconium-95-Niobium	$< 2.8 \times 10^{-2}$
Ruthenium-103	$< 3.1 \times 10^{-2}$
Ruthenium-106	$< 8.6 \times 10^{-2}$
Iodine-131	$< 5.2 \times 10^{-3}$
Cesium-134	4.8×10^{-1}
Cesium-137	1.0×10^0
Cerium-144	$< 3.8 \times 10^{-2}$

Source: Reference 1.

Table 18
Principal Radionuclides Released in Gaseous Emissions from Boiling Water Reactors

Radionuclides	Half-Life	Release Rate $\mu Ci/sec$
^{m}Krypton-85	4.4 h	3×10^2
Krypton-85	10.7 yr	1×10^{-1}
Krypton-87	76 min	7×10^2
Krypton-88	2.8 h	5×10^2
^{m}Xenon-133	2.3 day	1×10^1
Xenon-133	5.3 day	3×10^2
Xenon-135	9.1 h	8×10^2
Xenon-138	17 min	2×10^3
Hydrogen-3 (tritium)	12 yr	5×10^{-2}

Source: Reference 12.

LIMITS OF PERMISSIBLE RADIOACTIVE WASTE RELEASE

Under federal law, protection of the public from effects of radioactivity is the responsibility of the Atomic Energy Commission, and all reactors are subject to licensing procedures that govern their design, construction, and operation.

The AEC has relied on the National Council on Radiation Protection and Measurements (NCRP) to recommend the permissible dose for atomic energy workers and the public. The NCRP was founded in 1929 and, until recently, was headquartered in the Bureau of Standards. In 1964 the organization was granted a congressional charter and now operates as an independent organization financed by voluntary contributions from government, scientific societies, and manufacturing associations. There are 65 members on this Council and about 175 members of the numerous scientific committees that have the responsibility for developing the technical reports of the organization.

In 1928, one year before NCRP was formed, the International Society of Radiology sponsored formation of the International Commission on Radiation Protection (ICRP). This group has operated in close cooperation with our NCRP and receives support from the World Health Organization.

The recommendations of ICRP and NCRP were originally intended for protection of workers exposed to ionizing radiation. Prior to World War II, there was so little use of ionizing radiations that the need for standards to protect the public did not yet arise. Since 1959 the limit for whole body occupational exposure has been 5 roentgen equivalents man (rem) per year. Permissible exposure to contaminated air and water is calculated and is based on the requirement that the dose to the individual organs not exceed 5 rem per year for the whole body, gonads, or bone marrow. Certain tissues such as the skin and thyroid are permitted a somewhat higher dose.

The maximum permissible dose for exposure of the public has been suggested by ICRP and NCRP to be $1/30$ the permissible occupational dose.[4] The government regulations have assumed that this average will be achieved if the highest exposed individual in a given population is exposed to no more than $1/10$ of the permissible occupational dose. Since the permissible occupational dose is 5 rems/year, the *average* dose to the general population should not exceed 0.17 rem, and the dose to the *maximum exposed individual* should not exceed 0.5 rem.

Since leukemia, other forms of cancer, and genetic mutations are the potential effects of ionizing radiation exposure that are of greatest concern insofar as the general population is concerned, our discussion of current standards will focus on these.

Leukemia and other forms of cancer have been seen in increased incidence among several groups of humans exposed to relatively high doses of ionizing radiation. These include survivors of the atomic bombings of Hiroshima and Nagasaki, patients irradiated for ankylosing spondylitis, early radiologists exposed in the course of their work, and children irradiated *in utero* in the course of pelvic x-ray examinations. Additional human experience has been gained from the early misuses of radium, the massive fallout of radioactive dust in the Marshall Islands in 1954, and from studies of children irradiated for enlarged thymus and for ringworm of the scalp.[5,6]

This epidemiological experience has proved to be of much value in many respects, but the doses were much higher than those to which humans are exposed under normal circumstances. Moreover, the exposures involved mainly single or multiple exposures at high dose rates. To estimate the expected effect of doses of a fraction of a rad delivered in small bits, one must extrapolate from these epidemiological data involving doses in the range of hundreds of rads. In the interest of maximum safety, this is done by assuming there is no threshold and that the biological effect is proportional to the dose, and independent of the dose rate. The United Nations Scientific Committee on the Effects of Atomic Radiation,[6] the ICRP,[7] NCRP,[4] and the National Academy of Sciences [5] have emphasized that the estimates made in this way represent an upper limit of risk and that the actual risk may, in fact, be very much less.

Subject to these assumptions, the epidemiological evidence suggests that a dose of one rad delivered to 1 million people may produce a maximum of about 20 cases of leukemia and from 70 to 145 other forms of cancer during the lifetime of the population.[5]

We are faced with a number of difficulties when we attempt to establish such risk coefficients. One aspect of the problem is shown in Figure 27 in which are shown two basic types of dose-response curves. In Curve A there is a "threshold" below which no injury takes place; at higher doses, the curve assumes the form of a sigmoid in which the rate of change is relatively slow at low doses and then increases rapidly before again decreasing at high doses, by which time the entire sensitive population has been affected. In Curve B there is no threshold and the response is linear with dose. Curve B overestimates the effect relative to Curve A. However, it is not possible to differentiate between them in practice because the effects in either case occur so infrequently at low doses that unrealistically large populations would be required for study. We will see later that in practice we are concerned with effects that occur at frequencies smaller than 1 case per 10 million of population. Epidemiological or experimental studies at such low attack rates present such formidable problems that we are required to estimate the risk coefficients by extrapolations from very much higher doses.

Although it has been known since 1926 that ionizing radiations can produce genetic mutations in experimental animals, there is as yet no epidemiological basis for estimating the genetic effects of human exposure. Based on experiments with the fruit fly, it had been assumed until 1959 that the number of mutations produced is proportionate to total dose and *independent* of the rate at which the dose is delivered. It is now known, based on mouse experiments, that a given dose delivered over an extended period of time produces fewer mutations than if delivered in a short time.[8]

It is estimated that about 4% of live-born infants normally show evidence of hereditary defects. To what extent natural radiation contributes to this frequency is not known. However, it is currently thought that a radiation dose of about 20 to 200 rads delivered to an entire population for many successive generations would eventually cause the spontaneous mutation rate to double.[5]

Because of the assumption that there is no threshold for radiation injury, the recommendations and regulations of ICRP, NCRP, and AEC all admonish that radiation exposure should be minimized to the extent practicable and that no exposure should be permitted without commensurate benefit. AEC practice in its reactor regulatory program has been consistent with this "lowest practicable dose" concept, and exposure of the public has been a very small fraction of the permissible dose. The AEC has recently proposed that the maximum dose to a member of the public exposed to radiations from *light-water reactors* be reduced by a factor of 100, from 500 millirem (mrem) per year to 5 mrem per year. This proposed change is intended to reflect that the state of the art permits the lower limit to be specified and that power reactors generally have, in fact, been operating at less than 5% of the permissible level.

Figure 27
Two Possible Dose-Response Curves
(A, sigmoid curve; B, straight line)

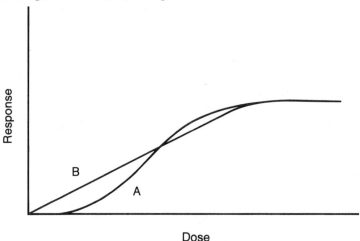

NATURALLY OCCURRING SOURCES OF IONIZING RADIATION

An appreciation of the kinds and amounts of ionizing radiation exposure due to natural sources will prove relevant to our discussion of the significance of reactor-produced radiation.

Radioactive substances are naturally present in the air we breathe and the food we eat. They become incorporated into our tissues in such amounts that on the average our bodies are literally disintegrating at a rate of about 500,000 times per minute due to the decay of radioactive species of carbon, potassium, and other naturally radioactive substances contained in our tissues.

The total body irradiation received by man in most parts of the world is about 0.1 rem per year. Deviations above the norm by as much as 20-fold occur in places such as Brazil and India, where the thorium or uranium contents of the rocks and soils are above normal.

The lung and skeleton are selectively exposed over and above the dose received by the body as a whole. A large component of the dose to the lung is due to the presence in the atmosphere of radon and its decay products. The concentration of this radioactive noble gas is variable, depending on geographical and meteorological factors. Under normal circumstances, radon can deliver a dose of about 1.3 rem per year to the basal cells of the bronchial epithelium, which is the tissue of the lung known to be particularly radio-sensitive. Higher doses are possible indoors, particularly when buildings are constructed of materials with a high radium content.

The radon has a half-life of 3.8 days and decays progressively through several shorter-lived progeny to 210 Pb, which has a half-life of 22 years. The atoms of 210 Pb become attached to the inert dust of the atmosphere and ultimately deposit on the earth's surface. The lead-210 decays to polonium-210, an alpha emitter with a 138-day half-life. Only in the last few years have we begun to appreciate that mankind has always been subject to this form of natural fallout and the broad-leafed plants, in particular, have relatively high concentrations of these isotopes. According to one investigator, this phenomenon contributes an additional 41 mrem per year to the lungs of individuals who smoke one pack of cigarettes per day.[1]

Two naturally occurring calcium congeners, radium-226 and radium-228, enter our bodies with food and water. Like calcium, these nuclides tend to deposit in the skeleton. Studies of food and water in various parts of the world have shown that there are wide variations in the amount of radium ingested. In certain parts of the Middle West the radium intake is elevated due to the presence of abnormally high amounts of radium in the drinking water, and the dose to the skeleton is increased by about 0.06 rem per year.

Thus, we can conclude that the whole body dose from natural radioactivity in most parts of the world is about 0.1 rem per year. The lung receives a greater dose due to the superimposed radiation from atmospheric radon, as does the skeleton in certain geographical areas where the radium content of food and water is elevated above normal. These dose rates provide a useful yardstick with which to assess the significance of exposure from reactor operation.

APPLICATION OF RADIATION STANDARDS TO REACTORS

It is convenient to divide radiation exposure into external and internal components. External radiation is that which is received from sources external to the body, such as from a cloud of radioactive gas overhead or from a deposit of radioactive material on the ground. Internal radiation is that received when a radioactive substance is absorbed into the body, as when ^{131}I deposits in the thyroid or ^{90}Sr deposits in bone.

The principal way in which the general population can be exposed to external radiation from reactors is from the cloud of passing radioactive gases discharged from the plant. Up to the present time, this source has been more significant for a BWR than a PWR. This source of exposure provides an opportunity to illustrate the subtle inherent safety factors built into the systems by which standards are administered. It will be recalled that the *average* dose to the population must be kept under 0.17 rem per year and that the *maximum* dose to any individual must be less than 0.5 rem per year. However, because the maximum dose is limiting, the average dose will be very much less than 0.17 rem per year.

For example, consider a hypothetical case in which a boiling-water reactor stack is located 100 meters from a 360° fence at which the dose is assumed to be 0.5 rem per year. Thus, people living right on the fence would receive the maximum permissible dose to individuals. From the known rates of diffusion of gaseous effluents from point sources, it can be calculated that the dose rate beyond the fence would, on the average, diminish inversely with the 1.8 power of distance from the stack. The per capita dose has been calculated for a population of 1 million people uniformly distributed around the fence at a density of 1,000 people per square kilometer. The annual per capita doses for such a population would be less than 0.00028 rem. The average dose to the population in the immediate vicinity would be 1/1,800 of the maximum, not 1/3 as is assumed in the AEC regulations.

The regulations for control over internal emitters include limits on the permissible concentrations of radionuclides in air and water. The regulations are frequently administered on the assumption that, if the maximum permissible concentration is not exceeded at the point of discharge to the environment, the dose to humans will not be exceeded anywhere beyond the site boundaries. The point of release in the case of a radioactive liquid effluent is the point at which the waste is discharged to the receiving body of water. As applied to gaseous effluents, the point of release is usually elevated above the ground. In most cases, this is a very conservative assumption, since dilution up to many thousandfold can take place before anyone is actually exposed to the air or water. However, it is also possible for biological concentration to take place, and, when this occurs, the risk can be increased correspondingly. Thus, it is known that iodine is concentrated in cow's milk, and many metals are concentrated in shellfish, sometimes 10,000-fold.

The AEC places upon the licensee the responsibility of demonstrating that such concentration does not take place. In the case of iodine-131, the maximum permissible concentration in air has been reduced by a factor of 700 to allow for the tendency of iodine to deposit on forage and eventually pass to cow's milk.

The AEC also requires the licensee to conduct monitoring programs in the vicinity of the reactor. This provides information about the concentration of radioactive substances in air, water, and biota, including whatever food products may be grown in the vicinity. Thus the question of environmental safety is not left to conjecture but is based on actual measurement of samples collected from the environment. The states, assisted by the U.S. Public Health Service, undertake independent monitoring programs as well and serve to evaluate the monitoring results reported by the licensee.

EXPERIENCE IN THE NUCLEAR POWER PROGRAM

Occupational Exposure

Since World War II, the AEC has reported regularly on the radiation exposure of its employees in statistical reports that also contain data on industrial accidents of all kinds—those that involve radiation exposure, as well as those in which radiation was not a factor.[9] The overall accident experience of the AEC and contractor employees, which employ about 100,000 persons, is shown in Figure 28, where the frequency of lost-time accidents of *all* kinds is compared with the national average accident frequency for all industry. The AEC accident record has been consistently between one half and one fourth the national average, which is all the more outstanding an accomplishment when one considers that the AEC program involves much heavy construction, chemical processing, and other types of industrial work that is potentially more hazardous than average industry. In recent years, of the 42 industries for which the National Safety Council publishes accident statistics, none has had a frequency of lost-time accidents lower than the AEC plants and laboratories.

Figure 28
Atomic Energy Commission and National Safety Council
National Industrial Average Injury Frequency Rates, 1943 to 1970

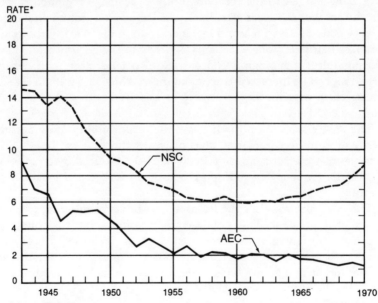

Source: Reference 9.
*Number of injuries per million man-hours

Despite the relative excellence of this 28-year-old program, there has been a total of 295 work-related fatal accidents, a large number of which (61%) occurred in construction activities because of falls or falling objects, motor vehicle mishaps, and electric shock. Of these 295 deaths, 6 were due to radiation. A seventh radiation-caused death occurred in a privately-operated industrial plant in 1964. Thus, during the 28 years from 1943 to 1970, fatalities owing to radiation exposure accounted for about 2% of all deaths due to occupational accidents. It is also significant that all but one of the fatal accidents were associated primarily with experimental programs. As of this writing, the last of the fatal accidents occurred in January 1961, more than 12 years ago.

In addition to the 6 fatalities, radiation accidents have resulted in 12 cases of clinically observable radiation injuries to employees during the 28-year period.

Except in uranium mining, there have been no known injuries from the delayed effects of radiation in the atomic energy industry. Ironically, uranium mining is the one part of the atomic energy program that had reason to take meticulous precautions, based on very early experience in European mines. Had the uranium mine atmospheres been controlled so as to meet the standards that were established by NCRP in 1941 to control the radon hazard in another industry, a tragic epidemic of lung cancer among the uranium miners of southwestern United States would have been avoided. Regrettably, regulation of the mines was not preempted by the federal government but was left to the states, which lacked either the means or the will to deal with the problem in an effective manner.

The absence of known cases of delayed injury from ionizing radiation exposure in the atomic energy industry is assuring. It is, of course, possible that isolated injuries or deaths due to chronic radiation exposure have occurred, or will occur; and a few cases here and there might not be recognized as such against the background of normal morbidity and mortality. However, one can find comfort in the records of personnel radiation exposure. During the 24-year period from 1947 to 1970, less than 0.2% of the employees received an annual dose of more than 5 rem, and almost 95% received an annual dose of 1 rem or less. It will be recalled that 5 rem is the maximum permissible dose recommended by ICRP and NCRP for radiation workers. There have been 44 annual exposures greater than 15 rem, most of which were associated with the accidents that caused the deaths and injuries noted earlier.

The accumulated mortality statistics of atomic energy workers at Oak Ridge have been examined for the purpose of comparing the death rates of this population of atomic energy workers with industrial workers generally.[10] Based on age-adjusted mortality rates, one would have predicted 992 deaths from all causes during the 16-year period included in the study, whereas 692 deaths actually occurred. This significantly lower death rate is, no doubt, attributable to many factors, including possibly higher mean educational level, a higher percentage of skilled people earning higher salaries, and other socioeconomic factors including the higher standards of medical care that one would expect in a modern planned community such as Oak Ridge. All one can conclude is that the additional occupational risk owing to ionizing radiation exposure in the nuclear energy industry is more than offset by other factors characteristic of the industry. Some of these factors, such as the highly selective personnel practices of the industry may, actually, be related to the dangers of radiation exposure. Biases in personnel selection that reduce the incidence of alcoholism or accident proneness are examples of factors that are likely to be associated with reduced mortality.

Exposure of the General Public

The gaseous and liquid releases from the operating civilian reactors during 1971 are summarized in Tables 19 and 20. It is seen that the releases were a fraction of those permitted by the AEC licensing procedures.[11] The data in these tables are expressed as percentages of the permissible releases in the license issued to the reactor operator. The actual doses received by the public are so small that they are difficult to quantitate. For this reason the reactor operators and the AEC have tended to measure the quantities of waste radioactive materials released, based on assurances from environmental studies that, if the release limitations are not exceeded, the dose to people will be within acceptable limits.

Table 19
Releases of Radioactivity in Gaseous Effluents from Nuclear Power Plants, 1971

Facility	Noble and Activation Gases		Halogens and Particulates with Half-Lives > 8 Days	
	Released (Ci)	Percent of Permissible	Released (Ci)	Percent of Permissible
Oyster Creek	516,100	6.2	2.14	1.7
Millstone Point	275,700	1.1	4.0	4.23
Indian Point-1	360	0.007	0.21	2.8
Dresden-1	753,000	4.3	< 0.67	0.9
Dresden-2/3	580,000	2.1	8.68	11.9
H. B. Robinson	0.018	< 0.0001	not detected	
Humboldt Bay	514,300	32	0.3	5.4
Fermi-1	< 180	< 20	< 0.001	< 0.04
Big Rock Point	284,000	0.91	0.61	1.6
Nine Mile Point	253,000	0.97	< 0.80	1.65
R. E. Ginna	31,850	~ 1	0.17	10.1
Saxton	437	11.7	0.007	0.07
Peach Bottom-1	122	0.06	< 0.0003	< 0.33
La Crosse	529	0.17	< 0.001	< 0.06
San Onofre	7,667	0.45	< 0.0001	< 0.012
Point Beach-1	838	0.035	< 0.0001	*
Monticello	75,800	0.89	0.052	0.5
Yankee-Rowe	13	0.058	< 0.0001	< 0.008
Conn. Yankee	3,250	1.12	0.031	15

Source: Reference 11.

*Included in noble and activation gases.

Table 20
Releases of Radioactivity in Liquid Effluents from Nuclear Power Plants, 1971

| Facility | Mixed Fission and Corrosion Products | | | Tritium | |
	Released (Ci)	Concentration Limit (10^{-7} $\mu Ci/ml$)	Percent of Limit	Released (Ci)	Percent of MPC
Oyster Creek	12.1	1	42.5	21.5	0.0026
Millstone Point	19.65	5.7	4.6	12.7	0.0006
Indian Point-1	81.12	10	22	725	0.063
Dresden-1	6.15	1	21	8.7	0.001
Dresden-2/3	23.2	1	17	8.5	0.001
H. B. Robinson	0.736	1	11.5	118.3	0.062
Humboldt Bay	1.84	1	11.4	< 7.5	< 0.002
Fermi-1	0.01	1	10	not measured	
Big Rock Point	3.46	5.8	5.9	10.3	0.003
Nine Mile Point	32.2	33	2.1	12.4	0.0009
R. E. Ginna	0.96	1	1.38	154	0.007
Saxton	0.01	1	0.54	4.14	0.007
Peach Bottom-1	0.007	1	0.38	14	0.025
La Crosse	17.1	300	0.16	91.4	0.009
San Onofre	1.54	1	2.4	4570	0.24
Point Beach-1	0.15	3	0.09	266	0.015
Monticello	0.014	1	0.054	0.59	0.0008
Yankee-Rowe	0.0115	1	0.041	1685	0.198
Conn. Yankee	5.88	6.3	1.3	5830	0.26

Source: Reference 11.

Such assurances can, in fact, be obtained from unusually detailed studies of the environs of three power reactors that have operated from 10 to 12 years. The Bureau of Radiological Health of the U.S. Public Health Service (now the Environmental Protection Agency) investigated the Yankee Nuclear Power Station in Rowe, Massachusetts, and the Dresden Nuclear Power Station Unit I in Illinois.[12] Indian Point Station Unit I, a PWR on the Hudson River, has been studied by my associates at the New York University Medical Center.

The Environmental Protection Agency (EPA) concluded, on the basis of its survey of the Dresden environs, that "exposure to the surrounding population through consumption of food and water from radionuclides released at Dresden was not measurable." This is a particularly significant conclusion in view of the fact that this plant had by then been in operation for about ten years and a considerable amount of fuel cladding damage was known to have occurred early in the life of the plant.

The EPA has also completed a study of the environs of the Yankee Nuclear Power Station, a PWR that has been in operation since August 1970.[13] No evidence could be found that operation of this plant had increased the exposure of the surrounding population above that received from natural sources.

The environs of the PWR at Indian Point, on the east bank of the Hudson River, have been studied since 1963 by my associates at New York

University.[14] Periodic surveys have also been made by the New York State Health Department and the Department of Environmental Conservation.

The main route of human exposure from the Indian Point releases would be consumption of fish, and the bulk of the dose would be due to ^{137}Cs and ^{134}Cs. Figure 29 illustrates the distribution of ^{137}Cs in the water, sediments, and biota of the Hudson. Similar data are available for other radionuclides, both artificial and natural. Since the most important exposure pathway would be consumption of fish, the dose received by an individual consuming 11 kilograms per year (kg/yr) of Hudson River fish has been calculated. For such a person, the whole body dose would have been 0.20 mrem/yr based on the 1971 data. To put these doses into perspective, it can be observed that the gamma radiation dose from igneous rock on the island of Manhattan exposes people to about 15 mrem/yr more than they would receive from the sandy terrain of Brooklyn, another borough of New York City. A dose of 0.20 mrem per year from a steady diet of Hudson River fish would be equivalent to the additional dose a Brooklyn resident would receive if he visited Manhattan for a period of about 120 hours per year.

Figure 29
Average Concentrations of Cs-137 Measured Annually in Hudson River Samples Collected at Northern Sites, 1962–1971

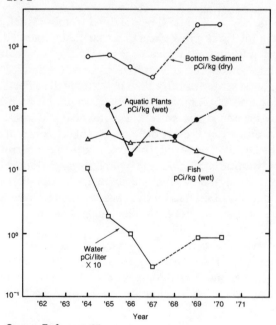

Source: Reference 14.

That the radiation exposures due to nuclear power stations are so low cannot be a surprise to anyone familiar with the quantities of fission products from weapons-testing fallout that have been present in the environment during the past two decades. The behavior of these radionuclides has been the subject of global research by investigators from many nations, and models have been developed of the pathways by which the more important radionuclides expose man. With only a few exceptions, all the radionuclides discharged in reactor effluents have previously been deposited on earth by weapons testing in much larger amounts. For example, during 1971, a total of about 200 curies/yr of mixed radionuclides, excluding tritium, was discharged to the aquatic environment by all U.S. civilian power reactors. In contrast, several hundred thousand curies of ^{90}Sr and ^{137}Cs have been deposited on the surface of the United States by nuclear weapons testing. This is illustrated with respect to the Indian Point site by Table 21, in which the weapons-testing fallout and reactor discharges are given for 1963 and 1971, the years in which the quantities were maximum for the two sources, respectively.

Table 21
Comparison of Discharges of the Principal Radionuclides from Indian Point I and Fallout from Weapons Tests*

	Curies			
	Sr-90	Mn-54	Cs-137	H-3 (tritium)
Annual discharge from Indian Point I (1971)	< 0.01	10.2	22.5	725
Fallout from Weapons On Hudson River watershed (35,000 km²)	825.0	1236.0	1320.0	205,000.0
On Hudson River surface	3.7	5.5	5.9	920.0
On mixing zone of river, 16 km above and below plant	0.58	0.87	0.93	144.0

*For purposes of comparison, the year of heaviest fallout (1963) is compared to the year of maximum reactor discharge (1971). These data have been assembled from several sources by my associate, M. E. Wrenn.

The Environmental Protection Agency has recently published [15] a study in which the reactor experience accumulated to date was extrapolated through the year 2000, by which time it is estimated that nuclear generating capacity in the United States will be about 500,000 megawatts (Mw). The EPA study also considered exposure of the public to other portions of the fuel cycle, including mining, milling, fuel fabrication, fuel reprocessing, and transportation. At the present time the per capita dose rate from nuclear power activities is estimated by the EPA to be about 0.002 mrem/yr. The study estimates that this dose will increase to about 0.4 mrem/yr by the year 2000. Table 22 shows the estimates of the per capita dose from nuclear power and other sources of radiation and a comparison of the 0.4 mrem/yr to 130 mrem/yr from natural background and 72 mrem/yr from the diagnostic uses of medical x-rays and radioisotopes. A modest reduction in the dose from x-ray examinations would more than offset the dose from nuclear power.

Table 22
Per Capita Dose Rates for 1970 and 2000

Source of Exposure	1970 (mrem/yr)	2000 (mrem/yr)
Natural	130.0	130.0
Occupational	0.8	0.9
Nuclear Power	0.002	0.2
Nuclear Fuel Reprocessing	0.0008	0.2
Weapons Fallout	4.0	4.0
Medical	72.0	72.0

Source: Reference 15.

It is now possible to return to the risk coefficients discussed earlier, in order to convert the exposure estimates to actual cases of radiation injury. Such calculations are, of course, highly speculative at best but, because of the underlying conservative assumptions, probably yield estimates that are on the high side.

If we assume with EPA that the annual per capita whole body dose will be 0.4 mrem by the year 2000, the dose integral for a population of 300 million people will be 120,000 man rem. Based on a risk coefficient of 100 cancers per million man rem, exposure from the nuclear power industry could produce a maximum of 12 cases of cancer per year in the U.S. population, assumed to be 300 million by the year 2000. Since the annual incidence of cancer in the U.S. is about 1,600 cases per 1 million persons, the 12 cases would occur against a background of nearly 500,000 cancers from other causes.

We thus conclude from the operating experience of civilian power plants that nuclear power involves but minimal and insignificant radiation exposure of the public. From the point of view of one concerned with the public health, nuclear power is a welcome alternative to power generated by combustion of fossil fuels. Environmental radioactivity should pose no limitation on the development of nuclear energy in the decades immediately ahead.

References

1. Eisenbud M: Environmental Radioactivity, ed 2, New York, Academic Press, 1973.

2. Eisenbud M, Petrow H: Radioactivity in the Atmospheric Effluents of Power Plants That Use Fossil Fuels, *Science* **144:**288, 1964.

3. Martin JE, Harward ED, Oakley DT, et al: Radioactivity from Fossil Fuel and Nuclear Power Plants, Rep SM-146/19, Environmental Aspects of Nuclear Power Stations, IAEA, Vienna, 1971.

4. National Council on Radiation Protection and Measurements, Basic Radiation Protection Criteria, NCRP Rep No 39, 1971.

5. National Academy of Sciences—National Research Council. The Effects on Populations of Exposure to Low Levels of Ionizing Radiation, Rep of Advisory Committee on the Biological Effects of Ionizing Radiations, Wash DC, Nov 1972.

6. United Nations Scientific Committee on the Effects of Atomic Radiation, 21st Session, Suppl No 14 (A/6314) and 24th Session, Suppl No 14 (A/7613), United Nations, New York, 1966 and 1969.

7. International Commission on Radiological Protection. Report of Committee I on the Evaluation of Risks from Radiation. *Health Physics* **12:**240, 1966.

8. Russell WL: Recent Studies on the Genetic Effects of Radiation in Mice. *Pediatrics* **41:**223, 1968.

9. US Atomic Energy Commission. Operational Accidents and Radiation Exposure Experience Within the US Atomic Energy Commission 1943–1970. Rep WASH 1192, USAEC, Wash DC, 1971.

10. Larson CE, Lincoln TA, Bahler KW: Mortality Comparison, Rep No K-A-708. Union Carbide Corp, Oak Ridge, TN, 1966.

11. US Atomic Energy Commission. Report on Releases of Radioactivity in Effluents from Nuclear Power Plants for 1971. Directorate of Regulatory Operations, 1972.

12. Kahn B, Blanchard RL, Krieger HL, et al: Radiological Surveillance Studies at a Boiling Water Nuclear Power Reactor, *Proc Environ Aspects Nucl Power Sta, 1971,* IAEA, Vienna, 1971.

13. Kahn B, Blanchard RL, Kolde HE, et al: Radiological Surveillance Studies at a Pressurized Water Nuclear Power Reactor. US Environmental Protection Agency, 1971.

14. Wrenn ME, Lentsch JW, Eisenbud M, et al: Radiocesium Distribution in Water, Sediment, and Biota in the Hudson River Estuary from 1964 Through 1970. *Proc 3rd Natl Symp of Radioecology,* Oak Ridge, TN, May 1971, (in press).

15. Environmental Protection Agency. Estimates of Ionizing Radiation Doses in the United States 1960–2000. Rep of Special Studies Group, Div of Criteria and Standards, Office of Radiation Programs, 1972.

14

Comparison Scales for Radioactive and Nonradioactive Hazards

Marvin Goldman, Ph.D.

Any comparative analysis of all the hazards to which man may be exposed consequent to generation of energy is a mind-boggling experience that few of us are prepared to undertake without serious misgivings. At the outset, I would like to establish some simple ground rules, which I hope are agreeable to you. I have assumed that for any agent, chemical, radioactive or otherwise, a toxic or hazardous level can be demonstrated. It is not my purpose to describe these qualitatively but to accept the fact that our products or effluents of concern have been identified and that our task is to define methods of quantifying these effects in rational objective studies—that is, our task is to learn what we can of the nature of the curve that best summarizes the relationship of biological effect to time and exposure. I have been told that Holmes, Sherlock not Oliver Wendell, said that it was a capital offense to theorize before you have the data. While I have to agree with that statement, I am often asked: How good or complete are the data available to us? Clearly some conclusions and decisions must be made in the absence of adequate data.

In reviewing data, particularly on health effects, I find that, in some cases, analyses have suggested certain associations and immediately the temptation to equate correlation with causality ensues. Quite often, I am told, epidemiologists uncover additional factors, relevant or otherwise, that can also be correlated with the effect under study, and it is then the obligation of the scientific experts to provide "hard" data in support of, or to refute, the original causal relationship. The discussion often generates proportionately more heat than light as the doses and possible effects under discussion get smaller and smaller.

This consideration leads me to my next assumption: that almost all of the agents of concern (i.e., radiation and chemicals and particulates) already exist in our environment at some, usually quite small, level. That is to say, in all likelihood, if our detection technology were perfect, we could quantify the normal or natural background level for just about any of the by-products of energy generation. For example, hazards to health from nonnuclear powerplants are primarily related to the products of fossil fuel combustion released to the environment. It is quite difficult to separate out that part of the air pollution problem that may be associated with electricity generating stations. Furthermore, it may not be realistic to consider each component contributing to "air pollution" as a single isolated hazard. In combination they may pose more of a problem than one might deduce from the sum of the effects of each taken alone. Thus, hydrocarbon, CO, NO_x, SO_2, and fly ash released in quantity to the environment may act synergistically to produce pulmonary function impairment or other toxic manifestations.

LOW-LEVEL SULFUR DIOXIDE EXPOSURE

A review of some of the extensive literature on biologic effects of air pollutants suggests to me that, while considerable data have been generated, much of it appears to be restricted to studies of the effects of acute exposure. By these effects I mean either temporary recuperable disability or a long-term effect from an acute and severe exposure. There is not much information yet available on the possible consequences of continual low-level exposures.

Of course, this statement depends on what one means by low-level. I would like to discuss this low-level concept briefly using SO_2 as an example. Our national primary ambient air quality standard sets a once-per-year, 24-hour concentration limit of 365 micrograms per cubic meter ($\mu g/m^3$) or 0.14 parts per million (ppm), plus an annual mean concentration limit of 80 $\mu g/m^3$ (about 0.03 ppm).[1] There have been reports of adverse health effects when 24-hour average levels of SO_2 exceeded about 300 $\mu g/m^3$ (about 0.11 ppm).[2] These effects were described in terms of increased hospital admissions of older persons for respiratory diseases.[3] Furthermore, when annual mean levels exceeded 115 $\mu g/m^3$ (about 0.04 ppm), adverse effects in terms of elevated frequencies of respiratory symptoms and lung disease in children and older persons have been noted.[3] Epidemiologic and animal experimental data suggest that SO_2 itself may be potentiated in its action when it is combined with particulates or aerosols. The toxicity of SO_2 is enhanced by those physical-chemical reactions that promote its formation into sulfuric acid.[4] It appears that effects may be expected after "brief" exposure to levels that are about three to five times higher than the comparably effective continuous exposure level. In both instances the standard is very close to the level at which effects might be expected.

Urban annual average SO_2 concentrations generally range between about 0.01 ppm (San Francisco) to 0.2 ppm (Chicago), with maximum one-day concentration values that are about tenfold higher (but occurring about 1% of the time).[2] The primary ambient air standards are intended to provide "an adequate margin of safety to protect the public health." [1] It is instructive to note that in some urban locations, the standard is exceeded for certain periods, and that abatement measures are probably being improved.[2] In terms of the effects on susceptible groups of the population, the margin between current average ambient levels and the standards are quite small (perhaps within a factor of 2 of the 0.03 ppm annual standard). A complication, mentioned above, is that most epidemiologic associations implicating SO_2 also imply an interrelationship with airborne particulates (perhaps both generated from the same fuel source). Some British investigators suggest that increases in lung cancer, adjusted for other factors such as smoking or socioeconomic class, might add to the mortality risks from SO_2 overexposures of long duration.[3]

Dr. Chauncey Starr and others have attempted to compare hazards from radioactive and nonradioactive sources.[5] He notes that the natural background level of SO_2 is about 1% of both the air quality standard of 0.03 ppm and the level associated with "medically perceivable effects." He has further computed risks for death from respiratory diseases in terms of the product of exposure time (in years), the concentration of ambient SO_2 (in ppm) and the particulate concentration (in $\mu g/m^3$). His analysis suggests that "lethal levels" are perhaps ten times higher than those that produce medically perceivable effects.

RADIATION RISK ASSESSMENTS

At this point I think it would be useful to attempt some comparisons and contrasts that may be reasonable with respect to the effects of radiation and radioactivity. Perhaps my choice of SO_2 alone does not provide the balance that would accompany a collective and integrated assessment of all fossil fuel emissions. In radiation risk assessments, all the radionuclides that may be released are included in the calculation of possible dose commitment to man. And unlike the fossil fuel source term, in radiation work we all use a common unit of dose equivalent to man, the rem (roentgen equivalents man). There is no chemical equivalent of the rem. An exposure-concentration-time unit, such as used by Starr is closer to the maximum permissible air concentration (MPCa) for respirable radionuclides, which is computed to result in a certain radiation equilibrium dose rate for continuous exposure to man or one of his critical organs. The background natural radiation level to which man has always been exposed, from external and internal sources, is about 0.15 rem per year.[6] While acute radiation lethality may result from doses over several hundred rem, recent experimental data suggest that chronic, continual radiation exposures may be less damaging. The data to date suggest that the most serious consequence of excessive radiation exposure, continual or acute, is an increased risk for cancer. Much of our data on man has come from studies of the survivors of the atom bombings in Japan and certain groups of patients whose therapy involved large doses of X-irradiation. Risks based on these acute exposures, generally in excess of about 100 rem, and extrapolated down to zero in a linear, nonthreshold fashion, suggest an excess cancer mortality rate of about 50 to 165 deaths per million people per year per rem.[6]

For many years national and international groups of experts have been evaluating data and providing recommendations, many of which are translated into regulatory limits. The International Commission on Radiological Protection (ICRP), in discussing risks, states that:

the data which are now available on the effects of radiation in the main relate to exposures at high dose rate received during a limited period, and all estimates of effects at low doses and low dose rates are made on the basis of linear dose-effect relationship below the doses at which quantitative information has been obtained. It must be borne in mind that, in some instances, this may lead to a gross overestimate of the incidence of effects from chronic low level exposure; indeed, some of the effects may not occur at all.[7]

DOSE-EFFECT PROPORTIONALITY

Since low level studies at small increments above background are likely to be inconclusive, our only recourse, lacking a validated theory, is to apply a prudent and conservative philosophy to extrapolate down into the unknown domain from that of the known. Note, however, that the dose-effect proportionality (linearity) is an assumption and not an established fact at these low levels and that the true effect may range from zero (nondemonstrable) to some upper level of effect.

Animal studies, using either external or internally deposited radionuclide exposures in careful gradations from quite low up to lethal levels, suggest that some dose-effect curves may indeed be sigmoidal, "S-shaped." The steeply rising portion, where significant excess cancers are seen, is often at doses above 0.1 rem per day (i.e., 30 to 50 rem per year). In quite a few of these studies with mice, rats, rabbits and dogs, the lower exposure groups show no change in lifetime cancer incidence relative to the unirradiated controls.[8]

In one instance we have some data on the effects of the same kind of radioactivity in man as well as in animals. I refer to radium toxicity, and, because its effects in man were recognized early, it constitutes one of the foundations in our setting of limits of exposure to radioactivity for man. The use of radium in the watch dial luminizing industry some 40 to 60 years ago resulted in exposure of several thousand persons. Some of these people, in orally "tipping" their paint brushes, ingested radium, a fraction of which was absorbed and deposited in bone. The consequent skeletal irradiation has induced sarcomas and carcinomas in some of the highest level cases.[9]

After cumulative skeletal irradiation estimated to be in excess of about 10,000 rem over a 40 to 60 year span (i.e., approximately 200 rem per year on the average), the risk for cancers appears to rise appreciably while in the several thousand cases under study no cancers have yet been seen at lower doses. The radioactivity equivalent in body burdens is about 0.5 microcuries of ^{226}Ra and this is five times higher than the maximum permissible level. Similar results have been obtained from animal studies and these provide a basis for scaling other radionuclides studied in animals to assist in estimating risks to man.[10] As in any toxicological quantitation, the precision of the data decreases as the dose and effect diminishes (i.e., sample sizes must be very large to demonstrate small differences).

"In view of the gaps in our understanding of radiation carcinogenesis in man, and in view of its more conservative implications, the linear, nonthreshold hypothesis warrants use in determining public policy on radiation protection; however, explicit explanation and qualification of the assumptions and procedures involved in such risk estimates are called for to prevent their acceptance as scientific dogma." [6] An application of this hypothesis to population risk estimations has generated the concept of the man-rem. This means that, if the product of numbers of individuals exposed times their average annual exposure are constant, the same number of cases in excess of natural incidence expectation would be predicted. For example, the same risk (number of cancers) is assumed if 10 million people receive 0.1 rem per year as if 1 million people received 1 rem per year. Of course, these are practical limitations on population size and on dose. This provides a means of expressing risk as cancers per 10^6 people/rem/year. Although the populations are comparatively small, most animal experiments at low dose rates have shown considerably lower cancer incidence than a nonthreshold, linear dose-effect proportionality would predict.

Although there are some differences in methods of data analyses, most investigators seem to be in agreement that in the radium cases manifesting tumors and blood dyscrasias, terminal radium body burdens were at least 5 to 15 times above the permissible level and that the initial burdens were even ten or more times higher (i.e., about 100-fold above the 0.1 microcurie limit).[9] The apparent existence of a "practical threshold" in the data (i.e., no cancers below a 0.5 microcurie terminal burden with incidence seeming to rise steeply at higher levels) is interesting but caution should be used in interpretation until the study is completed. It is also of interest that a general similar response curve has been seen in mouse and dog experiments, if one corrects for the different species-dependent skeletal uptake patterns.[10] As with the SO_2 problem, animal experimental models were utilized in radium studies after human effects were noted.

The experiments have shown that skeletal cells at greatest risk appear to be most concentrated on bone surfaces and that following radium deposition an increasing fraction of the radioactivity is, with time, buried by appositional bone growth and remodelling. With increasing time and at low concentrations, these deposits seem to be less hazardous as more of the radiation energy is expended in "cell poor" osteoid and mineral than initially when more of the "cell rich" endosteum was being irradiated. Although the time scale for relating interspecies-similar effects ranges from 50 or more years in man to about 3 years in mice or 15 years in dogs, an estimation normalized to comparable initial bone concentration of radium (i.e., similar dose rates), suggests that, within a factor of ten, there is good agreement between the curves fit to the cumulative incidence of tumors in these three studies.[10] Such comparisons are useful in design and execution of animal studies on other radionuclides that may be potentially hazardous to man.

In general, the animal studies to date have shown: (a) that deleterious effects, especially tumor production are seen when the doses are 100 to 1,000 times the background rate; (b) that the effects are largely confined to the tissues that concentrate or accumulate the radionuclide (and thus receive the greatest radiation dose); (c) that although the data analyses methods vary, the response curves, especially for the fission product radioelements, are nonlinear, usually sigmoidal in shape; and (d) that the data are similar to the limited amount of information available from studies in man.

RADIATION PROTECTION STANDARDS

Despite the evidence demonstrating repair and recovery from both radiation and nonradioactive pollutants, practical limits of epidemiological analyses will preclude any determination of an absolutely safe threshold or noneffective level. In the real world all we can do is to reduce risks as much as practicable. In setting radiation protection standards for the general public, the National Council on Radiation Protection and Measurements (NCRP) recommendations provide our basic guidance criteria. Their dose limiting recommendation is 0.17 rem/year per person.[11] The AEC is currently considering criteria for light-water cooled nuclear reactors to quantify the requirement to keep radioactivity in effluents as low as practicable. The intent is to utilize available technology to provide reasonable assurance that individuals living near the site boundary will receive less than 0.005 rem per year. This is about 3% or 4% of the natural background radiation level in most parts of the country. Background levels in the United States range from less than 0.1 rem per year to over 0.25 rem per year.

Several estimates of risk from nuclear fueled powerplants have been made. A recent National Academy of Sciences report, using a projection of about 800,000 Mw (nuclear) in the year 2000 with a 0.005 rem/year site boundary dose limit, quotes an average radiation dose increase to the U.S. population of about 0.1% of the natural background level.[6] A further assumption is that radiation risks are linearly proportional to dose and that 0.1 rem/year to our current population might likely increase cancer deaths by about 1% (about 3,000 to 4,000). If this is translated to the year 2000, with a population of 320 million, the comparable calculation for the nuclear plants might predict an additional 10 to 20 deaths per year added to the 500,000 cancer deaths that might be expected if current natural rates remain constant. This amount of radiation and assumed risk is comparable to an increase from cosmic radiation associated with living about 20 feet higher above sea level than we now do. If these estimates are converted to cancer deaths per year per unit Mw, one might quantify this health cost in as 20 cases/320 million people/800,000 Mw or a risk of about 8×10^{-14} per person per year per Mw.

Dr. Starr has compared a nuclear with an oil fueled plant and, by integrating all effluents and assuming operation at regulatory limits, calculated a ratio of 60 deaths annually (from respiratory disease) for the oil fueled plant for each cancer death from nuclear fuel for the same power production.[5]

I have tried to indicate that a hazard comparison or scaling in terms of deaths per year per unit power produced is difficult to perform. Since fossil fuel combustion is not solely associated with electrical power, it is difficult to use epidemiologic methods. Research to date is quite limited, especially with regard to chronic low-level effects, but a threshold for effect seems implied. A dose equivalent unit, a "chemical rem," does not exist that might be useful in relating effects of different nonradioactive effluents.

Radioactive effluents have been studied directly and indirectly, by analogy from other radiation studies, often at high doses and dose rates. In setting standards, threshold for effects has been rejected in favor of a more conservative straight line dose-effect proportionality,[6] despite much data suggesting that the risk at low dose rate and low total doses may be overestimated by this assumption. Finally it may be useful to consider the criteria that might be appropriate to apply some of the experimental approaches and methods of analyses used in radiation protection work to assessing the risks from other sources of energy.

References

1. *Federal Register* **36(No 84):**8186–90, April 30, 1971.

2. Terrill JG Jr, Harward ED, Leggett ED Jr: Environmental Aspects of Nuclear and Conventional Powerplants, *J Ind Med & Surgery* **36(6):**412–19, 1967.

3. *Air Quality Criteria for Sulfur Oxides,* Publ AP-50 EPA-NAPCA. US Department of Health Education and Welfare, 1970.

4. Murphy SD: *Use of Laboratory Animals to Assess the Health Effects of Air Pollution.* Prepared for the NIEHS Task Force on Research Planning in Environmental Health Sciences. On deposit at the National Library of Medicine, Bethesda, Maryland, 1970.

5. Starr C, Greenfield MA: *Public Health Risks of Thermal Powerplants,* UCLA-ENG-7242, May 1972.

6. *The Effects on Populations of Exposures to Low Levels of Ionizing Radiation,* BEIR Report. National Academy of Sciences—National Research Council, Washington, DC, November 1972.

7. *The Evaluation of Risks from Radiation,* ICRP Publ 8, International Commission for Radiological Protection, 1966.

8. *Ionizing Radiation: Levels and Effects,* Public E72.IX.18, United Nations, Vol 2, pp. 379-401, New York, 1972.

9. Finkel AJ, Miller CE, Hasterlik RJ: Radium-Induced Malignant Tumors in Man in *Delayed Effects of Bone-Seeking Radionuclides,* Mays CW, et al, (eds), U of Utah Press, pp. 195–224, 1969.

10. Goldman M, Rosenblatt LS, Hetherington NW, Finkel MP: Scaling to Man of Dose, Time and Incidence of Radium-Induced Osteosarcomas of Mice and Dogs, in *Radionuclides Carcinogenesis,* Sanders CL, Busch RH, (eds): USAEC Symposium Series, 1973.

11. *Basic Radiation Protection Criteria,* Report No 39, National Council on Radiation Protection and Measurements, Washington DC, 1971.

15

Power Plant Reactor Safety and Risk Appraisal

Peter A. Morris, Ph.D.

Nuclear reactors for electric power generating plants are made up of large, complicated, advanced technology equipment and systems. Because of the extensive nuclear chain reaction taking place in the reactor cores, there are very high radiation fields and very high levels of radioactivity involved in the operation of such plants. Because of the goal of achieving economic production of electricity, the steam-generating aspects of the plants require high power, high temperature and high pressure of water and steam, which leads to the storage of an immense quantity of energy in the reactor system. The combination of a very large amount of stored energy in conjunction with a very large amount of radioactivity presents a potential hazard to the public and to the environment in the vicinity of a nuclear power plant. This paper discusses what the risk really is and how nuclear power plant safety is achieved.

Many different kinds of nuclear reactors have been designed and operated for use in electric power plants. All of them depend upon the fissioning of uranium and plutonium for operation. The major differences are in the design of the fuel elements and in the choice of materials used to cool the fuel elements and to control the average energy of the neutrons produced from fission. Fuel element designs have used natural uranium, enriched uranium dioxide, and uranium metal alloys. Moderators, the materials used to absorb energy of fission neutrons, principally have been graphite, ordinary water (called light water), and heavy water (which has an extra neutron in the nucleus of the hydrogen atom). The primary coolants have been light water, heavy water, liquid sodium, carbon dioxide, and helium gas. Within the United States the great majority of the power reactors in operation today, as well as those to be built in the foreseeable future, are of two basic designs; the rest of this discussion will be confined to these two designs. Both use uranium dioxide pellets, slightly enriched in the isotope uranium-235, and light water as both moderator and primary coolant. In the boiling-water reactor (BWR) type, the pressure in the reactor system is designed to be approximately 1,000 pounds per square inch (psi). The water is

189

heated sufficiently to form steam in the reactor vessel itself and this steam is piped to the turbine. In the pressurized-water reactor (PWR) type, the pressure in the reactor system is designed to be approximately 2,200 psi. In this design, the water is piped to heat exchangers (i.e., steam generators) in which the heat is transferred to a secondary water system at lower pressure in which steam is generated to drive the turbine. The BWR design is called a direct cycle system and the PWR design is called an indirect cycle system.

The light-water reactor systems are made up basically of the fuel elements in the reactor core, a reactor pressure vessel and associated pipes, pumps and valves, control and auxiliary systems, engineered safety features, and a containment building. Of course, designs for both systems have a large turbine and generator.

ROUTINE RADIOACTIVE RELEASES

Aside from the problems of high pressure and high temperature steam—which are common to any steam-turbine system whether fueled with uranium, gas, oil, or coal—the different potential hazard from a nuclear plant arises from the possible release of radioactivity either as a routine effluent or as a result of an operational transient or accident. The fuel elements themselves, which are made up of columns of small, pill-box shaped pellets, become intensely radioactive. The uranium dioxide pellets contain some of the products of fission and transmutation and some of the products, particularly the gaseous isotopes, escape into the spaces between pellets and between the pellets and the tube-like containers in which they are located. Some of these radioactive materials diffuse through the fuel cladding (i.e., the walls of the tubes) into the primary coolant water, and some leak out through pin-holes or other defects in the cladding. In addition to this source of radioactivity during normal, routine operation, radioactive materials are also formed by the irradiation of the coolant water and any impurities, such as corrosion products from pump seals, that might be in the water.

As just described, it is, therefore, expected and normal that the primary coolant water, after the reactor has been operated for any appreciable time, will contain a certain amount of radioactivity. It is also expected and normal that a certain amount of water, gas, or steam containing radioactivity will escape the reactor primary coolant system. Some will escape during normal operation as a result of the irreducible low leakage that occurs from high pressure systems with many valves, pumps, flanges, and seals. Some will escape when the reactor vessel is opened up—by removing the vessel head—to permit replacement of fuel elements (about once a year) and some will escape during the time that newly discharged fuel elements are stored underwater in a storage pool before shipment off-site to a fuel reprocessing plant. There are other minor sources, such as from water chemistry sampling procedures, that we need not concern ourselves with in this discussion.

Deferring discussion of nonroutine or accidental releases for the time being, why is it acceptable to design and operate nuclear plants that routinely release radioactivity? The answer is fundamental to the entire question of use of radiation in this country and abroad. Hardly anyone doubts the benefits to be derived from medical uses of radiation in diagnosis and in therapy. In each such use, however, the doctor recognizes that there is potential for damage. In each such use he is, in effect, making a cost-benefit analysis—balancing the potentially deleterious effects of radiation against the potential gains and advantages.

In the nuclear power business a cost-benefit analysis is also made. The difference, however, is that the analysis is done, to a large extent, on a generic basis. The general conclusion is that for small releases of radioactivity, the potential benefits of nuclear power (e.g., lower cost power, conservation of natural resources, less pollution) justify the relatively small risk. More specifically, there has been a world-wide professional effort since 1928 to try to give quantitative guidance on what levels of radiation, or what average doses to both radiation workers and the general public, might be accepted without undue risk to health and safety. Other papers in this conference deal at greater length with this subject. Pertinent here, however, is the fact that, in addition to the numerical guidance given, there has always been the admonition by the professionals to keep radiation exposures as low as practicable. The implementation of this admonition depends, of course, on the state of technology at any particular time. But let me emphasize that the admonition and the guidance is not that one should make every effort to keep radiation levels absolutely zero, but to keep them as low as practicable in the perspective of what is potentially to be gained.

An important consideration in maintaining perspective on assessing the risk of radiation is the relationship of incremental radiation dose from a voluntary activity to that which is involuntary (i.e., that from natural background from cosmic radiation, geologic activity, and potassium-40 and carbon-14 in the body). Still another important consideration is the risk level accepted from other activities, many of which are voluntarily assumed, such as driving a car or smoking, or from the carcinogenic or genetic effects of a myriad of substances less well understood than radiation; or from naturally occurring disasters, such as earthquakes, floods and tornados, from which we are generally protected only partially.

To answer the question, then, it is considered acceptable to build and operate nuclear power plants with the knowledge that they will discharge some radioactivity on a routine basis only because, first, it also has been judged that the technology permits the resulting radiation exposures to be kept as low as practicable; second, it has been judged that the risk from such exposures is acceptable in order to achieve the benefits of nuclear power. In practice this means, for routine releases, that doses to the public or to the environment at the worst possible off-site location near a nuclear plant are kept at levels below approximately one tenth of natural background, and the average dose to the public in the vicinity of a nuclear power plant will be kept to less than 1% of natural background. In round numbers, average background radiation in the

United States produces a dose of 100 millirem (mrem) to an individual each year, roughly equivalent to that received from a single chest x-ray. Average doses to individuals living near nuclear power plants are expected to be less than 1 mrem per year.

LARGE ACCIDENTAL RELEASES

First, it is very easy to conceive of accidents in which large amounts of radioactivity might be released. Second, the character of the consequences and the magnitude of the conceivable consequences of a very large release of radioactivity are clearly more severe than for the consequences of accidents in nonnuclear activities that normally are considered. In nonnuclear catastrophes one thinks of explosions, fires, collisions, ship sinkings, aircraft crashes, and the like in which a hundred or a few hundred people might be killed and damage that might cost in the tens or hundreds of millions of dollars. For natural catastrophes, such as floods and earthquakes, one might think of consequences of thousands killed and costs exceeding hundreds of millions of dollars. Such events are not generally expected to produce severe genetic consequences or to render uninhabitable large areas of land, however. Nevertheless, they are serious accidents that have occurred and will occur well within the span of human history.

The consequences of several hypothetical large releases of radioactivity from a nuclear power plant were studied and reported by the Brookhaven National Laboratory in 1957 in a report known as WASH-740. The results of this study are frequently misrepresented to the public by those who are critical of the nuclear community. The largest release—for which no mechanism was postulated—assumed the most of the radioactivity contained in the fuel and that could be released from the fuel if all of it were in a molten state was in fact not only released from the fuel, but also completely escaped the primary system, completely escaped the containment building, and was transported by unfavorable weather conditions to regions of high population. These conservative assumptions, assumed to apply simultaneously, constitute an almost impossible situation. No estimate of probability of such a release was made in the Brookhaven report except to characterize it as very small. While the study did quantitate the upper limit of consequences that could be conceived for such a hypothetical accidental release of radioactivity (3,400 deaths and the equivalent of $7 million damage, maximum), it did not, and was not intended to, characterize the risk of nuclear power plant operation. The upper limit of theoretical consequence calculated in the Brookhaven report was used as a basis for the maximum level of third party liability insurance to be provided by the government under the Price-Anderson Act but was never intended to imply that there was any meaningful probability that such a release would, in fact, occur. Any evaluation of risk needs to discuss not only conceivable consequences, but also probability or frequency of occurrence of such consequences.

In answer to the second question, then, it is considered acceptable to build and operate nuclear power plants with the knowledge that conceivable accidental releases of radioactivity would have very serious consequences—at least as bad as severe natural disasters—only because it has been judged that the probability of such events is acceptably small.

To recapitulate, potential hazards to the public and to the environment could arise either from the routine release of small amounts of radiation or from the accidental release of a large quantity of radioactive material. As previous AEC chairman Dr. James Schlesinger said to the Congressional Joint Committee on Atomic Energy in January 1973, we do not live in a riskless society. Thus, in accepting nuclear power plants, the public is tacitly accepting the government and industry conclusion that the risk is not zero but is acceptably small. More explicitly, the public is accepting the conclusion that the consequences of low level, routine releases from nuclear power plants are sufficiently small and that the probability of an accidental release is sufficiently small.

REVIEW AND REGULATION

First, what are the procedures by which proposed nuclear power plant design, construction, and operation are reviewed? As required by the Atomic Energy Act—and all the rules and regulations that implement it—there are several steps in the safety review and licensing process, and several different organizational units are required to make such reviews. The applications for permits or licenses filed by utilities, together with the results of all of the reviews, are required to be made public. A construction permit is required before a site is cleared or any construction work is begun. An application for a construction permit—nowadays a stack of papers about a yard high in eight or nine volumes— is first reviewed by the Regulatory Staff of the Atomic Energy Commission for completeness and adequacy of content. Completeness is determined not only in relation to information needed for nuclear safety review, but also for review of environmental impact and for review of possible anti-trust considerations. The AEC has issued guides to the content considered necessary for such applications, based on its experience in safety review matters over the last 30 years; for anti-trust and environmental matters, the experience is far less.

When an application is accepted for review, a specific schedule and review plan is drawn up that takes into account the priorities of all other work, both in progress and planned, and the availability of professional staff and consultants having the many technical skills required for such a review. The basic review is conducted by the regulatory staff with the use of whatever consulting and technical assistance is required from national laboratories, private industry, or educational institutions. During this review, frequent meetings are held with the utility and its suppliers and consultants to explain or amplify information in the application. Also, formal written questions are asked of the applicant and formal replies are filed to supplement the application, all of which are submitted under oath. The results of the staff review are reported in a public safety evaluation document that is made available to the public, sent to the statutory Advisory Committee on Reactor Safeguards (ACRS), and to the Atomic Safety and Licensing Board (ASLB) appointed to hold a public hearing and to render an initial decision with respect to whether or not a construction permit should be issued.

The Advisory Committee on Reactor Safeguards is made up of 15 part-time experts from various technical disciplines bearing on safety of reactor design and operation. Initial review is made by a specially appointed subcommittee. Final review is made by the full committee, which normally meets once a month. The subcommittee always visits the site for firsthand evaluation and identifies those issues that it feels merit the attention of the full committee. Meetings are held with both the staff and the applicant, and all three groups use whatever consultants deemed appropriate. Following its review, which is mandatory at both the construction permit and operating license review stages, the committee is required to make its findings public, which it does in the form of a letter to the chairman of the AEC. Based on the advice received, the AEC staff may modify or supplement its safety evaluation, which becomes the principal staff testimony at the public hearing.

The licensing board is composed of three experts, selected from a special licensing board panel, including a chairman with legal competence and two technical experts. The parties involved in the hearing are the applicant, the commission staff, and any intervenors who are admitted by the board on a showing that their interest would be affected by the licensing action. In addition to these parties, who may submit testimony and cross-examine witnesses, limited participants are allowed to present unsworn statements, and the states are allowed to participate fully as a special consideration. Procedures have now been developed to allow early definition of the issues and parties and to accelerate discovery and other information exchange and stipulations so as to minimize delay of the hearing process on purely procedural matters. As an aside, the commission also has begun holding rulemaking hearings on generic issues as a way of dealing with common problems or technical issues outside the context of a hearing for a specific nuclear plant. The individual plant hearing procedures are generally adjudicatory in nature, whereas the rule-making hearings now are more legislative-type hearings; that is, the licensing hearings involve cross-examination by the parties and other trial-like procedures, whereas the rule-making hearings are generally restricted to questioning by the board.

The initial decision of the hearing board is reviewed as a matter of course by the Atomic Safety and Licensing Appeals Board acting as agent for the commissioners, who also have the right to review decisions of both the board and the appeals board. If the appeals board or the commission takes no action, either on its own initiative or because of an appeal by one of the parties, the initial decision of the licensing board becomes final and the staff takes the licensing action (e.g., issues a permit or license), acting for the commission.

The basic purpose of the required ACRS review of individual cases is to provide an expert technical opinion on the merits of an application independent of the technical conclusion of the AEC staff. The basic purposes of the licensing board hearings are to provide an opportunity for public participation in the individual decision-making process for a particular case and also to provide an audit of the staff review to assure that it was conducted in accordance with commission procedures, criteria, and requirements. Notwithstanding these independent checks on the staff review, the burden of proof of the adequacy of the proposed plant location, design, and operation rests with the applicant. In the case of a contested hearing, the board is to resolve those issues in contest.

In parallel with the staff review of the radiological safety aspects of the proposed plant, review for anti-trust considerations is undertaken and the staff prepares a draft environmental impact statement, in accord with the requirements of the National Environmental Policy Act of 1969. This draft is circulated to other federal and state agencies having jurisdiction or interest in environmental matters for comment. A final impact statement is prepared by the staff and is submitted to the President's Council on Environmental Quality, to the hearing board, and to the public.

At the operating license stage, the same review procedures are followed, with the exception that a public hearing is not mandatory. In effect, a finding must be made that a substantially new safety development had occurred since the construction permit was issued in order to hold a hearing, which automatically would be a contested hearing.

At the construction permit review stage, emphasis is placed on the acceptability of site-related matters, overall plans and preliminary design. At the operating license review stage, emphasis is placed on the acceptability of the final design, proposed operating procedures, and the technical specifications that become incorporated into the license and that put technical limits on the allowable variations in plant operating parameters, and other matters, which may not be exceeded without further review by the AEC.

Throughout the construction period and throughout the lifetime of a nuclear plant, the AEC makes inspections, on site and at vendor and manufacturer facilities, to ascertain compliance with commission rules and regulations and to make on-the-spot assessments of the quality and safety of construction and operation. Such inspections include visits to the shops of the reactor pressure vessel manufacturers, observation of concrete and steel placement, review of welding procedures and inspections, witnessing of preoperational and start-up tests and routine operation and maintenance, review of operating procedures and emergency plans, and assessment of overall management organization and effectiveness.

While the basic regulatory process involves the licensing of the utility to own and operate the reactor, the Atomic Energy Act also requires that the AEC license the individual operators who manipulate or direct the manipulation of the controls. Written and demonstration examinations lasting many hours are administered to each person seeking such a license. At present, there are more than 2,000 licensed operators and senior operators in the United States.

LICENSING CRITERIA

The objectives of safety reviews are to assure that proposed reactor design and operations are such that (1) routine releases of radioactivity are maintained as low as practicable; and (2) accident probabilities and consequences are maintained acceptably low, as discussed before. Attaining these objectives is necessary to assure that the risk posed by nuclear power plant operation is sufficiently small that the benefits are worth achieving.

There are three general concepts used in assuring that the objectives are obtained: (1) conservative design, construction, and operation, (2) defense-in-depth; and (3) quality assurance. Clearly the best way to avoid unforeseen and unacceptable consequences resulting from nuclear plant operation is to be sure that unforeseen performance and accidents do not happen in the first place. This leads to the requirement that designs be conservative, even though extra cost is incurred. Conservative designs are achieved by careful selection of materials and design principles, by use of redundant systems in parallel and systems using diverse principles of operation and physical separation of backup systems.

Similarly, conservative construction is more likely to lead to reliable systems, and conservative operation reduces the chance for mistakes or deterioration in operating conditions. Even though conservative design, construction, and operation are mandatory and do produce a relatively small chance for unacceptable performance, the degree of assurance needed that public health and safety are protected has led to the requirement of defense-in-depth (i.e., even though accidents should not happen, equipment and systems are built into the plant, first, to detect reliably any abnormal or impending abnormal condition and, second, to provide reliable and positive control measures). The most important example of this is the elaborate control system and automatic independent fast acting and separate slow acting shutdown systems that are always provided in each nuclear plant to shut down the nuclear chain reaction should this become desirable. In addition to control and safety systems, engineered safety features are always provided to mitigate the consequences of an accident should it occur. Such features might include, for example, filters or sprays to remove radioactivity from the reactor building atmosphere.

Another way of thinking about defense-in-depth is to consider the barriers that impede release of the radioactivity in the fuel to the environment. First, even when molten, not all of the radioactivity escapes from the fuel itself and the fuel cladding, when intact, retains most of the activity. That activity that does escape to the primary coolant is retained in the primary system, unless there is a significant breach in that system. That which escapes the primary system will be retained, to a large extent, by the containment building (which is required in all cases). Finally, all plants are required to have an exclusion area, of some 600 yards radius or more, and are located in a low population zone of radius generally in the range of 2 to 5 miles, which serves to isolate the source of radioactivity from the public.

The third general concept, quality assurance, as used in the nuclear industry, is extremely important and is, perhaps, unique. It is defined to comprise "all those planned and systematic actions necessary to provide adequate confidence that a structure, system, or component will perform satisfactorily in service." As such, it means a rigorous discipline throughout design, construction, test, operation, and maintenance on the part of all concerned to give a very high degree of assurance that objectives are indeed met. Frequently, quality assurance programs provide an independent check of everything that is done by front line organizations to see that the job is done and is done properly.

In addition to the general concepts, the bases for reactor technical safety reviews include the following:

GENERAL DESIGN CRITERIA. There are 55 general design criteria listed in Appendix A to 10 CFR Part 50, which is the AEC's rule on Facility Licensing. These criteria are grouped in relation to overall requirements, protection by multiple fission product barriers, protection and reactivity control systems, fluid systems, reactor containment, and fuel and radioactivity control.

RADIATION PROTECTION STANDARDS. These are provided in 10 CFR Parts 20 and 50 of the Commission's rules and are discussed further in other papers in this Congress.

SITE CRITERIA. Site criteria for reactors are provided in 10 CFR Part 100. No fixed requirements are listed, but procedures are described by which the suitability of a site is determined.

SAFETY GUIDES. In many areas, requirements of the Commission's rules are general. To give additional guidance on implementation of the rules, regulatory guides have been developed (a) to describe and make available to the public methods acceptable to the AEC regulatory staff of implementing specific parts of the Commission's regulations and, in some cases, to delineate techniques used by the staff in evaluating specific problems or postulated accidents; and (b) to provide guidance to applicants concerning certain of the information needed by the regulatory staff in its review of applications for permits and licenses. The guides are not intended as substitutes for regulations, and, therefore, compliance is not required. There are ten divisions of the guides dealing with different facets of the licensing process; Division 1 deals with power reactors.

INDUSTRY CODES AND STANDARDS. The Commission strongly believes in the increased use of codes and standards to improve the quality of design and construction and to accelerate the safety review process. Where such codes and standards meet Commission requirements, this is explicitly stated in Commission rules.

LETTERS OF THE ADVISORY COMMITTEE ON REACTOR SAFEGUARDS. These letters comment not only on the acceptability of specific designs, but also on generic matters, including such things as research and development.

DECISIONS BY THE ATOMIC SAFETY AND LICENSING BOARDS, THE APPEALS BOARDS, AND THE COMMISSION. These decisions may very well deal with policy matters and therefore set precedents for future licensing actions.

Aside from the bases and requirements contained in the material just described, licensing decisions are based on the technical analysis of the proposed plant design and proposed operation to evaluate the ability of the plant to perform as designed for both routine and transient conditions. For the nonroutine conditions, a number of "design-basis accidents" are postulated. The consequences of such accidents are calculated conservatively and the resulting calculated doses at the site boundary are compared with the guideline dose values that are provided in the Commission's site criteria and that are used in evaluating the suitability of a site. Thus, for a low probability but very severe postulated accident, such as the instantaneous break of the largest pipe attached to the reactor pressure vessel, the site and the reactor design must be such that an individual at the site boundary would receive a calculated whole body dose less than 25 rem and a calculated dose to the thyroid from iodine less than 300 rem in two hours following the accident. While these guideline dose values may appear large compared to background and to those acceptable normally, they are still only in the range where biological effects can begin to be observed.

With respect to environmental review, the development of criteria and bases is just beginning. The matters that are routinely considered, however, include the following:

1. biological effects from entrainment through cooling systems and ecological significance
2. design and siting of water intake and discharge structures to minimize entrapment and entrainment
3. impacts to aquatic environments from heat effluents
4. toxicity of biocides and other chemical wastes
5. impact of cooling tower releases on local ecology
6. ecological health
7. prediction of environmental effects on population
8. behavioral information on important species
9. regional planning for nuclear power facilities

To assure itself that plant construction and operation really are as they are supposed to be, the Commission, in an operating license, includes license conditions, in the form of technical specifications, that are required to be met by the licensee. These specifications, for both nuclear and environmental control, include items in the following categories:

1. safety limits and limiting safety system settings
2. limiting conditions for operation
3. surveillance requirements
4. design features
5. administrative controls

Second, the Commission has a program for periodic, and mostly unannounced, inspection of licensed facilities. As part of this program, independent measurements of radioactivity levels are carried out, in some cases in cooperation with state agencies and with the Environmental Protection Agency. Also, systematic appraisals are made of the management effectiveness of the operating organizations, including senior executive officers.

NUCLEAR POWER PLANT SAFETY

This is a very difficult question to answer precisely and quantitatively. This does not mean that the plants are unsafe; it does mean that the chance of a serious accident is sufficiently small so that it is difficult to put an error band on the very small number that expresses the unreliability of a reactor plant. We do not have, and never will have, frequency data, as we have for automobile accidents, that permit a statistical answer to the question. We have to estimate, therefore, based on experience with pipes and pressure vessels, knowledge of heat transfer mechanisms, nuclear reactions, chemistry, metallurgy, meteorology and much more. Several attempts have been made to synthesize the overall risk; usually such studies discuss the probability of release of different quantities of radioactivity. A sort of consensus conclusion might be that the chance for a bad accident that would result in the release of 1 million curies or more of fission products (related to ^{131}I) is in the range of 1 in 10 to 100 billion (i.e., 1 in 10^{-10} to 10^{-11} per reactor year).[1] Thus, even with 1,000 reactors in operation, the chance of a bad accident is less than approximately 1 in 10 million per year.

In conclusion, then, let me offer my personal opinion on reactor safety and risk appraisal. I think that reactors can be built and operated safely, and I think that the risk to the public presented so far, by a limited number of reactors operating for a relatively few years, has been minimal—that is, far offset by the advantages I believe are certain to be derived.

On the other side of the coin, though, I would like to quote Lord Kelvin, who said, "I often say that when you can measure what you are speaking about and express it in numbers you know something about it; but when you cannot measure it, when you cannot express it in numbers your knowledge is of a meager and unsatisfactory kind: it may be the beginning of knowledge, but you have scarcely, in your thoughts, advanced to the stage of science. . . ." In this sense, while I am comfortable today, based on a community consensus judgment that reactors are safe, for tomorrow, with hundreds of reactors to be operated for tens of years, I believe that concerted efforts continue to be needed to develop quantitative risk assessment techniques so that more and more of the public can understand and participate meaningfully in the risk-benefit-cost decisions that need to be made.

Reference

1. See EG, Otway HJ, Erdman RC: Reactor Siting from a Risk Viewpoint, *Nuclear Engineering and Design* **13**:365–376, 1970.

Discussion

Dr. Mario Battigelli: Dr. Goldsmith, I think we all may benefit from your efforts in calling attention to the need of distinguishing between correlation and causation. As I think Dr. Goldman suggested, there is always the risk of oversimplifying in translating the language of correlation into one of logical acquisition. I wonder if you would care to comment briefly.

Dr. Goldsmith: The process of drawing a socially relevant interpretation from epidemiologic work requires a judgment as to the extent to which statistical association can be interpreted causally. The perfection of that interpretation is never really available to the epidemiologist. But the convergence of experimental and epidemiologic information on a quantitative relationship, such as we have shown for lead and for carbon monoxide exposures, tends to make each of those types of data appear to be more significant with respect to causing a health effect. The convergence of studies in differing populations on the same general relationship also tends to make one believe that causation is nearer. However, Dr. Battigelli has raised a second question having to do with the validity of the materials being monitored as being the agents which produce the effects. Clearly, if you are living in an ideal circumstance, you want to have the epidemiologic association with a pollutant with which you are also carrying out the experiment. In the case of sulfur oxides and particulate matter, the more relevant pollutant may be an acid aerosol rather than SO_2 or black suspended particulate matter. The active agent is probably neither sulfur dioxide alone nor any single definable chemical-physical species in the mix of suspended particulate matter. But in public health we have, over the years, used indices. We use the coliform count as an index of fecal pollution and, therefore, of the need for control in water pollution. We use various indices in radiology and radiological health, such as rems and rads. Indeed, Dr. Goldman raised the need for new units which reflect an index of exposure. There is nothing terribly offensive to building environmental health policy around the applicability of indices of exposure. We are living in a sufficiently sophisticated era so that we can use joint exposures to two indices, in this case sulfur oxides and suspended particulate matter, as a guideline to what is a reasonable level, a hazardous level, or a probably innocuous level of power plant emissions.

Q: I would like to address this to the panel. Assuming for the moment that society needs or desires more electricity, and assuming that we have two practical methods, fossil fuel and nuclear, what is your qualitative and/or quantitative estimate of the risk relationship of the two in light of our present knowledge?

Dr. Goldman: I do not know the extent to which any real options still exist. Each of the preceding papers identified some limitations, so that by the time we establish the appropriate quantification to assess and balance the relative cost of one type of fuel to another in terms of health costs, the costs of obtaining it or utilizing it may change the entire equation. I attempted to get away from the more political or economic aspects and just concentrate on the relative ways of handling risk. In terms of mortality, a statistic over which there seems to be less dispute, I quoted the value that Chauncey Starr derived for oil—possibly 60 to 1 in favor of the nuclear. For coal the ratio may be higher. The assessment was based on one or a pair of the constituents of the effluent stream when in fact combustion of fossil fuels, by definition, will produce a mix that is going to be modified by the fuel source and the local environment. This is similar to computing the nuclear risk based solely on the strontium or cesium or the tritium radionuclides when in fact the total assessment is the weighted average of the mixture that is released.

Another point is that, to my knowledge, there are no effects demonstrated for consequences on health of nuclear power plant operations. There have been quite a few consequences alluded to with respect to other fuel sources. We have an unbalanced equation in terms of our "retrospectroscope" as it were, and we can only go at this by indirection. Thus there will be dispute depending upon the type of assumptions that go into making that assessment. On balance, I tend to agree with the studies that I quoted, that, if the standards are used, and solely on the basis of available experimental data plus what little epidemiological information there is, I feel more comfortable that a 60-to-1 ratio or an order of magnitude difference in assessment may not be totally out of reason.

Dr. Goldsmith: Dr. Goldman, many of whose statements I fully agree with, has cited Chauncey Starr's 60-to-1 assessment with which I totally disagree. Starr has constructed this ratio by citing some oral reports on Conley that were not published, for which the author is no longer connected with the agency, and for which the agency itself has withdrawn its endorsement. He has contrived a series of implausible events and has talked about the health hazards of large-scale oil fires that were not relevant to power generation. In short, I think that the 60-to-1 ratio is not based on science but is based on the value system of Mr. Starr. This question involves both science and values, both evidence (the objective and critical evaluation of which is the qualified scientist's responsibility) and the social and the political processes of deciding what society ought to do. Chauncey Starr is as well qualified to evaluate air pollution health effects as I am to design a safe power plant—and I am not proposing to design power plants.

On the other hand, this task is not one that should be left to casual disputation or to people whose interests are on one side or the other. I am not a proponent or opponent of either fossil fuel or nuclear power plants. I believe that the process and problem of getting a comparative statement of these yardsticks, for which is better and which is preferable from the health point of view, is a very serious undertaking. As far as I can tell, it has not been seriously engaged in by the people who are qualified to be objective in it. I feel that the decisions and the evaluations have to take into account not only the difference between fossil fuel and nuclear fuel but where the plant is located, how it is designed, how it is operated, how the effects are monitored, and the need for the resources that go into the plant as well as the energy that comes out of it. Now that process has got to be engaged in systematically, objectively, and with plenty of opportunity for critical evaluation.

Dr. Goldman: I would like to comment briefly on this ratio of 60 to 1 before it gets set into stone. The data that I utilized were not based solely on Starr's analysis but on the fact that, per megawatt of electrical energy production, the only viable fossil fuel option ahead seems to be our coal resources and none of the other fossil fuels. And if, under normal operations, the radioactivity emission from coal burning equals the radioactivity emission of nuclear power plants, then an additional amount of risk or health costs is going to be associated with some number higher than that for equal risks from radiation sources for all of the additional effluents—the SO_2 and NO_x. Therefore one adds to the comparable base radiation value any further risk that you wish to associate with the particulates and oxides. It was on the basis of this that I felt at least an order of magnitude or more difference would be reasonable and prudent at this time.

Dr. Charles Gaylord: Dr. Morris, I am from Colorado and I have just listened to a lengthy group of hearings before the State Board of Health of the State of Colorado. CER Nuclear takes the position that in phase one of the Rio Blanco project there is absolutely no risk whatsoever. This refusal to assign any risk shook up the Board of Health considerably and struck some of the staff of the health department as being scientifically unacceptable. I think the board was left with the impression that they also refused to discuss full field development, and it was related to the fact that, if you assign any risk to the first shot, by the time you got up to 400 or 500 shots there may be,an unacceptable risk. But the question I had is simply this: The amount of money that has gone into the building of nuclear reactors and making them safe, as you detailed so well for us, represents a fantastically large investment on the part of the people of the United States. We are concerned about the Rio Blanco affair in Colorado because if you do not assign any risk to it, there is nothing to discuss about it as far as safety is concerned. But, should CER Nuclear be wrong, what would be the impact on the nuclear reactor program of a large escape of radioactivity from the Rio Blanco project, which offers rather relatively small gains in terms of energy resources with reference to the nuclear reactor problem?

Dr. Morris: I am totally unqualified to talk about the gas stimulation project, and I could not begin to talk about its risk. Really your question is what would be the effect of the nuclear power industry if there were a release there, and any answer would have to be speculative. I am sure we would have some impact, but I would also point out, just as a layman, that there have been many tests at the Nevada test site; so one does have some experience and one should be able to estimate the risks. Let me make this personal statement, I am surprised that any technically competent organization would say there were zero risks and mean absolute zero.

Dr. Rose: Over the last year or two, it has been my unhappy experience to come across a number of places in the United States where the combination of particulates (SO_2, NO_x, and things like that) has been very, very much different from the normal and, in my personal opinion, much in excess of the ambient standards. These places tend to have been in Appalachia, in Rockwood, Tennessee, Charleston, West Virginia, and very lately a place with the strange name of California, Pennsylvania, which is a college town of 6,000 students in the Monongahela Valley. But when one goes there it does not take a very complex analysis to discover there is something seriously wrong in those places. The people complain of it, and you can see it with your own eyes and feel it with your own throat. People there have personal histories of wretched circumstance living in such valleys. You said this morning that there are really no overall studies going on as to the epidemiology of such places. Is that really true? To a layman like me the evidence seems so close to the surface. Could anybody comment on that?

Dr. Eisenbud: I think the thinness of our epidemiological base is nothing short of a national disgrace. I put this failing squarely on the shoulders of the governmental medical research community because of its failure to appreciate the enormous economic impact of the decisions that are being made and the need to train young people to go out and undertake the necessary studies. Now there has been some good epidemiology done, and John Goldsmith has done much of it, but it has been a case of driving a spike with a tack hammer.

Let me tell you about New York City. In 1965 the hourly maximum SO_2 concentration was 2.3 ppm. That pattern had been repeated year after year for many years. The annual average SO_2 concentration was close to 0.3 ppm. We decided long before the federal EPA was formed that this was too high. On the basis of the advice that we had, we set 0.1 ppm as a target level for an annual ambient figure and an hourly maximum of something like 0.5 ppm. We had essentially achieved that goal in 1969, when we were told by the federal government that the target that we established was not good enough, and that we would be required to lower it to an annual average of 0.03 ppm. We demonstrated that the city was already spending about $50 million a year in additional fuel costs in order to achieve the level that we had reached by that time. For a relatively modest additional investment we could get to 0.06 ppm. Governor Rockefeller and Mayor Lindsay sent representatives to Washington to see if 0.06 ppm would be acceptable on an interim basis while epidemiological studies were conducted in New York City to determine if there was any need for further reduction. It was argued that to move the standard from 0.06 to 0.03 would cost perhaps $100 million a year in a city where we could not get enough money for rat control, elimination of lead poisoning, and correction of deficiencies in housing. We were told that the city would be required to go to 0.03 ppm, for which 0.3% sulfur oil would be needed. In my opinion, this has imposed enormous additional costs on both the private and public sectors for a commensurate benefit which has not been identified to my satisfaction. In answer to your question, Dr. Rose, if we cannot get the kind of epidemiology we need in the face of a decision to spend $100 million per year for increased desulfurization, what can one expect in the communities you mentioned?

Dr. Forrest E. Rieke: Dr. Goldsmith, one of the things that impressed me in England last summer and this winter was that they did double their use of electricity. They have not changed the power station situation much. They have 180 coal burning and 14 nuclear stations. I was interested in your bronchitis figure because you certainly cannot get around in London anymore with automobiles because of the huge build up of motor cars. If bronchitis has changed, quite possibly it is because they did pass a law that said, "You have to quit using coal in homes for space warming and space heating." Now, Dr. Goldman, how can one compare the impact of oil spill on the ocean all around England with what happened to bronchitis because they quit using coal to heat and to cook with. These things are extremely complicated and extremely difficult to measure.

Dr. Goldsmith: First, I think much more epidemiologic work is needed. I think it has been grossly inadequately supported, and if we make decisions in its absence, we are making them at peril either to health or resources. Secondly, I was speaking to the problem of what kind of new power plants we build. I was not speaking to the effects of existing heat and power generation by small inefficient poorly managed operations. There is detectable damage from the existing use of energy resources in this country, even though efforts to detect it have been inadequate. But the fact that this is true does not mean that we do not know how to build good power plants and operate them with relatively little health risks. Those are my major points.

Q: Dr. Eisenbud, did I hear you correctly when you said that solid waste is not a pollutant?

Dr. Eisenbud: The technology for handling the low radiation level solid wastes generated by the reactor is well in hand, and the packaging and transportation techniques are regulated sufficiently well so that the public is not being exposed. I think you can say the same thing for the shipment of the spent fuel from the reactor to the fuel reprocessing center. The shipping casks have been designed in such a way that if necessary they could withstand catastrophic accidents without releasing radioactive material to the environs. The problem with which some people are concerned and which I, at this particular point in time, cannot accept as a problem, is the philosophical question of how one goes about storing the high level wastes, many components of which have half-lives on the order of 10,000 years or longer, in literal perpetuity, recognizing that there may be social upheavals, there may be natural disasters, glaciations, who knows what, that could redistribute the material which is being stored. Now the reason I feel that it is not a problem yet is that, first of all, the total amounts of material that we are talking about are very small. With the kinds of packaging requirements established by the AEC, the high level wastes generated by the nuclear power industry will be in a solid refractory form that would occupy a volume much smaller than the volume of this room by the year 2000.

The various techniques for converting the wastes to a refractory form and storing the wastes, with provision for retrieval if necessary, are being studied. One of the techniques that has been proposed is storage in dry salt mines. Other techniques are available. My own view is that the safest method on an interim basis would be to simply convert them to a refractory form, glasslike or ceramic, and store them above ground where you can get at them if necessary during the next several decades. We are dealing with relatively small volumes. Let's study the problem and then, in that interim period, perhaps we can think through the philosophical problems associated with the question of how one goes about storing something in perpetuity.

V

SOCIOECONOMIC
CONSIDERATIONS

16

Health Costs to the Consumer per Megawatt-Hour of Electricity*

Lester B. Lave, Ph.D. and Linnea C. Freeburg, Sc.B.

     Miners, other fuel workers, and the general public experience adverse health effects due to electricity generation. During the 20th century, much has been done to lower the occupational hazards and curb emissions, but the results have not been satisfactory as shown by federal, state and local legislation and by professional and public interest. The problem is not one of getting more stringent legislation to lower these risks; indeed, current legislation is quite sufficient to handle these "externalities." Instead, the problem is to gain the knowledge that will enable us to make intelligent decisions about the amount of power we want, the locating of generating facilities, and the type of fuel that should be used. These are not problems that can be answered by slogans such as "no environmental degradation," "only the cleanest fuel will be acceptable," and "no adverse health effects will be tolerated." To answer these questions well we must have detailed knowledge of the effects of alternative methods of generating electricity, including the cost of each. We view this study as a small part of this larger analysis.

     This study is focused on the public health effects of electricity generation, including a detailed comparison of the effects of the three principal fuels. Only light-water reactors (LWR) will be considered. Before describing these public health effects, we summarize the occupational hazards associated with extracting coal, uranium, and oil and with refining the latter two fuels to get them into the proper form for generation.

     The accident and chronic disease rates for coal miners are high.[1-16] Similar problems plague uranium miners, although their chronic disease stems from silicosis and cancer, rather than pneumoconiosis.[1,17-26] Oil drilling, production, and refining do not have important chronic disease rates, although the

---

* This study was supported by a grant from Resources for the Future, Inc. A longer version of the paper will appear in *Nuclear Safety*. Any errors and opinions are those of the authors. We thank Charles R. Adkins, Robert W. Dunlap, Andrew P. Hull, Claude G. Poncelet, and Edward S. Rubin.

210

accident rates are significant.[27] Elsewhere we have analyzed the accident and disease rates for these fuels.[28] Per megawatt-hour of electricity, the accident disability rates for uranium mining and milling and for oil drilling, production, and refining are similar, although coal mining offers ten times the risk. Per megawatt-hour of electricity, the excess mortality from chronic disease among coal miners appears to be about 18 times that among uranium miners.

In addition to extraction accidents and diseases, other occupational health effects stem from the transportation of fuels, the generation of the electricity itself, and, for light-water reactors, the fuel processing, reprocessing, and waste storage.[29-39] Accident and chronic disease rates are not available for many of these activities. However, some data exist on radiation exposure to employees in the nuclear power industry,[40] from which radiation-induced cancer rates may be estimated. In looking at all occupational health effects for which data are available, coal has a considerably higher health cost than either uranium or oil per megawatt-hour of electricity generated. Comparing the occupational health effects of the latter two fuels is more difficult; however, miner silicosis and radiation exposure in the nuclear power industry appear to tip the balance toward greater health risks for uranium, per megawatt-hour.

The chronic disease comparisons above are for coal and uranium mined underground under current conditions. Improved safety measures stemming from recent legislation, the increase in strip mining, and the development of automated deep-mining techniques may have significant effects in reducing the occupational health risks for coal. Regulations governing the exposure of uranium miners to radioactivity should lower their chronic disease risk. All of our data and comparisons concern existing facilities. While this means that the comparisons are already out of date,[41-47] they still provide the best evidence of the health effects of each process.

The normal operation of electric power plants, both nuclear and fossil-fueled, results in the release of heat, radioactivity, and chemical pollutants. The latter two effluents have direct public health effects, which will be compared. Venting heat has ecological effects, but, since no direct human health effects are produced, this effluent is not analyzed here.

RADIOACTIVE AND CHEMICAL EFFLUENTS

The generation of electricity from burning coal produces a major proportion of the SO_2, NO_x, and suspended particulates in those cities where coal is the principal fuel.[48-52] In addition, trace amounts of heavy metals and carcinogenic hydrocarbons, such as benzo(a)pyrene, are released.[53-55] Trace amounts of radioactivity in the form of thorium, uranium, and radium are present in coal ash; the amount emitted into the air is inversely proportional to the efficiency of the ash collection mechanism.[56-57]

Most nuclear reactors currently being built are either of the boiling-water type (BWR) or the pressurized-water type (PWR). Most currently operating BWRs release much more gaseous radioactivity, generally in the form of noble gases, while PWRs release more liquid radioactive waste, principally tritium. A small amount of radioiodine is also released in gaseous effluent, particularly by current BWRs.* [58-62]

A number of studies have attempted to compare the radioactive and chemical pollutants released per unit of electricity generated from fossil fuel-burning and nuclear plants.[50,51,56,57,63-66] These releases depend on the type of reactor, the composition of the fuel, the efficiency of the ash collection equipment for fossil fuel-burning plants, and the differing waste treatment systems.

Martin, Harward, and Oakley [57] presented a careful comparison of radioactive stack releases from power plants, extending earlier work by Eisenbud and Petrow.[56] The amounts of radioactive material released by oil-burning generators are almost undetectable. In comparing coal-burning generators with nuclear generators, problems arise because the radioactive release takes such different forms. Some of the radium and thorium isotopes released from coal combustion are extremely long-lived and chemically active. The radionuclides in the ash that are water soluble are assumed to pose a threat to bone, while those that are insoluble are considered to present a threat to the lungs. For nuclear plants, the whole-body exposure from noble gases released from the stack is considered most significant. These isotopes are relatively short-lived compared to ^{226}Ra in coal ash.

For coal-fired and nuclear power plants, Martin et al [57] calculated the dose that a new 1,000-megawatt of electrical power (Mw(e)) plant would give to individuals in the vicinity of the plants under specified meteorological conditions. To take account of the different forms of radioactive effluent, they calculated the dose as a fraction of the maximum permissible dose recommended by the International Commission on Radiological Protection (ICRP), with a correction for the effect of different stack heights on distribution of radioactivity. Their results, based on 1968 and 1969 data, indicated that a coal-burning plant would apparently pose about 410 times the threat of a PWR, while a BWR would pose about 180 times the threat of a coal-burning plant, in terms of radioactive releases through the stack.

Terrill, Harward, and Leggett [51] compared power plants in terms of the volume of air that would be required to dilute their stack effluents each year in order to meet conventionally accepted concentration standards. Hull [63] updated these dilution factors, making use of radioactive emissions from a much larger sample of plants and imposing a more stringent standard on the concentration of chemical pollutants.† Based on 1969 releases, these factors cor-

---

* The most recently designed BWRs are expected to release much lower quantities of gaseous effluent, as provision has been made for much longer holdup of these effluents before release to allow most of the radioactivity to decay, as is currently practiced at operating PWRs. In addition, application of the recently proposed stricter discharge limits can be expected to reduce the quantities of radioactive effluents discharged from the light-water reactors having the highest release levels.[44] Similarly, coal gasification and air pollution abatement measures will lead to much lower releases of air pollutants from plants burning fossil fuels.

† These studies, based on quantities being emitted from the stack rather than on doses provided, do not allow for differential residence times of pollutants in the atmosphere.

roborated the conclusion reached by Martin et al that the radioactivity released from coal-burning plants was more significant than that from PWRs, but less significant than that from BWRs. Since that time, however, Hull has further updated these factors to reflect 1967 to 1971 nuclear power plant releases and more recent standards for air pollutant concentrations.* Included in his study were SO_2, NO_2, CO, hydrocarbons, particulates, and various radionuclides; however, only SO_2, particulates, and the radionuclides will receive attention in this report. The updated dilution factors for these pollutants are presented in Table 23, except that the discharge quantities for light-water reactors have been

Table 23
Volume of Air Required to Meet Concentration Standards for Yearly Emission from a 1,000-Mw(e) Plant

Type of Plant	Pollutant	Standard**	Discharge Quantity	Dilution Volume (10^9 m^3)	
Coal	SO_2 (3.5% S)	80 $\mu g/m^3$	3.06×10^8 lb.	1.77×10^6	
	Particulates (97.5% Removal) (15% Ash)	75 $\mu g/m^3$	9.9×10^6 lb.	6.0×10^4	
	Particulates — ^{226}Ra	2 pCi/m^3	0.0172 Ci	8.6	
	Particulates — ^{228}Ra	1 pCi/m^3	0.0108 Ci	10.8	
Oil	SO_2 (1.6% S)	80 $\mu g/m^3$	1.16×10^8 lb.	6.58×10^5	
	Particulates (0.05% Ash)	75 $\mu g/m^3$	1.6×10^6 lb.	9700	
	Particulates — ^{226}Ra	2 pCi/m^3	1.5×10^{-4} Ci	0.075	
	Particulates — ^{228}Ra	1 pCi/m^3	3.5×10^{-4} Ci	0.35	
Gas	SO_2	80 $\mu g/m^3$	3×10^4 lb.	170	
	Particulates	75 $\mu g/m^3$	1.0×10^6 lb.	6050	
Nuclear (LWRs)	^{85}Kr and ^{133}Xe Short lived radioactive	3×10^5 pCi/m^3	1.6×10^4 Ci	55	PWR
	noble gases	3×10^4 pCi/m^3	1.33×10^6 Ci	4.4×10^4	BWR
	^{131}I	100 pCi/m^3 (Inhalation)	0.15 Ci	1.5	PWR
			6.6 Ci	66	BWR
		0.14 pCi/m^3†† (Air-Grass-Milk)	0.15 Ci	1060	PWR
			6.6 Ci	4.7×10^4	BWR

** Environmental Protection Agency National Primary Ambient Air Quality Standards,[67] and Atomic Energy Commission "Standards for Protection Against Radiation," 10 CFR 20.[68]

†† A reduction factor of 700 is applied to the inhalation standard for ^{131}I to allow for reconcentration via the air-grass-milk route.

recalculated to reflect only 1971 releases. According to these more recent calculations, SO_2 from coal-fired plants is the residual requiring the most dilution.† The SO_2 from oil-fired plants requires less than half as much dilution; that from gas-fired plants, substantially less. Particulates from coal-fired plants and radionuclides from a BWR lacking extended stack gas hold-up also require a

* Personal communication from Andrew P. Hull, Brookhaven National Laboratory.
† The figure for sulfur dioxide emissions from coal combustion, based on coal with a 3.5% sulfur content, overstates the level of emissions that is currently tolerated in major cities.

significant amount of dilution. However, the 1971 radioactive releases from both PWRs and BWRs would appear to be more significant biologically than that from coal-fired plants (unlike previous comparisons), but less important than the release of SO_2.

The above comparison is based on concentration standards that are not necessarily equally stringent for chemical air pollutants and radionuclides. Relative to concentrations at which effects on human health have been inferred from epidemiological studies, the concentration standards for radionuclides appear to be more conservative than those for chemical air pollutants.[66] In order to meet this difficulty, an attempt will be made to evaluate the relative hazards to individuals of long-term exposure to these pollutants at the specified concentration standards, by using mortality risks derived from such epidemiological studies. The relative mortality risks of airborne effluents from fossil-fueled and nuclear power plants will then be estimated. While morbidity (illness) risks would be expected as well, they are more difficult to quantify, and will not be included in the analysis for this reason.

HEALTH EFFECTS OF RADIOACTIVITY

The amounts of radioactive material released from power plants are typically very small relative to background and medical radiation. While large doses of radiation have been found to increase risk of death from leukemia and other cancers, as well as the risk of genetic damage, little work has been done which gives evidence for effects of such low-level dosage.[69-71]

A number of investigators have attempted to quantify the relationship between radiation dose and cancer, on the basis of data on Japanese survivors of the atomic bomb, noncancer patients treated medically with radiation, and occupationally exposed groups. Assuming a linear dose-response relationship, the National Academy of Sciences' Committee on the Biological Effects of Ionizing Radiation has estimated that an additional 100 milliroentgen equivalents man (mrem) of radiation above background per year per person would produce between 2,000 and 9,000 extra deaths from cancer per year in the United States, the most likely estimate being 3,500.[72] It is estimated that 1 rem to bone from ^{226}Ra will produce 0.11 to 0.16 cases of bone cancer per million irradiated adults per year. The risk to bone from ^{90}Sr is considered to be lower. The estimate for 1 rem to the stomach is 0.32 to 0.64 deaths per million per year; for 1 rem to the remainder of the gastrointestinal tract, 0.22 to 0.44 deaths per million per year. No estimate was made by the NAS Committee for the risk to skin because there is insufficient evidence for skin cancer induction by low-dose levels. For the lung, 1 rem to the bronchi is estimated to produce 1 case of bronchial cancer per million per year. For a dose to the thyroid, Otway and Erdmann have estimated a mortality risk per rem of one person per million exposed for all ages, with a 1 rem threshold.[73] Calculations of radiation effects in this paper will be based on these estimates, except that no threshold will be assumed.

The 10 CFR concentration standards utilized in the Martin et al and Hull studies have been set by the Atomic Energy Commission at levels which would limit dosage to exposed individuals from any one radionuclide to 500 mrem per year, in the case of exposure to the whole body; for many radionuclides, the standards reflect limits on doses to particular organs, with doses higher than 500 mrem per year permitted in some cases.[68,74] Thus, continuous exposure to whole body radiation from noble gases at the concentration limit would entail a mortality risk to individuals of 90×10^{-6} per year (according to the National Academy of Sciences mortality estimate). The concentration standard for ^{131}I limits the dose to the thyroid from inhalation of this radionuclide. However, a stricter limit by a factor of 700 is applied to ^{131}I when allowing for reconcentration via the air-grass-milk route. At the latter concentration of ^{131}I in the air, there is a potential dose to the thyroid of 500 mrem per year to infants from milk, with a lower dose to older individuals; [75,76] the average mortality risk for all ages from this concentration would be less than 0.5×10^{-6} per year.

HEALTH EFFECTS OF AIR POLLUTION *

The association between air pollution and ill health is well documented.[78-80] It is easy to document the adverse health effects of high concentrations of chemical pollutants in laboratory experiments, but it is much more difficult to show that ill health results from the low levels of chemical pollutants currently present in our air. In order to prove that the observed association between air pollution and ill health is not spurious, every factor known to affect health would have to be controlled, experimentally or statistically.

Lave and Seskin have explored this relationship, beginning with an examination of the association between the total mortality rate and air pollution in 117 U.S. cities in 1960.[79,81-85] The basic regression, taken from Reference 77 is shown in Table 24. In this ad hoc regression, 82.7% of the total variation in the mortality rate across the 117 cities is explained. The relation is a linear equation that predicts the mortality rate in a city on the basis of air pollution in the city (particulate levels and SO_2 levels as reflected in sulfate data), the population density, the proportion of nonwhites in the population, and the proportion of the population 65 years of age or older.[86-88] Values are given for the estimated coefficients of the variables; the figures in parentheses are the *t* statistics for a test that the explanatory variable has no effect (the estimated coefficient is not significantly different from zero). With the exception of population density, all coefficients are extremely significant. Another way of viewing the estimates is to ask how much the mortality rate varies with a 10% increase in one of the variables used in the analysis; these values are shown as "sensitivity coefficients" in Table 25. These results show that the mortality rate is significantly related to air pollution and that a 10% increase in air pollution (particulates + sulfates) is associated with an increase in the mortality rate of 0.90% (0.53 + 0.37).

---

* Only health effects will be discussed here. Air pollutants have many other deleterious effects, as discussed in Reference 77.

Table 24

$$MR_i = 19.607 + 0.041 \text{ mean } P_i + 0.071 \text{ min } S_i + 0.001 \text{ P/M}_i^2 + 0.041\% \text{ NW}_i + 0.687\% \geqslant 65_i + e_i \quad (1)$$
$$\quad\quad\quad (2.53) \quad\quad\quad (3.18) \quad\quad\quad (1.67) \quad\quad (5.81) \quad\quad\quad (18.94)$$

Where MR_i = total mortality rate (per 10,000 people) in city i,
 mean P_i = arithmetic mean of suspended particulate readings in city i,
 min S_i = smallest biweekly sulfate reading in city i ($\times$10),
 P/M_i^2 = population density in city i,
 % NW_i = proportion of the population which is nonwhite in city i ($\times$10),
 % $\geqslant 65_i$ = proportion of the population 65 and older in city i ($\times$10),
 e_i = error term for variation in the mortality rate not explained by the equation

Table 25

Independent Variable	Estimated Increase in Total Mortality Rate
Mean P	0.53%
Min S	0.37%
P/M²	0.07%
% N-W	0.57%
% ≥ 65	6.32%

This basic relationship has been elaborated and explored in a number of ways. Equation (1) was replicated with 1961 and 1969 data; 28 different age-race-sex specific mortality rates and 14 disease specific mortality rates were explored for 1960 and 1961, and explanatory variables for various socioeconomic phenomena were added. The form of the relationship was checked for linearity and split sample analyses were performed; it was found that various mortality rates and disease rates that one would not expect to be caused by air pollution were not statistically associated with it. In addition, daily time series data were explored, the analysis tending to corroborate the cross-section data. A possible interaction between sulfates and particulates was investigated but not found to be significant for these data.

The implication in Equation (1) is that a 50% decrease in air pollution is estimated to lower the mortality rate by 4.5%. Another way of translating the results is to note that if we assume that the reduction in air pollution would have the same effect on morbidity as on mortality (which is certainly a very conservative estimate), we could reduce the economic cost of morbidity and mortality by just under $9 billion per year.[77]

The estimates of the effect of air pollution that will be used are those from the 1969 replication, using data for 89 cities, with SO_2 data substituted for sulfates. The regression coefficients will be used to estimate the mortality risk of exposure to air pollutants at the Environmental Protection Agency (EPA) primary concentration standards utilized in Hull's study. According to these coefficients, an additional microgram per cubic meter of mean particulate concentration is associated with an increased mortality of 0.085 per 10,000 per year, while an additional microgram per cubic meter of mean SO_2 concentration is associated with an increased mortality of 0.039 per 10,000 per year.* Thus, long-term exposure to mean concentrations of these pollutants at the EPA primary standards implies an increased mortality risk to individuals of 638 X 10^{-6} per year for particulates and 312 X 10^{-6} per year for SO_2. The primary standards for SO_2 and particulates thus appear to carry many times the mortality risk of the AEC standards for radionuclides.

RELATIVE MORTALITY RISKS FROM AIRBORNE POWER PLANT EFFLUENTS

An abstract comparison will be made between the airborne emissions of a 1,000-Mw(e) coal-burning power plant and a 1000-Mw(e) light-water reactor based on the mortality risks estimated above. The method used by Terrill et al and Hull will be followed in that an arbitrary dilution volume will be assumed for the emissions of both plants, 1.77 X 10^{15} m³ of air per year, the dilution at which the SO_2 from a 1,000-Mw(e) plant burning 3.5% sulfur coal is assumed to meet the primary standard. The dilution volume chosen is not important to the conclusions since both chemical air pollution and radiation dose-response relationships are assumed to be linear over the range under consideration, only relative risks are being estimated, and both plants are assumed to be occupying the same site.

The mortality risk per year for individuals continuously exposed to gaseous effluent at the specified dilution from a plant burning 3.5% sulfur coal with 15% ash is estimated to be 334 X 10^{-6} (312 X 10^{-6} from SO_2 and 22 X 10^{-6} from particulates). The inclusion of other pollutants in this estimate, such as benzo(a)pyrene, would be expected to add an increment to this risk, and synergistic effects would also play a role. For gaseous effluent from a BWR with 30-minute hold-up, the estimated risk per year at the same dilution is 2.25 X 10^{-6} (2.24 X 10^{-6} from noble gases and less than 0.013 X 10^{-6} from ^{131}I, via the air-grass-milk route), and from a PWR less than 0.0031 X 10^{-6} (0.0028 X 10^{-6} from noble gases and less than 0.0003 X 10^{-6} from ^{131}I). Thus, within the limits of the assumptions made, the emissions from the coal-burning power plant are estimated to present a mortality risk approximately 150 times the risk from airborne effluents of a BWR and approximately 110,000 times the risk from the airborne effluents of a PWR. For emissions of a plant burning 1.5% sulfur coal, the corresponding figures are estimated to be 69 and 50,000 times, respectively (assuming the same ash content), and for emissions of the same plant removing 75% of the SO_2 via stack gas scrubbing methods, the estimates are 24 and 18,000 times, respectively.

---

* The measure of ambient SO_2, which was most significantly associated with mortality in 1969, was the minimum biweekly reading. However, since the mean concentration was of greater interest in the above calculation, the relationship was reestimated by using the SO_2 reading. While the regression coefficient for mean SO_2 was not statistically significant, its magnitude was reasonably relative to the coefficient for minimum SO_2 concentration.

At the same dilution, the emissions from a plant burning 1.6% sulfur oil with 0.05% ash would present an estimated mortality risk to exposed individuals of about 119×10^{-6} per year (116.0×10^{-6} from SO_2 and 3.5×10^{-6} from particulates), about 53 times the risk from BWR stack effluents, and about 39,000 times the risk from PWR stack effluents. For 0.2% sulfur oil, the corresponding figures would be 8.0 and 5,800 times, respectively, and for 0.2% sulfur oil with 75% of the SO_2 removed, the estimates would be 3.2 and 2,300 times respectively.

The dilution factor method of comparing power plant emissions can provide only a first approximation of their relative health effects, as any other factors affecting pollutant concentration or dispersion, such as different residence times in the atmosphere or different stack heights, are completely ignored. Another problem of the comparison is the crudeness of the dose-response estimates for both radiation and air pollution. For the above reasons, not much confidence can be placed in the difference between the calculated mortality effects of emissions from fossil fuel-burning plants and most current BWRs. However, the difference between the estimates for fossil fuel-burning plants and PWRs is strong enough to justify a conclusion that the airborne emissions of PWRs (and BWRs, if they are provided with longer hold-up facilities) are substantially less dangerous to human health.

Ideally, a comparison of health effects of generating power from different fuels would consider not only the quantities of pollutants emitted per year but also their dispersion patterns, half-lives, and ambient concentrations in the environment. Meteorology and terrain would be important factors to take into account. Population distribution at various distances from a site would have to be known in order to estimate average doses received by the public.

Such a procedure requires extensive data collection regarding actual sites. Numerous studies have measured concentrations of air pollutants at various distances from fossil fuel-burning plants.[89] With respect to nuclear power plants, Gamertsfelder has estimated a maximum value for the average annual radiation doses received from 1969 noble gas effluents by members of the public within various distances of 13 plants.[90] These calculations were based on the percent of noble gases released relative to the amount permitted that year for each plant, the latter being the quantity which, under adverse meteorological conditions, would have been expected to deliver a dose of no more than 500 mrem per year to individuals located at the plant boundary. Population distributions and wind speeds were taken into account. While comparison of the results of these separate studies for fossil-fueled and nuclear power plants would be desirable, it would be difficult to carry out because of differences in meteorology and other factors at the individual sites and, accordingly, will not be attempted here.

However, these comparisons are precisely what should be done in an environmental impact statement for a new power generating facility—that is, the effluents of power plants of alternative designs and fuels should be more carefully evaluated to estimate the doses of noxious materials that would be experienced by the public. These doses must be evaluated for their public health effects by using dose-response curves, such as those previously presented.

An attempt in this direction has been made by Bergström,[65] who compared anticipated emissions from power plants of alternative designs being considered for sites in Sweden. Expected population exposure to radiation from a nuclear power plant and to SO_2 from a plant burning 1% sulfur oil were compared for a range of sites by means of dose-response curves, which he estimated for both types of exposure. According to his calculations, the health effects of the nuclear power plant would be smaller than those from the oil-fired station by a factor of 10^4 or more. Since the dose-response curves that he estimated were derived from acute rather than long-term effects, and since population exposure to SO_2 was calculated indirectly, on the basis of dispersion characteristics of tritium, these estimates need to be further refined. However, they serve to indicate the type of comparison that needs to be made.

A maximum value for mortality from noble gas effluents of nuclear power plants can be obtained by using Gamertsfelder's calculations, referred to above. Adjusted according to 1971 release rates, the average dose per year received by the population within 50 miles of a 1,000-Mw(e) plant at a typical site would not be expected to exceed 0.36 mrem per person for a BWR or 0.020 for a PWR, with an estimated risk of 0.065 or 0.0036 extra death from cancer per million exposed persons per year for a BWR and PWR, respectively. For an average population of 2.5 million within 50 miles of the LWRs, 0.16 extra death or less from cancer would be expected per year from noble gases from a typical 1,000-Mw(e) BWR and 0.009 extra death or less in the case of a PWR.*

The maximum dose to individuals from ^{131}I, via the air-grass-milk route, can be estimated in the same way. In 1971 the estimated maximum dose (to the thyroid) from ^{131}I discharged by a nuclear power plant averaged about 0.6 and 2 times the maximum dose (to the whole body) from noble gases from a BWR and PWR respectively.† If the average doses from ^{131}I and noble gases are assumed to be in the same ratio as their maximum doses, the ^{131}I doses would be expected to add less than 1% to the mortality from light-water reactors.

LIQUID EFFLUENTS FROM NUCLEAR POWER PLANTS

Liquid releases for reactors were not treated in the above analysis because of the difficulty of estimating dose rates. The short-run problem does not

---

* These calculations are based on very conservative meteorological assumptions. More realistic assumptions would reduce the mortality estimates. The proposed restriction of maximum dosage from LWR effluents to 5 mrem/year would also serve to reduce the mortality estimates.[44] A number of systems are under development which may virtually eliminate either liquid or gaseous radioactive release to the environment from nuclear power plants.[45]

† While radiation from noble gases has been detected in the air in the vicinity of Dresden I Nuclear Power Station, corresponding to a dose rate of 5 to 15 mrem/year, the concentrations in milk of ^{131}I from either Dresden I or Yankee Nuclear Power Stations have been too low to be detectable.[61,62,91]

seem important, relative to the doses from airborne releases; [61,62,91-94] however, the longer-lived radionuclides from both liquid and airborne releases accumulate over time and will present more of a problem in the future.[45]

OTHER PUBLIC HEALTH EFFECTS OF NUCLEAR FUEL

Accidental releases from light water reactors are a possibility,[73,74,95-100] even though there is no possibility of an atomic-bomb-type of explosion. Some estimates have been published of the probability of accidental releases of specified amounts of radionuclides.[73] While it is difficult to estimate and work with really small numbers of the sort cited, it does seem evident that the health risk associated with accidental releases is small relative to that from routine releases.[66]

The vast proportion of radionuclides produced in light-water reactors are not released, but are concentrated and stored. As the number of reactors grows, so will the amount of stored wastes (some of which have half-lives of millions of years). Several ways have been proposed to store this material,[30,101,102] but there is not yet any way that has proved satisfactory.

The reprocessing of spent fuel elements at the only commercial reprocessing plant in operation has resulted in the release of relatively large amounts of ^{85}Kr, tritium, ^{90}Sr, and ^{137}Cs.[46,103-108]* Detectable amounts of the exceedingly long-lived ^{129}I have also been released.[107] While these releases appear to be more significant than those from a light-water reactor, a substantial amount of uranium is recovered from the spent fuel.[30,105] The health effects of these releases do not appear to be as important as the occupational health effects of mining, milling, and processing an equivalent amount of uranium.[28]

Radioactive effluents are also released from uranium mines and mills, and plants involved in feed materials production, isotopic enrichment, and fuel fabrication.[30,40] However, population exposure from these effluents is considered to be much less significant than that from power and reprocessing plants.

SUMMARY AND CONCLUSIONS

To compare the health effects of generating electricity from alternative fuels, the systems effects of the fuel cycles must be considered. For example, the cycle for coal consists of exploration, mining, transportation, power generation, and ash removal; for nuclear fuel, the processes of exploration, mining, milling, fuel preparation, transportation, power generation, and disposal of radioactive wastes are included (as well as a subcycle in which reprocessing of spent fuel substitutes for the mining and milling of fresh ore). The entire cycles, rather

---

* Recently installed equipment has reduced the amount of ^{90}Sr and ^{137}Cs released.[46,105] In addition, other reprocessing plants under construction have been designed in such a way that there will be no routine discharge of liquid effluents to the environment. (Tritium will continue to be released, through the stack.) [47]

than simply the power generation phase, must be compared for their health effects.

Some tentative conclusions emerge from a comparison of the main components of the cycles for coal and uranium. Occupational health effects from accidents and chronic disease are substantially greater for coal mining than for uranium mining and milling per megawatt of power generated. While complete data are not available on accident and disability rates for other phases of the fuel cycles, the differences between coal and uranium are unlikely to be important compared with the estimated differences from mining and milling.

Comparing the effluents from power generation is more difficult. Both nuclear and coal-burning power plants discharge radioactivity into the environment in amounts that have little effect on background radiation levels; the small proportion of radium and thorium in coal that is released into the air seems to be less significant than the noble gases and ^{131}I from a BWR or PWR. When liquid effluents and effluents from reprocessing plants and other phases in the uranium cycle are added to the comparison, it becomes still clearer that the total radioactive release from the uranium cycle is more significant than that from the coal cycle. However, coal-fired generators are a major source of chemical air pollutants, which have been shown to be harmful to health.

Thus, a comparison of the total health effects of generating electricity from the two fuels depends on weighing the adverse effects of air pollution from coal combustion and the excess accident and chronic disease disability from coal mining against the excess radioactivity released from the atomic power industry. To accomplish this, one would need dose-response curves for both the radioactive and chemical effluents. Estimates of both dose-response curves have been published, although there is still considerable debate on the effect of low-level, long-term exposure to either air pollution or radiation.

In the work reported here, airborne releases were compared in terms of the dilution volume of air that would be required to meet recommended concentration standards and in terms of relative mortality risks to individuals exposed to these effluents at a specified dilution, as estimated from the dose-response curves. In the most conservative comparison considered, a PWR appears to offer 18,000 times less health risk than a coal-burning power plant, while a BWR with a 30-minute hold-up of stack gases appears to offer 24 times less health risk. Including effluents from other processes in the uranium cycle does not change the nature of the comparison, even when atmospheric build-up of ^{85}Kr from spent fuel reprocessing is considered. In view of uncertainties in the dose-response curves and differences in atmospheric residence times, which were omitted from the comparison, the factor of 24 between coal-burning plants and existing BWRs must be viewed as suggestive rather than conclusive.

Liquid releases from light-water reactors were not fully evaluated, since there is uncertainty about the size of the populations exposed by the various pathways and about the average doses received. However, since the population dose from these effluents is considered to be much smaller than the dose from airborne releases, it is unlikely that they would have much effect on the comparison.

The conclusion can thus be drawn that uranium offers lower risk than coal as a fuel, in both the extraction phase and the generation phase.

In comparing coal and oil as fuels, it is clear that the latter offers lower risks in both the extraction phase and the generation phase. Comparison of low-sulfur oil and uranium is less clearcut. The differences in the public health risks from power plant emissions favor the PWR; however, the lack of complete data for many phases in the fuel cycles makes it difficult to compare the occupational health risks from these fuels. Nevertheless, the occupational health risk per megawatt-hour appears to be higher for uranium because of miner silicosis and radiation exposure to employees in the nuclear power industry. Which of the two fuels has the more serious over-all health effects is difficult to determine because of the limitations imposed by the available data and the many assumptions, some of them arbitrary, made in comparing power plant emissions; therefore, such a comparison will not be attempted.

The relative health risks of airborne power plant effluents need to be compared for actual sites, controlling for such factors as stack height, meteorology, terrain, population distribution, and atmospheric half-lives of the pollutants emitted. Improved measures need to be obtained for the population doses received by various pathways from liquid effluents. More complete data are needed on radiation exposure to employees in the nuclear power industry. Also necessary are better dose response curves for both radioactivity and chemical pollutants. Much more work needs to be done to explore the toxic, mutagenic, and teratogenic properties of radionuclides in low concentrations. This work is not likely to be susceptible to laboratory experimentation; rather, careful epidemiological work is needed to measure the age-sex-race mortality rates and disease specific death rates for various groups, as well as their exposure to various radionuclides and other environmental insults.

The above comparisons have been based on current data and operating practice. Changes in such areas as mining techniques, mine safety regulations, reactor design, and effluent control methods can be expected to alter both occupational and public health risks from electricity generation in the future.

222

References

1. *Minerals Yearbook: 1970,* Government Printing Office, Washington, DC, US Bureau of Mines, 1972.

2. Crofton EC: A Study of Lung Cancer and Bronchitis Mortality in Relation to Coal-Mining in Scotland. *Brit J Prev Soc Med* **23:** 141–144, 1969.

3. Higgins ITT, et al: Respiratory Symptoms and Pulmonary Disability in an Industrial Town. *Brit Med J* **2:** 904–910, 1956.

4. Higgins ITT, Oldham PD: Ventilatory Capacity in Miners. *Brit J Ind Med* **19:** 65–76, 1962.

5. Higgins ITT, Cochrane AL: Chronic Respiratory Disease in a Random Sample of Men and Women in the Rhondda Fach in 1958. *Brit J Ind Med* **18:** 93–102, 1961.

6. Ryder R, et al: Emphysema in Coal Workers' Pneumoconiosis. *Brit Med J* **3:** 481–487, 1970.

7. Enterline PE: Mortality Rates among Coal Miners. *Amer J Pub Health* **54(5):** 758–768, May 1964.

8. Enterline P: The Effects of Occupation on Chronic Respiratory Disease. *Arch Environ Health* **14:** 189–200, 1967.

9. Enterline P, Lainhart W: The Relationship between Coal Mining and Chronic Nonspecific Respiratory Disease. *Amer J Pub Health* **57(3):** 484–495, 1967.

10. Enterline P, et al: Synopsis of the Work Session Proceedings, International Conference on Coal Workers' Pneumoconiosis. *Ind Med Surg* **39(3):** 19–28, March 1970.

11. Henschel A: Ventilatory Function and Work Capacity in Appalachian Bituminous Coal Miners and in Miners and Nonminers in Two West Virginia Communities, Lainhart WS, et al (eds), pp. 77–111 in *Pneumoconiosis in Appalachian Bituminous Coal Miners,* Public Health Service, Cincinnati, 1969.

12. Hyatt RE, Kistin AD, Mahan TK: Respiratory Disease in Southern West Virginia Coal Miners. *Amer Rev Resp Dis* **89:** 387–401, 1964.

13. Lainhart WS: Prevalence of Coal Miners' Pneumoconiosis in Appalachian Bituminous Coal Miners, Lainhart WS, et al (eds), pp 31–60 in *Pneumoconiosis in Appalachian Bituminous Coal Miners,* Public Health Service, Cincinnati, 1969.

14. Pemberton J: Chronic Bronchitis, Emphysema, and Bronchial Spasm in Bituminous Coal Workers. *Arch Ind Health* **13:** 529–544, 1956.

15. Rasmussen DL, Nelson CW: Respiratory Function in Southern Appalachian Coal Miners. *Amer Rev Resp Dis* **103:** 240–248, 1971.

16. Pichirallo J: Black Lung: Dispute about Diagnosis of Miners' Ailment. *Science* **174:** 132–134, 1971.

17. *Guidance for the Control of Radiation Hazards in Uranium Mining,* Rept No. 8 (Rev), Washington, DC, US Federal Radiation Council, Sept 1967.

18. Archer VE, Brinton HP, Wagoner JK: Pulmonary Function of Uranium Miners, *Health Phys* **10:** 1183–1194, 1964.

19. Trapp E, et al: Cardiopulmonary Function in Uranium Miners. *Amer Rev Resp Dis* **101:** 27–43, 1970.

20. Archer VE, Lundin FE, Jr: Radiogenic Lung Cancer in Man: Exposure-Effect Relationship. *Environ Res* **1:** 370–383, 1967.

21. Flinn RH, et al: *Silicosis in the Metal Mining Industry: A Revaluation. 1958–1961.* Public Health Service Publication No. 1076, Washington, DC, US Government Printing Office, 1963.

22. Lundin FE, Jr, et al: Mortality of Uranium Miners in Relation to Radiation Exposure, Hard-Rock Mining and Cigarette Smoking—1950 through September 1967. *Health Phys* **16:** 571–578, 1969.

23. Saccomanno G, et al: Lung Cancer of Uranium Miners on the Colorado Plateau. *Health Phys* **10:** 1195–1201, 1964.

24. Saccomanno G, et al: Histologic Types of Lung Cancer Among Uranium Miners. *Cancer* **27:** 515–523, March 1971.

25. Wagoner JK, et al: Radiation as the Cause of Lung Cancer among Uranium Miners. *New Eng J Med* **273:** 181–188, 1965.

26. Wagoner JK, et al: Cancer Mortality Patterns among US Uranium Miners and Millers, 1950 through 1962. *J Nat Cancer Inst* **32:** 787–801, 1964.

27. *Petroleum Facts and Figures,* 1971 Ed. Washington, DC, American Petroleum Institute, 1971.

28. Lave LB, Freeburg LC: Health Effects of Electricity Generation from Coal, Oil, and Nuclear Fuel, to appear in *Nuclear Safety,* 1973.

29. *Statistical Abstract of the United States: 1972,* ed 93, Government Printing Office, Washington, DC, US Bureau of the Census, 1972.

30. *Environmental Survey of the Nuclear Fuel Cycle,* Directorate of Licensing, Fuels and Materials, USAEC, Washington, DC, US Atomic Energy Commission, 1972.

31. Archer VE, Wagoner JK, Lundin FE: Cancer Mortality Among Uranium Mill Workers. *J Occup Med* **15(1):** 11–14, January 1973.

32. Dunn JE, Jr, Weir JM: A Prospective Study of Mortality of Several Occupational Groups. *Arch Environ Health* **17:** 71–76, July 1968.

33. Scott LM, Bahler KW, De La Garza A, et al: Mortality Experience of Uranium and Nonuranium workers. *Health Physics* **23:** 555–557, October 1972.

34. *Work Injuries in Atomic Energy, 1970,* Bureau of Labor Statistics Rept 411, Government Printing Office, Washington, DC, US Dept of Labor, 1972.

35. Brobst WA: Transportation Accidents: How Probable? *Nuclear News* **16(5):** 48–54, May 1973.

36. Cummings LG: Third Party Liability Insurance and Government Indemnity Associated with the Transportation of Radioactive Material. *Third International Symposium on Packaging and Transportation of Radioactive Materials,* 1971, vol 2, pp 516–531.

37. Rogers L: Transport of Radioactive Material—Accidents and Insurance Coverage. *JAMA* **215:** 1333–1334, 1971.

224

38. *Environmental Survey of Transportation of Radioactive Materials to and from Nuclear Power Plants,* Directorate of Regulatory Standards, USAEC, Washington, DC, US Atomic Energy Commission, 1972.

39. Yadigaroglu G, Reinking AG, Schrock VE: Spent Fuel Transportation Risks. *Nuclear News* **15(11):** 71–75, November 1972.

40. Klement AW, Jr, et al: *Estimates of Ionizing Radiation Doses in the United States 1960–2000,* Rockville, MD, Office of Radiation Programs, Environmental Protection Agency, 1972.

41. Hammond AL: Breeder Reactors: Power for the Future. *Science* **174:** 807–810, Nov 19, 1971.

42. Squires AM: Clean Power from Coal. *Science* **169:** 821–828, Aug 28, 1970.

43. *General Description of a Boiling Water Reactor,* San Jose, Nuclear Energy Division, General Electric Company, 1973.

44. Radiation Discharge Limits. *Nuclear Industry* **18(6):** 17–19, June 1971.

45. Belter WG: Recent Developments in the United States Low-Level Radioactive Waste-Management Program—A Preview for the 1970s. *Management of Low- and Intermediate-Level Radioactive Wastes,* pp 155–182, IAEA, Vienna, 1970.

46. Logsdon JE, Hickey JWN: Radioactive Waste Discharges to the Environment from a Nuclear Fuel Reprocessing Plant. *Radiol Health Data Rep* **12:** 205–312, 1971.

47. Russell JL: A Review of the Actual and the Projected Offsite Doses at Fuel Reprocessing Plants, paper presented at the Seventeenth Annual Meeting of the Health Physics Society, Las Vegas, June 1972

48. *Environmental Effects of Producing Electric Power,* Hearings Before the Joint Committee on Atomic Energy, 91st Cong, 1st Sess, Part 1, National Air Pollution Control Administration, 1969, pp 810–823.

49. Cuffe ST, Gerstle RW: Emissions from Coal-Fired Power Plants: A Comprehensive Summary, Public Health Service Publication 999-AP-35, 1967.

50. Gibson AS: Ecological Considerations and the Fast Breeder Reactor, paper presented at IEEE Region Six Conference, Sacramento, CA, May 11–13, 1971.

51. Terrill JG, Jr, Harward ED, Leggett IPaul, Jr: Environmental Aspects of Nuclear and Conventional Power Plants. *Ind Med Surg* **36:** 412–419, 1967.

52. Wright JH: The Role of Electric Power in Minimizing Total Pollution from Energy Use. *Proc Amer Power Conf* **33:** 602–610, 1971.

53. Watson DE: Goals of Cost-Benefit Analysis in Electrical Power Generation, UCRL-73567, 1971.

54. Billings CE, Matson WR: Mercury Emissions from Coal Combustion. *Science* **176:** 1232-1233, 1972.

55. *Engineering for Resolution of the Energy-Environment Dilemma,* Washington, DC, National Academy of Engineering, 1972.

56. Eisenbud M, Petrow HG: Radioactivity in the Atmospheric Effluents of Power Plants That Use Fossil Fuels. *Science* **144:** 288–289, 1964.

57. Martin J, Harward E, Oakley D: Comparison of Radioactivity from Fossil Fuel and Nuclear Power Plants, Environmental Effects of Producing Electric Power, Hearings Before the Joint Committee on Atomic Energy, 91st Con, 1st Sess, Part 1, 1969, pp 774–809.

58. Report on Releases of Radioactivity in Effluents from Nuclear Power Plants for 1971, Directorate of Regulatory Operations, USAEC, Washington, DC, US Atomic Energy Commission, 1972.

59. Logsdon JE, Chissler RI: *Radioactive Waste Discharges to the Environment from Nuclear Power Facilities,* Public Health Service, Rockville, MD, Bureau of Radiological Health, Environmental Health Service, 1970.

60. Logsdon JE, Robinson TL: *Radioactive Waste Discharges to the Environment from Nuclear Power Facilities, Addendum-1,* Washington, DC, Office of Radiation Programs, Environmental Protection Agency, 1971.

61. Kahn B, et al: *Radiological Surveillance Studies at a Boiling Water Nuclear Power Reactor,* Rockville, MD, Radiological Engineering Laboratory, Environmental Protection Agency, 1971.

62. Kahn B, et al: *Radiological Surveillance Studies at a Pressurized Water Nuclear Power Reactor,* Cincinnati, Environmental Protection Agency, National Environmental Research Center, 1971.

63. Hull AP: Radiation in Perspective: Some Comparisons of the Environmental Risks from Nuclear- and Fossil-Fueled Power Plants. *Nucl Safety* **12(3):** 185–196, May–June 1971.

64. Schikarski W, Jansen P, Jordan S: An Approach to Comparing Air Pollution from Fossil-Fuel and Nuclear Power Plants. *Environmental Aspects of Nuclear Power Stations* pp 877–890, IAEA, Vienna, 1971.

65. Bergström SOW: Environmental Consequences from the Normal Operation of an Urban Nuclear Power Plant. *Proceedings of the Fifth Annual Health Physics Society Midyear Topical Symposium,* vol 1, Idaho Falls, Idaho, November 3–6, 1970, pp 29–55.

66. Starr C, Greenfield MA, Hausknecht DF: A Comparison of Public Health Risks: Nuclear vs Oil-Fired Power Plants. *Nuclear News* **15(10):** 37–45, October 1972.

67. *Federal Register* **36(84):** 8186–8187, US Natl Arch, April 30, 1971.

68. *Code of Federal Regulations,* Title 10, Part 20, Appendix B, Government Printing Office, Washington, DC, US Natl Arch, 1972.

69. Lave L, Leinhardt S, Kaye M: Low-Level Environmental Radiation and US Mortality, working paper, Carnegie-Mellon University, 1972.

70. International Commission on Radiological Protection, The Evaluation of Risks from Radiation, *ICRP Publication 8,* Oxford, England, Pergamon Press 1969.

71. Stannard JN: Evaluation of Health Hazards to the Public Associated with Nuclear Plant Operations. *Nuclear Power and the Environment* pp XII–1 to XII–16, University of Wisconsin, Madison, Wisconsin, 1970.

72. *The Effects on Populations of Exposure to Low Levels of Ionizing Radiation,* Report of the Advisory Committee on the Biological Effects of Ionizing Radiations, Washington, DC, National Academy of Sciences, 1972.

73. Otway HJ, Erdmann RC: Reactor Siting and Design from a Risk Viewpoint. *Nucl Eng Des* **13:** 365–376, 1970.

74. Morgan KZ, Struxness EG: Criteria for the Control of Radioactive Effluents. *Environmental Aspects of Nuclear Power Stations* pp 211–236, IAEA, Vienna, 1971.

75. Burnett TJ: A Derivation of the "Factor of 700" for [131]I. *Health Physics* **18(1):** 73–75, January 1970.

76. Background Material for the Development of Radiation Protection Standards, Rept No 2, Government Printing Office, Washington, DC, US Fed Radiation Council, 1961.

77. Lave L: Economic Implications of Trace Contaminants in the Air, presented at Symposium on Trace Contaminants in the Environment, 65th Annual AIChE Meeting, New York, November 1972.

78. Anderson DO: The Effects of Air Contamination on Health. *Can Med Assoc J* **97:** 528–536, 585–593, 802–806, 1967.

79. Lave L, Seskin E: Air Pollution and Human Health. *Science* **169:** 723–733, 1970.

80. *Air Quality Criteria for Sulfur Oxides,* Government Printing Office, Washington, DC, US Natl Air Pollution Control Admin, 1969.

81. Lave L: Air Pollution Damage: Some Difficulties in Estimating the Value of Abatement in *Environmental Quality Analysis,* Kneese A, Bower B (eds), pp 213–242, Johns Hopkins University Press, Baltimore, 1972.

82. Lave L, Seskin E: Does Air Pollution Shorten Lives? *Proceedings of the Second Research Conference of the Inter-University Committee on Urban Economics,* University of Chicago, Sept 10–11, 1970.

83. Lave L, Seskin E: An Analysis of the Association between US Mortality and Air Pollution, to appear in *Journal of the American Statistical Association,* June 1973.

84. Lave L, Seskin E: Health and Air Pollution: The Effect of Occupation Mix. *Swedish J Econ* **73(1):** 76–95, March 1971.

85. Lave LB, Seskin EP: Air Pollution, Climate, and Home Heating: Their Effects on US Mortality Rates. *Amer J Pub Health* **62:** 909–916, 1972.

86. *Vital Statistics of the United States, 1960,* Government Printing Office, Washington, DC, US Public Health Service, 1962.

87. *Air Pollution Measurements of the National Air Sampling Network, Analyses of Suspended Particulates,* Government Printing Office, Washington, DC, US Public Health Service, 1962.

88. *County and City Data Book, 1962,* Government Printing Office, Washington, DC, US Bureau of the Census, 1962.

89. *Air Pollution Aspects of Emission Sources: Electric Production. A Bibliography with Abstracts,* Government Printing Office, Washington, DC, US Environmental Protection Agency, 1971.

90. Gamertsfelder CC: Regulatory Experience and Projections for Future Design Criteria, paper presented at Southern Conference on Environmental Radiation Protection at Nuclear Power Plants, St. Petersburg Beach, Fla, April 21–22, 1971.

91. Lieberman JA, Harward ED, Weaver CL: Environmental Surveillance Around Nuclear Power Reactors. *Radiol Health Data Rep* **11:** 325–332, 1970.

92. Bond VP: Evaluation of Potential Hazards from Tritiated Water. *Environmental Aspects of Nuclear Power Stations* pp 287–300, IAEA, Vienna, 1971.

93. Elwood JW: Ecological Aspects of Tritium Behavior in the Environment. *Nucl Safety* **12(4):** 326–337, July–August 1971.

94. Weaver CL, Harward ED, Peterson HT, Jr: Tritium in the Environment from Nuclear Powerplants. *Public Health Rep* **84:** 363–371, 1969.

95. Fontana MH (ed): Core Melt-Through as a Consequence of Failure of Emergency Core Cooling. *Nucl Safety* **9(1):** 14–24, January–February 1968.

96. Gillette R: Nuclear Reactor Safety: A Skeleton at the Feast? *Science* **172:** 918–919, 1971.

97. Gwaltney RC: Missile Generation and Protection in Light-Water-Cooled Reactors. *Nucl Safety* **10(4):** 300–307, July–August 1969.

98. Morgan KZ: Acceptable Risk Concepts, lecture presented at the University of Florida, Gainesville, Nov 4, 1969, and before the Pittsburgh Section of the American Nuclear Society, Pittsburgh, Pa, Nov 18, 1969.

99. Palladino NJ: Safety of Nuclear Reactors. *Nuclear Power and the Environment.* University of Wisconsin, Madison, 1970, pp VI–1 to VI–15.

100. Starr C: Benefit-Cost Relationships in Socio-Technical Systems. *Environmental Aspects of Nuclear Power Stations* pp 895–916, IAEA, Vienna, 1971.

101. Schneider KJ, et al: Status of Solidification and Disposal of Highly Radioactive Liquid Wastes from Nuclear Power Plants in the USA. *Environmental Aspects of Nuclear Power Stations* pp 369–384, IAEA, Vienna, 1971.

102. Goldman M: Management of Nuclear Fuel Reprocessing Wastes. *Nuclear Power and the Environment* pp VIII–1 to VIII–7, University of Wisconsin, Madison, 1970.

103. Cochran JA, et al: *An Investigation of Airborne Radioactive Effluent from an Operating Nuclear Fuel Reprocessing Plant,* Public Health Service, Rockville, MD, Northeastern Radiological Health Laboratory, 1970.

104. Magno P, Reavey T, Apidianakis J: Liquid Waste Effluents from a Nuclear Fuel Reprocessing Plant, USAEC Report BRH/NERHL-70–2, Northeastern Radiological Health Laboratory, 1970.

105. Wenstrand TK, Wilcox DP: Environmental Reports No. 10 and 11, January–June 1971 and July–December 1971, Nuclear Fuel Services, Inc., West Valley, N.Y., 1971–2.

106. Kelleher WJ: Environmental Surveillance Around a Nuclear Fuel Reprocessing Installation, 1965–1967. *Radiol Health Data Rep* **10:** 329–339, 1969.

107. Martin JA, Jr: Calculations of Environmental Radiation Exposures and Population Doses Due to Effluents from a Nuclear Fuel Reprocessing Plant. *Radiation Data and Reports* **14(2):** 59–76, February 1973.

108. Shleien B: *An Estimate of Radiation Doses Received by Individuals Living in the Vicinity of a Nuclear Fuel Reprocessing Plant in 1968,* Public Health Service, Rockville, MD, Northeastern Radiological Health Laboratory, Bureau of Radiological Health, 1970.

17

The Relation of Power Needs to Population Growth, Economic and Social Costs

Vic Reinemer

At the outset, I should discuss briefly the control and decision-making process in the energy sector. Then we can better evaluate the costs involved in meeting needs. In important respects, public policy regarding energy is not decided by public officials, at either federal or state levels. In all but one of the states, utilities have one of the most powerful rights of government, eminent domain.

A few oil companies—not the government—deal with Middle East nations regarding availability and cost of oil and gas. A few pipelines—not the government—deal with the Soviet Union for Siberian natural gas. A few oil companies—not the government—decided that the oil from Alaska's North Slope should go not to the oil-short Midwest, but to an Alaskan port from which it can easily be shipped to Japan, whose premier happily reported last year that Japan would be buying some of it. The pipes to Valdez were quickly laid down along the right-of-way. The push is on now to change the legal right-of-way width and thus legalize the venture.

THE ENERGY MONOPOLY

We have all heard the litany that energy companies are regulated by dozens of government bureaus. Let us remember that the "regulation" of utilities was invented in Chicago, by Samuel Insull. He devised the scheme so as to appear to be controlled by government and thus stop the growth of municipal power systems. Then he sent his lawyers to Springfield to set up the Illinois Commerce Commission. All the government energy regulatory bureaus collectively can be likened to the wizened mountaineer who had seven huge, strapping sons. The mountaineer boasted that they did not disobey him. "Of course," he added, "I'm right careful what I ask them to do."

Energy companies are, in reality, governments. Primary control of the energy industry rests, as it does in other major sectors, with a few large banks.

229

This corporate government—"corpocracy" if you prefer—exercises its control through the three branches of corporate government. One is the legislative branch, through which the bankers vote other people's stock. The second is the money branch, through which the banks extend credit and hold the mortgage. The third—and certainly the most fascinating—is the interlock branch. The big banks maintain large stables of vice presidents—Chase Manhattan has 298—for service on the boards of companies in which they have financial interests and on the boards of the funds, universities, and foundations which have money to invest. A second tier of interlocks functions through government bureaus such as the Federal Power Commission (FPC), which last year created 30 new advisory committees. You could hide all of the FPC auditors and accountants among its official industry advisers. Their corporate reports become government writ regarding, for example, the natural gas shortage, a subject about which neither the FPC nor any other government bureau has independent knowledge. The third tier of interlocks is comprised of the men who come into government from energy companies and their law firms for the full tour, four or five years. After their tour, they are pastured out to the big remuda of energy company lobbyists, who constitute the fourth tier of interlocks. This recycling of commissioners is especially characteristic of the FPC and the Interstate Commerce Commission (ICC). I mention the ICC because it is supposed to regulate conglomerates such as the Burlington Northern and the Union Pacific which, although often thought of as railroads, have the most fabulous coal reserves of all corporations. And so it goes.

It is important to distinguish between the power *needs* of this country and what the energy corpocracy *wants.* The companies want development of the energy sources that they control; those are the fossil fuels (oil, gas, and coal) and uranium for their nuclear reactors. They are also anxious for development of other energy sources subject to monopoly control—oil shale and geothermal steam. These companies raised the national fuel bill by about $6 billion and contributed significantly to the energy crisis by persuading a president, 14 years ago, to turn down the spigot of cheap Middle East oil, through the import quota system. The same companies also use their vast influence among elected officials to channel tax dollars into programs that will facilitate development and depletion of the energy sources they control. In support of their goals, the energy companies have generated a corporate advertising program that is continuous, costly, and pervasive.

UNDEVELOPED ENERGY SOURCES

The *wants* of the energy industry contrast with the public's *need* for development of alternative power sources that are not subject to monopoly control. These alternate sources have low operating costs. They do not present the environmental hazards endemic to coal, oil and uranium. The alternate sources are elemental: the sun, the wind, and water. And in a related category is the fastest-growing energy source of all, solid waste, the utilization of which will enhance the environment.

Energy companies generally downgrade these alternate sources. Solar power and wind power raise the specter of competition, of customer independence; so does hydropower, insofar as it is developed at federal projects subject to the preference clause, under which public and cooperative power systems have first call on the power.

Additional hydropower potential is limited. But hydro could constitute an important increment in areas such as the Missouri Basin through installation of additional generators at existing main stem dams. Unfortunately, for four years now, the White House Office of Management and Budget has stymied the Corps of Engineers' work on this environmentally ideal power development.

Wind power and solid waste conversion still suffer from disregard by too many scientists and engineers. But solar power is at a stage where substantial research funding would make it significant within five years.

The energy companies' rush to strip and burn coal, at plants with only 30% to 40% efficiency, severely impedes development of magnetohydrodynamics (MHD), the direct conversion process for getting approximately twice as many BTUs per ton of coal while reducing its pollution materially. We are far behind the Russians, the Germans, and the Japanese in MHD technology. But industry, and consequently the federal government, have not assigned a high priority to MHD.

The big problem in developing alternative, economical, environmentally attractive and unmonopolized energy sources is to obtain recognition for them in the federal budget, which reflects the short term interests of the energy corpocracy. The needed research would be marvelously assisted by the equivalent of the cost of one Trident submarine, which is about $1.2 billion.

A rational energy system would include an integrated electrical transmission system, which would reduce by an estimated 20% or 25% the new construction of plants needed to meet electric energy needs. Our present transmission system can be compared with an interstate highway interspersed with one-lane gravel roads. An integrated private and public transmission system would permit rapid transfer of power where needed, depending on peak loads that vary according to season, time zone, and time of day.

A rational energy system would provide for public development of energy resources on public lands and thus reduce monopoly control and its adverse effects on both price and supply. A rational energy system would reinstitute rail passenger service and copy or even improve upon the Japanese pollution emission control systems. A rational energy system would apply the common carrier concept to all energy transmission systems. And a rational energy system would provide the public with as much talent and information, before regulatory commissions and courts, as the companies buy and bill us for.

But these proposals are strongly opposed by the energy companies, which means that they will not be permitted in the near future. Given corpocracy's entrenchment and public lassitude, we are in for years of higher prices, less fuel, more inconvenience, greater pollution, and growing alienation of American citizens who dimly but surely perceive the paralysis that grips the public government. Economic power in the energy sector is now becoming even more concentrated as the independent gasoline and oil distributors, unable to obtain supplies, close their stations. A growing population, concentrated in urban areas, becomes increasingly restive as the costs of essential energy-related services increase while service deteriorates. The market for night lights and night sticks will increase—the President's budget for them has already been augmented. And the Middle East will become even more explosive as we arm and advise Iran in exchange for its oil.

What the energy corpocracy needs is The Pill. As recently as last month the presidents of the American Gas Association, American Petroleum Institute, Atomic Industrial Forum, Edison Electric Institute, and National Coal Association, jointly declared against restricting the growth rate of energy use which as they project will almost triple energy consumption by the year 2000. The industry leaders foresee a doubling of rates and prices in 10 years. Their program rests wholly on exploitation of the fuels which their corporate governments have monopolized. *I say that we have to stop these market-mad men from selling such a disastrous policy.*

They plead for deregulation of natural gas, in order to increase supplies. Yet theirs are the same companies whose *unregulated* oil enterprises have run us short of fuel. Furthermore, Texaco has admitted, in a current FPC proceeding, that it would oppose any attempt by the Commission to force producers to plow back into exploration and production any part of new higher gas prices they are seeking. And the hand of the regulator is already so light that the FPC does not even publicize the handsome return on equity of the gas pipeline companies.

The President at last delivered his energy message on April 18, 1973, just as Congress was recessing for Easter. The timing was no surprise to seasoned Washington observers. Pronouncements contrary to public interest are usually made when Congress and the press are diverted. Over holidays, corporate government is as busy as the highway patrol. On Christmas Eve before last the railroads tried to slip through an "emergency" rate increase, and the Federal Communications Commission tried to quit altogether the job it has never done of regulating AT&T. That was too much for the public to forgive even at Christmas. So the FCC simply waited until last Thanksgiving to give Ma Bell what she wanted.

The most recent Christmas-New Year's holiday featured regal pronouncements of executive privilege and unskilled surgery on the statutes, the budget, and, perhaps, the Constitution itself. As momentous issues rise to a divided Supreme Court, some of us are more grateful than anyone can know for the medical technology that implanted a Pacemaker in the heart of a great Justice.

The heavy hand of the energy industry is imprinted on every page of the President's energy message: Raise prices. Cut taxes. Stretch out compliance with environmental standards. Strip the prairie. Burn that coal. Pipe that oil to the coast. Ease regulation. Lease out *all* energy resources on public lands. Triple the leases on the Outer Continental Shelf. Energy prices should reflect their true costs, he said. Yet he asked for more tax relief for energy companies, and did not mention rate structure. Nor did he recognize the lower environmental and operating costs of the alternate energy sources. He again advocated, and deserves credit for urging, that local officials be allowed to use money from the highway trust fund for mass transit purposes. But, all in all, it's a "burn, baby, burn" message, with only mild pleas for "voluntary" conservation: Turn out the lights. Tune up the car.

One of the most crucially important problems involved in developing energy policy is obtaining independent data, including information that companies would rather not share but should be required to divulge because of the public service nature of their business and its overriding importance to the nation. Neither the executive nor the legislative branch, neither the Democrats nor the Republicans, have dedicated themselves to this fundamental proposition of obtaining the facts upon which intelligent policy can be based. The President's approach, in his energy message, is to say that the Department of the Interior "is to develop capacity for gathering and analysis of energy data." Well, the director of the Department of the Interior's Office of Oil and Gas recently transferred to the Lone Star Gas Company. He was succeeded by a Conoco man. My hunch is that Interior will gather and analyze energy data by asking the National Petroleum Council, its most prestigious, all-industry advisory committee, to put out another report.

The President barely recognized development of alternative energy sources. The budget for solar energy research and development is a mere $12 million. His approach to developing magnetohydrodynamics is to make it a joint project with the Russians. They have a pilot MHD plant in operation and we haven't even begun to design one. We are not even going to work with the Russians or the Chinese on solid waste conversion, hydro, or wind power.

Perhaps I am old-fashioned. Maybe there are ways to develop alternate, economical, and environmentally attractive energy sources in this era. We could lease Litton Industries exclusive rights to the sun. We could organize a wind division of ITT. We could send another team to the moon, to evaluate its tug on the tides of Passamoquoddy, where a hydro facility should have been built long ago. And a public relations firm could be hired to propose that the environment and the image be enhanced by transforming the Watergate into a solid waste conversion plant.

A PUBLIC ENERGY POLICY

There are ways in which individuals who wish to can help limit the growth sought by the energy hucksters. I don't mean riding the bike or bus, or insulating the house and turning down the heat, although such practices are to be commended. I refer to participation in the small but growing groups, active in most states, which, working within the system, seek to make it responsive to the needs of people. One of the most effective groups is in St. Louis, thanks in good measure to the remarkable Dr. and Mrs. Slavin. Their interests include revision of retail rate structure, a matter handled by state commissions, and sponsorship of consumer counter-ads on TV and radio.

In a typical retail rate structure, electricity used to produce aluminum for bombers over Cambodia costs one third as much as the electricity that a doctor uses for providing health care. The industrial customers are similarly subsidized by the low-income family that lives in a densely settled area where the cost of electric service is low, but rates are high. State commissions are concerned about this inequity. But they need testimony from persons who will counter the arguments of the batteries of company lawyers, experts, and kept professors whose retainers and salaries you pay as part of your utility bill.

State commissions also need to hear from those who object to free advertising by utilities. Many state commissions permit advertising and sales promotion to be written off as operating costs of the cost-plus utilities. Those companies, on the average, spend three and a half times as much on advertising and sales promotion as they spend on research and development. (Commonwealth Edison, I am pleased to report, spends slightly more on research and development than on advertising and sales promotion.)

Utility research and development is an allowed operating cost. In fact, sometimes utilities make money from research and development by getting it included in the rate base. They are trying to obtain tax incentives for research and development expenditures as well. Yet the annual research and development effort of the nation's largest industry, the investor-owned electric utilities, is less than the amount Exxon spent to put up and merchandise its new name.

Then there is the lighting project, which could use the services of pro bono oculists. Some years ago a group of electrical equipment and utility salesmen formed the Illuminating Engineering Society. They have by now jacked up the lighting standards in many states to the extent that schools, libraries, government offices, and other buildings use much more electricity for lighting than is necessary. A Georgia Power official bragged to his colleagues that the lighting standards have become so high that the air conditioner had to run year round to keep down the heat from the lights.

Finally, corpocracy itself needs attention from stockholders. They, more likely than government, will make constructive changes in corporate affairs during the next few years. The job of affecting corporate policy is indeed awesome. The agenda and candidates considered at an annual stockholders' meeting are determined well in advance by corporate management. Great effort and considerable expense, months prior to the meeting, are required to obtain consideration of the most modest proposals that have not been offered by management. If the attempt to get on the ballot is successful, identification of the voting stockholders and timely communication with them is difficult or impossible. The big voters, usually the banks and other institutional investors, often hide their identity behind multiple "street names" or "nominees."

Most everyone has probably received proxies from companies that will not even permit you to cast a negative vote against management's single slate. You vote "da" or withhold your vote. *The corporate election process in America today is as rigged as elections are in the Soviet Union, the outcome as predictable, and the accompanying propaganda as self-serving.* But that is the structure with which we must deal, in attempting to ameliorate the undesirable social and economic consequences of explosive energy growth. In the energy business the structure is the policy. Changing that structure involves an extraordinary investment of time and energy by thousands of individuals who decide to become active public citizens. It is that kind of investment, costly in both social and economic terms to each public citizen, that is required to relate energy policy to public needs rather than to the profligate goals of corpocracy.

18

Esthetic Effects of Power Systems

Garrett Eckbo

What are the esthetic effects of generating and transmitting electricity? By esthetic effects we mean: how do these processes and facilities affect people's qualitative experience of their environment? This experience takes place through a complex process. Environment is everything in the world that impinges in some way on the life of a person or other organism. There are a number of environmental contact zones or gradations: daily; weekend, holiday, vacation; proxy, via communication media. At any given moment environment is everything perceived or sensed by a person. Qualitative experience is subjective as well as objective, emotional as well as rational. How does the environment make the person feel?

Environmental experience is cumulative. Each moment's experience is conditioned by all of the experiences and reactions that have preceded it. Experience is moderated and manipulated by education and communication. In a verbalizing society, people tend to see things as they are taught to see them or to wait for interpretation by experts. Except for very young children, some old people, designers, and artists, few people see the environment directly, as it actually is. Most see it through a screen of words, associations, and symbols.

Experience takes place through a sequence of perception, comprehension, interpretation, reaction. This sequence runs through the screen of cultural indoctrination and experiential memory which is each person's interface with the environment.

Electricity is generated and transmitted through a complex of physical facilities that are important components of the physical environment. Basic elements of these complexes are generating plants based on water power, the burning of coal, oil, or gas, nuclear reactors, or limited geothermal energy. Other sources of power—solar energy, tidal and wind energy, burning garbage—are recognized as theoretically possible but are considered impractical at this time by the power establishment. Environmental impacts of these latter possibilities have never been seriously investigated. They may prove to be more serious than impacts by contemporary methods of energy production.

Generating plants and substations are buildings, architectural elements

237

with normal problems of relations to the landscape. High tension lines and service lines are those networks of wires and supporting structures that link all of our urban, suburban, and rural communities together in one continuous continental network of urbanism. Transformer stations are those elegant jungle gyms of structure and wire that mediate between buildings and wire systems.

A further dimension of power systems is their contribution to pollution. The new West Four Corners system in the Southwest, now building the second of six generating plants, is an archetype of the problem. Burning coal, the first plant pollutes the air of its entire four-state region, in spite of the installation of modern pollution control equipment. The coal is being strip-mined in the Black Mesa area. The plants are consuming staggering quantities of water from inadequate river systems and underground reservoirs. To cap it all, the Indians, through whose reservations the system operates, have been bamboozled, deceived, and manipulated by the power entities.

SITE AND LANDSCAPE INTRUSIONS

Now to return to the question: what are the esthetic effects of these systems? They are visual and psychological. Visually, generating plants, substations, and transformer stations may be well designed in relation to site and surrounding landscape. Pollution problems may or may not be subject to design control. Structures in urban, suburban, rural, or wild settings will have different kinds of design problems, but all are subject to creative solutions.

With high tension lines, we move from site to landscape scale. Together with other utilities, railroads, highways, freeways, and water systems, these are the most conscious systematic visual evidence of man's conquest of nature and the landscape. They are also, in crude and oversimplified form, direct symbols of man-made ecosystems competitive with those of nature.

The design and development of the American landscape have been dominated by two basic concepts:

1. That man and nature are separate entities, and that it is man's God-given prerogative to conquer, use, exploit, and change nature as he sees fit. Nature is seen as a passive feminine recipient of man's masculine conquest and as a bottomless reservoir of resources and goodies. This concept remains dominant in spite of a persistent strong conservation minority.

2. That the environment is an arena, and that environmental development is a competitive process in which any number of single-purpose systems, entities, and agencies compete for space and resources. The terms of the competitive game are political and economic.

With these concepts dominant, the design of systems such as high tension lines has been totally single-minded. Their technical functions and structural requirements are paramount and mature, and other systems must give way and adjust to them. Cost-benefit ratios, in which there are no figures covering losses of amenity or natural systems, determine the engineered form and alignment of the system. Many battles by citizen and conservation groups have failed to change this monolithic process.

Current questioning of all environmental decision-making processes, because of the inescapably monumental accumulations of pollution and destruction they have produced, has added some new dimensions to the scene. Environmental protection legislation, impact statement requirements, young environmental law groups, new radicalization of conservation groups have all forced the power, utility, transportation, and water establishments to slow down and adjust their tactics to this new input. Thus, Tucson Gas and Electric Company hires the Environmental Systems Department of Westinghouse Electric Corporation to prepare the Environmental Analysis for its current application for a 424-mile transmission line corridor from Waterflow, New Mexico, to Tucson, Arizona. This document appears thorough and competent but, on examination, proves to be a narrative rationalization of what TG&E wants to do for reasons of its own. Unable to ignore or repress the demands of environmental planning and design, the establishment now sets out to co-opt those processes.

Studies done by professionals, such as Eckbo, Dean, Austin & Williams' studies for Pacific Gas & Electric in California, attempt seriously to grapple with the transmission line corridor problem by the use of current techniques of ecosystematic analysis and computer or manual mapping, plus overlay manipulations involving creative insights and judgments. Data maps, covering 27 physical landscape factors resulting from natural and/or human processes are boiled down to five constraint maps—visual, physical, social-cultural, economic, and ecological—which, in turn, are boiled down to one final suitability map that determines the best possible routing.

The basic implication of this experience is that regional-scale systems such as high-tension lines must become integral elements in a regional survey-analysis-planning-design process. The PG&E studies were advanced in that they dealt with the broadest regional area that might be affected by, or affect, the power lines. But they were still limited in that they did not deal with complete regional units.

ENVIRONMENTAL PLANNING AND DESIGN

We need a process that will make it possible, once and continuously thereafter, to integrate completely all natural and man-made systems in region-wide ecosystematic concepts. We need this because of the basic lesson of ecology itself that all elements and systems within any contiguous area are interconnected and interdependent. Change in any one affects many others in ways we have never learned to predict. Prediction of the ecosystematic effects of environmental change can only be accomplished within a coordinated regional process.

This process would include well-known steps:

1. Organization of continental landscapes into macro-, midi-, and mini-regional patterns.
2. Survey and inventory of regional resources, amenities, assets, liabilities, physical and social structures, and processes. This list creates a regional data bank to which all groups and agencies have equal access. It must be an ongoing effort, kept continually up to date.
3. Establishment of present and future standards of environmental quality for man and nature.
4. Analysis and evaluation of the inventory in relation to such standards.
5. Projection and testing of alternative coordinated ecosystematic responses to existing regional problem structure and to proposals for development, change, or management.
6. Selection of most likely alternatives by continuous testing and continuous refinement.
7. Design, development, and/or installation of final selected alternatives, with continuous testing of their environmental impacts.

This is a crude statement of a complex and subtle cyclical process. Each stage goes on continuously, with constant feedback to previous stages.

It may be said that this scheme is only a description of existing processes. That is true with the major and fundamental difference that present processes are fragmented into as many separate efforts as there are private and public groups seeking control of change in the environment. None of these efforts is complete or adequate because none has the vision or the resources to carry out steps one through four with any approximation of adequacy.

REGIONALIZED ENVIRONMENTAL CONTROL

The proposal here is for an unprecedented centralization and coordination of these efforts that use the combined energies and resources of regional communities to solve environmental problems which they share. Called regional planning and regional government, this process leads to political conflicts so well known that I need not elaborate them here. Suffice it to say that, whatever the objections (and many are legitimate), the regionalization of environmental control has to come. The nature and structure of the problems is such that no other form of solution will work. The alternative is to continue down the mindless, competitive, fragmented path that we have followed to date. To this may be added monumental governmental rhetoric and corporate rationalizations. But unless we actually do change our ways, putting both our wealth and our power where our mouths are, we will all end on the same dust heap of history, exploiters and conservationists together.

There are innumerable detailed refinements embodied in the implementation of regional control processes for environmental change. High tension lines, once corridored and routed, can be designed into the landscape in many reasonably convincing patterns. Careful study of traditional landscape relationships—sight line, topography, vegetation (both existing and possible), relations between line and mass, accent and rhythm, sequence and interruption—brings out many unexpected qualitative potentials. More detailed and specific consideration leads us to recognize that they do often pass through landscapes that are not purely natural, in the nonhuman sense. They must feed urban centers by passing through agricultural and suburban zones. As urbanization increases, construction becomes more dense and land values go up. These are more effective obstacles to high tension lines than are natural or rural amenities. At critical points the major lines terminate in transformer stations and substations. Here begins that ragged, dilapidated, archaic web of service lines that so exasperates all those who feel that cities and suburbs should be felicitous environments for people.

High tension lines have grand scale, magnificent geometry, consistent simplicity, constant directional qualities. Service networks have none of these qualities. They are improvised, expedient, without visual order, rhyme, or reason. Undergrounding has been the war cry of urbanists, conservationists, and improvement associations for many years. Out of sight, out of mind. Present underground technology has not yet solved the problem for high tension lines. Even if it had, in other than urban areas the environmental benefits of undergrounding in many cases would be only minor, not warranting the difference in cost. When the extent of clearing, grading, multiple trenching, and special underground facilities are taken into account it is apparent that under many conditions undergrounding could result in greater deleterious impacts on the environment.

For service lines within urbanized areas, it is clear that undergrounding or integration with continuous construction is the answer. In other words, as the environment becomes dominated by man-made construction, it becomes more essential to integrate service systems with basic urban construction. In intermediate suburban and exurban areas this may become impractical. But even free-standing low-tension service lines can be so designed and routed as to be environmental assets rather than liabilities.

However, in all of these areas of design, we cannot escape the confrontation between two fundamental attitudes:

1. The *doctrine of original sin* says that man-made construction is inherently ugly, inappropriate in the landscape, and destructive of natural beauty. At best it can be designed into the

landscape so skillfully as to appear integral and harmonious with it. Since the 18th-century romantic revolt against Renaissance geometric formalism in England, this attitude has been basic to all sorts of rusticated, informal, naturalistic, park-like, preservationist, conservationist, and now ecological efforts in the landscape. The word *park* is a key symbol. We automatically assume that a park is natural and informal. Efforts to co-opt the word, as in Industrial Park, Car Park, Educational Park, Residential Park, to rationalize un-park-like environments, testify to the strength of the symbol. This attitude is deep-seated and emotionally persistent among Americans and North Europeans. Japanese, and probably Chinese, apply it in more subtle and complex forms.

2. On the other hand, the *doctrine of manifest destiny* says that man is master of his fate and captain of his soul. Today we see this doctrine as basic to the frontier conquest of nature and the rationale for commercial-industrial-military-engineering exploitation and destruction of natural and historical environments. We tend to forget that it was basic to all of the glories of the Renaissance in Europe from the fourteenth through the seventeenth centuries. It is basic to great urbanism, great city-building, great architecture, great engineering, and great landscape architecture when it goes beyond naturalistic vocabularies.

For 300 years or more, attitude No. 2 has dominated environmental development in North America. Attitude No. 1 has remained a persistent and aggressive underdog. Now its influence is expanding rapidly. Do we want to swing completely from attitude No. 2 to No. 1?

There are, of course, few pure and consistent examples of either No. 1 or No. 2. Attitudes tend to cluster near them, and to filter out through a broad transitional zone between them. High tension lines, and comparable engineering systems, present crucial tests for this range of attitudes. No. 1 will say that there is no place in natural landscapes for such overtly man-made structures, that they automatically destroy the beauty of the scene and are at best a necessary evil that must be concealed, minimized, and camouflaged as skillfully as possible. No. 2, on the other hand, will not be put off by the idea of a high tension line in the landscape per se. It will see the line as either, or both, a demonstration of advanced engineering and technological skill and a magnificent web of man-made architectural geometrics. The former will feel that nature is of secondary importance and must adjust to the line. The latter will see the line as a potentially creative contrasting addition to the landscape, if properly routed and designed.

Confrontations between these polar attitudes are inherent throughout the entire range of American environmental planning and design, particularly at regional scale. They are not necessarily rigid positions. Constructive dialogue between them is essential to the development of a badly needed new ecologically oriented planning-design vocabulary.

Esthetics are more, much more, than the visual or pictorial quality of a power line or plant in the landscape. Beginning with those qualities, they have to do with symbolism, understanding, participation, and similar subjective values. If the physical elements of a power system are seen as representing a beneficial system that brings us needed amenities without destroying environmental quality or depleting scarce resources, we can then view it with sympathy and appreciate the contrast and interaction between its clean geometry and the natural surroundings. If, however, these elements represent a system that is fouling the air and the regional landscape, depleting and wasting its water and soil, and destroying natural amenities and traditional cultural values, all in the course of selling power we may not truly need, then no amount of careful handling of topography and vegetation will counteract those bad associations.

Esthetics exist whenever any single human being, of whatever color or background, is related to a landscape and reacts to it. They do not necessarily increase in importance as the number or status of people related to that landscape increases. Only their physical and political impact increases.

All of this brings us, perhaps, to the heart of the problem—the relationship between the exploiting, consuming, antiplanning society we have been and still are, and the steady state, ecologically harmonized, carefully planned and designed society that all of the environmental literature projects or implies is essential to survival. The form and detail of the latter are a vast ambiguity, once we look behind the rhetoric. The ways and means for transition from where we are to that ambiguous new society—over the dead bodies and through the barricades of entrenched governmental corporate power structures and bureaucracies—are even less clear.

In relation to power systems and their physical facilities, certain changes seem unavoidable. The power companies:

1. must stop selling the public the idea of constantly expanding power consumption;
2. must stop defining wants, generated by such selling and the normal American cornucopia expectations, as needs that must be met;
3. must stop rationalizing expansion plans on the basis of straight-line projections from the past growth patterns motivated by past normal expectations;
4. must begin to recognize actual trends in population growth, consumer attitudes, resource management, and conservation policies; and
5. must begin to support, and participate in, coordinated efforts for developing regional ecosystematic planning and design processes.

If this analysis of the esthetic effects of generating and transmitting electricity seems oversimplified, it is only because the physical elements involved are basically simple. Complications emerge from the application of these systems to the complexities of local situations.

Discussion

Dr. Weinberg: Mr. Reinemer, you very properly pointed out the possibility of solar energy and MHD, and you particularly mentioned the Russian experience with MHD. I wonder if you are aware of the fact that, in point of fact, the Russian 25,000-kilowatt (kw) MHD plant really does not work very well and has been on the line very intermittently.

Mr. Reinemer: Of course, the Fermi plant did not work very well, either. But we kept putting money into nuclear research.

Dr. Weinberg: I think the situation is really different, Mr. Reinemer. There have been several fast reactors of the general type of the Fermi plant that have run very reliably. But the MHD problem is a very, very difficult one, and I think that it is really a disservice to imply that MHD is simply a matter of research. It is a very difficult problem that may not be soluble.

Q: Mr. Eckbo, as our resident architect this afternoon, you talked about transmission lines, and I was impressed to see the detailed considerations and the ecological point of view. But I am going to ask about another aspect of architecture where I think the architect can have a very large input into the practices of efficient energy use and that is his being aware of energy efficient systems in the design of structures, especially those for commercial and residential use. I am aware that this can be done esthetically but I have had a recent experience with a very nicely designed addition to my own home that was just about as energy unconscious as it could be. But architects do not think this way and they might very well take a leading rather than a following role in making the public energy conscious and in doing a lot to save energy in the structures that they design.

Mr. Eckbo: I should point out that there has been a semantic slip; I am a landscape architect not an architect. But you are right that this kind of building design is needed because the home building industry and the architectural profession have been victims of the idea of unlimited energy for a long time. We now tend to design buildings in the same way in any region no matter what the climate may be, and we leave it to the mechanical engineers to solve the interior climatic problems. There is beginning to be a change in that the better architects are now trying to develop buildings that will conserve energy. This effort has two aspects, the design of the building itself, and the design of site improvement around it. Within the building there are complex relations between structure, insulation, mechanical equipment, size and orientation of glass areas and door openings, etc. In site selection and improvement, much ancient wisdom and ecological knowledge becomes relevant once again—cool north slopes versus warm south slopes, cold and warm air drainage patterns, providing space adequate for major tree planting (nature's air conditioner), surrounding buildings with planted ground rather than paved surfaces, handling drainage so that water goes into the soil rather than running off from it.

VI

PRESENT-DAY
ENERGY
USE
POLICIES

19

A Role for the Medical Community in Rationalizing the Energy Crisis

Edward E. David, Jr., Sc.D.

It is encouraging to me that the American Medical Association is taking an interest in energy and the environment and in the health matters related to them. There are three reasons for which the AMA is especially suited to tackle this issue: first, the medical community is foremost among professions in practicing the balance between risks and costs on one hand, and benefits on the other. The use of drugs in therapy is a classic instance where the benefits must be balanced against the risks in the decision to prescribe a drug or treatment for a patient. In addition, the physician has to consider the cost to the patient. Thus, the medical community knows that balancing the desirable against the undesirable is essential to human progress. So, too, this balancing act is the key to progress in the so-called energy crisis.

Second, the medical community is accustomed to dealing with the federal government in regulatory matters. The Food and Drug Administration (FDA) and the legislation behind it have long been features of the medical scene. Through dealing with the FDA and with other government agencies, you know both the strengths and weaknesses of government. That experience will be increasingly useful as federal activity expands to encompass energy and environmental matters. Much of the legislation administered by the Environmental Protection Agency (EPA) is based upon health effects as the criteria for action. For example, the primary air quality standards under the Clean Air Act are to be set so that there is "no risk to health." That is a sobering thought considering the risk-benefit trade-off, for zero risk can imply zero benefit or infinite cost. Esthetics are secondary to health in the Clean Air Act in setting air quality standards.

Finally, as representatives of medical research, you know very well the uncertainties in measurement of health effects and the difficulty of establishing cause and effect. Perhaps the single most discussed topic in environmental health science is the health effect of low exposures over long time periods. That is the crux of the matter in the lead-in-gasoline controversy as well as in the regulation of chemical carcinogens. There is, as yet, no accepted answer to the perfectly rational question, "Is there a threshold effect in such instances?" We ask other related questions that have no answers at the present time: how does a health effect change with the dose size, as well as with the weight of the subject, and its position on the phylogenetic scale? Even more basic, we do not understand the physiologic or pharmacologic mechanism of low-level health effects well enough to predict answers to such questions. Thus the medical community and its research arm can play a central role in convincing the public and its representatives that biological science is, at present, inadequate to set precise and unchanging standards to protect the public health and safety. Flexibility in regulation is needed, particularly as measurement advances to detect lower and lower levels of chemicals, drugs, and food additives in consumer products and the environment. Furthermore, it is up to you to convince Congress and the public that public policy requires much more effort on such critical basic questions as the ones that I have raised about threshold effects of carcinogens. Establishment of the National Center for Toxicological Research (NCTR) at Pine Bluff, Arkansas, is a hopeful sign. At facilities of that sort, it is possible to undertake "kilomouse" experiments that can help us answer empirically questions that depend on the statistics of large populations. More importantly, NCTR's charter includes basic work on physiological mechanisms. Hopefully, too, basic research activity by the National Institutes of Health (NIH) will throw light on these matters. The results could eventually relieve much of the burden of massive experimentation and data analysis.

It is only through such efforts that the public can be protected against real threats. On the other hand, it is just as important, in my view, that the public not be denied the benefits of drugs and chemicals and other products of technology. It is in this context that the nation is fortunate in having had a first-class health-effects effort in at least one field—namely, nuclear energy. The Atomic Energy Commission programs have been the largest and most persistent of any in environmental health. There is much basic knowledge on hand that can help answer the sort of questions that I have posed and can help us in quantifying the health effects of exposure to ionizing radiation.

The medical community also knows of the insensitivity of epidemiological analyses in looking for subtle effects on large populations. Here, too, there is the inevitable uncertainty of cause and effect. Logically, but fortunately not operationally, the cause of an observed effect epidemiologically cannot be proved but, of course, with additional evidence it can be inferred with a relatively small risk of error. So, for all these reasons, I see the medical community and the life sciences as a principal resource for the nation in resolving the conflict between energy and the environment with its involvement with human health.

RESOURCE STRATEGY

Now let me spend a moment or two giving you my views on the overall energy situation. The energy crisis is really self-inflicted. For example, the Clean

Air Act restricts the emission of sulfur oxides into the air and places a premium on the availability of low-sulfur fuels. So, though there is no basic shortage of fuel, there is a shortage of low-sulfur fuels. The National Environmental Protection Act (NEPA) requires environmental impact statements before beginning construction on power plants or refineries. There is red tape galore in the siting of other major facilities, such as the trans-Alaska pipeline, not only from NEPA, but from other sources as well. There are constraints in tapping offshore oil and gas supplies. This is not to say that these bills and the constraints they impose are uncalled for or unwise, but the energy crisis does stem from those actions.

But there are other causes, too (e.g., regulation of prices and of imports). With the regulation of gas prices at the wellhead, there has been little incentive for new gas exploration. Oil import quotas have prevented the country from importing oil in the quantities that are required to meet demands in an expeditious way. Quotas have also discouraged exploration in other parts of the world since the United States is the largest market. So there has been a lack of incentive to explore for oil and gas both here and abroad. The recent Presidential message has removed both oil import quotas and has recommended that the Congress remove gas price regulations. The most recent messages on energy, one in April and one in July this year, were preceded by an earlier one in 1971. Shortly thereafter, the Administration submitted a bill on power plant siting. Each of these proposals and messages was aimed at sources of the energy crisis.

The nation's overall strategy is necessarily complex, but it can be outlined relatively simply. In the near future, much more fuel will be imported. The trade deficit that will be created for the country is very serious indeed. Perhaps you have heard the figures before, but they are startling to me. Last year, the United States imported some $50 billion worth of all goods and services in total. Oil imports represented 10% or less. Looking ahead to 1980, it has been estimated that we will import fuels worth some $30 billion a year. Most of that money will accrue to the countries of the Middle East. The potential of those foreign dollar holdings for disruption of the world's monetary and industrial systems by reinvestment or by speculation will make the "American Challenge" to Europe or the recent monetary crisis seem like child's play.

To combat this developing situation, we must make much more of our domestic resources which we have not used fully. Coal is certainly a major resource. It is clear that we have enough coal in this country to sustain our energy supply for several centuries. However, coal is a dirty fuel. A great deal of it has a high sulfur content. We need new technologies to remove that sulfur. There are a number of promising approaches including both liquefaction and gasification. Also, we require technologies to tap marginal resources, such as oil shale and tar sands, and to gassify coal. The synthetic fuels that can be generated from such resources can become major resources. With today's technology, however, they are not economical. Nor are they competitive with oil imported from the Middle East or the Soviet Union or with liquified natural gas from Algeria or the Soviet Union. Nevertheless, whether these resources are economic or not at the present time, it is prudent to stockpile technologies so we can use them as bargaining chips to obtain the resources we require. These technologies can put a lid on the prices that we will have to pay for gas and oil in the future. Thus, the stockpiling of technologies promises to be a powerful tool for the future.

However, the use of coal, oil shale, and tar sands and the generation of synthetic fuels runs into a number of difficulties. I have already mentioned economics. In addition, there are problems in obtaining the basic resources, particularly in mining. The National Environmental Protection Act and bills now in Congress would regulate strip mining of coal. It is not at all clear that we will be able to use our resources in the years ahead. Again, we may create constraints for ourselves that are either wise or foolish, depending on your point of view, but which will effectively prevent us from using our great coal and shale resources of the West.

Oil shale is a very good example of how severe the environmental impact can be. About two thirds of a barrel of oil can be obtained from a ton of oil shale. In order to make a significant contribution to the oil supply of this country, literally tens of thousands of tons of oil shale *per day* would have to be mined, handled, and retorted. There is some possibility that this could be done without taking the shale out of the ground, but that is only a gleam in the eye as of now. A complication is that the volume of retorted shale is greater than the raw shale. Thus, the disposal problem is compounded, and this is the kind of problem that we have not excelled in solving in the past.

NEW TECHNOLOGIES

In the longer run, nuclear power is the chosen path as we see it from Washington. It certainly has the highest probability of success. We have more human resources in the nuclear field and a much larger backlog of science and technology. Nuclear power is clearly the preferred direction.

Present nuclear reactors burn nuclear fuel and extract only 2% to 3% of energy from the uranium. Nevertheless, these reactors are major resources and undoubtedly will be utilized. The fast-breeder reactor program, which promises a full scale demonstration plant by 1980, is based upon liquid-metal technology. That program seems to be progressing technically, but success is not assured. Thus it would be wise to have alternatives to the liquid-metal approach. A promising one relies on gas cooling.

We know that there are safety problems in the fission technology. We have heard a great deal about the possible failure of emergency shutdown and cooling systems that are designed to prevent catastrophic accidents. Also, there is the nuclear waste disposal problem, and there is the problem of controlling massive amounts of plutonium, which is potentially a nuclear explosive. But even admitting these problems, the preferred direction is nuclear, and, in my view, it is a sound direction since I believe these problems can be solved without adding significantly to public risks.

There are longer range alternatives. A promising one is thermonuclear fusion, and there are two current approaches. The first is the containment approach, which has been moving along slowly for 25 years or so. Enough of the basic physics is becoming understood that researchers now stand a chance of fashioning a machine that can achieve a "break-even" experiment to demonstrate feasibility. The AEC estimates that we may be able to achieve break-even by 1978 or 1979, and that we might have commercial fusion reactors by the turn of the century.

More recently, we have seen a new approach to fusion with use of a high-power laser to irradiate a small pellet of fuel to create a "mini-hydrogen-bomb" explosion. The explosion would be contained, as in an internal combustion engine, and its energy captured to generate power. It is an intriguing approach, but there is a great deal of physics about it that is not understood. An encouraging aspect is that the private sector has begun to invest in this approach. Though there has been some friction with the AEC because this technology has weapons implications, work has proceeded. I am quite encouraged since the competition between public and private sectors seems to be producing progress at a much more rapid rate than we had any reason to expect a few years ago. Some people close to the situation predict a break-even experiment this year and ignition of fuel within a few months.

Beyond fusion, there are some other interesting possibilities—namely, solar and geothermal energy. They may be important sources in the future. However, I believe that the backlog of technology and experience that we would need to use these as major resources in our energy economy in the near future is not available. We should be working hard to acquire this backlog.

ENERGY CONSERVATION

Conservation impacts very strongly upon lifestyle and has much less to do with technology than do new energy sources. Nevertheless, there are some scientific fundamentals beyond life-style arguments. There are fundamental difficulties with increasing the efficiency of energy production that arise from the laws of thermodynamics. These laws mean that obtainable increases in the efficiency of heat engines are quite limited. Yet even relatively small efficiencies, for example 10% better auto gas mileage, would be welcome. However, any large-scale conservation effort will hinge upon changes in American life-styles. Such changes will not come easily; yet there are a few steps that can be taken. For example, we might give the consumer a greater ability to compare the first cost of an appliance or an automobile against the operating and maintenance costs over the lifetime of that equipment. With better information, we might find consumers willing to put more into first costs while minimizing operation and maintenance costs. Ways of giving the consumer a chance to balance those factors could be very important in energy conservation.

I have tried to outline the research and development component of the nation's energy strategy. What are we spending on this overall strategy? We are spending about $1 billion a year. The federal government contributes about

$750 million; utilities, about $100 million; and the manufacturers of energy equipment, the remainder, to make up something slightly over $1 billion a year. Oil companies and other fuel industries spend perhaps $250 million in addition. This represents a substantial effort. In my opinion, larger amounts of money are not going to cure the problems that I have outlined here much faster. However, as programs mature, greater spending will be required.

The funding profiles of technological programs begin typically at a low level, then grow until they reach a peak. At that time demonstration equipment or prototype production equipment is being built. Many energy programs are in the early stages where funding is appropriately low. As these develop, more funding will be appropriate. I hope to see growth based upon that philosophy rather than an Apollo-style approach. I would like to see more industrial input into the picture rather than more federal input, because I think that the former will provide a degree of competition with federal activities that is needed to invigorate them. I would like to see industrial financing at least equal federal financing within five years.

HEALTH RISKS VS. BENEFITS

Overall, however, I think that the energy crisis is not basically a technological crisis. The causes, as I have indicated, are social and are aggravated by political opportunism. There is no quick technological fix as there was in the case of Sputnik and the missile gap of the early 1960s. I do not favor the Apollo approach to the energy crisis that has been put forward in a Senate bill to make "the United States self-sufficient in energy by 1983." I think that proposals of this kind avoid the major issues, which are social, economic, and political, and not technical. Resolution of these issues is going to depend very heavily, much more so than is generally realized at the present time, on health and on ecological matters. The life sciences are going to have a larger hand in the solution of this crisis than the physical sciences will. This is in contrast to the missile gap and the Sputnik challenges. The life sciences are going to be much more central than in the past.

As an input to public policymaking, how do we judge the risks to public health and safety, and what should the criteria for action be? This is a major question that has not been answered in a forthright way, and yet it is at the basis of progress in the energy crisis. In answering it, we must take the public temper into account. Today, the public temper is such that the benefits technologies can bring are less emphasized than are the risks these technologies impose upon people. With that in mind, I would propose two criteria: first, in setting out on some technological direction such as the breeder reactor, we must insist that we not add significantly to the existing health risks that are encountered by the population at large; second, we should allocate resources, research and otherwise, in proportion to the threats to health. We should put our greatest resources on our greatest problems. I was very interested in some statistics which were recently drawn up by the President's Science Advisory Committee panel.

They estimated that the threat to health from cigarette smoking in the United States was about 100,000 times greater than that from contaminated swordfish. They also estimated that the threat from bad choice of dietary composition is 2 million times that from DDT. There are other necessary considerations beyond such comparisons including, importantly, voluntary versus involuntary exposure. Yet, this distinction is not as clear as it first seems. Consider the involuntary exposure and possible health hazards to nonsmokers from smokers' air pollution, or deaths and injuries caused by drunken drivers. So, regardless of such factors, quantitative comparisons of relative risk to public health are essential when we are addressing the benefits and risks in actions aimed at the energy crisis. It will not be easy to project that viewpoint to the public and the Congress. It is there that the medical community can, and should, play a major role.

20

Energy and Environment

Senator John V. Tunney

I am very happy to be here today and to have a chance to talk to you about something that I consider very important. I was asked to talk not only about the environment but also about energy. I am more familiar, as a practical matter, with the fields of environment because, during my six years in the House and my first two years in the Senate, I concentrated primarily on environmental problems. But in the last six months, I have been assigned to the Commerce Committee, and the Commerce Committee has the major responsibility for the development of our energy resources. So I feel fortunate, at least insofar as my committee assignments, to have an overview of both aspects of what I consider to be perhaps the most critical domestic problem that we have and which affects all levels of society.

In the discussion of the energy crisis, we have to be aware that there has recently been a major campaign by the producers of energy, the petroleum industry, particularly, to demonstrate to the American people that there is a very serious energy crisis and that there may be gas rationing this summer. Clearly, the industry is making some valid points—the nation does have some serious energy problems. But there is a great potential danger if, we are panicked by this expensive advertising campaign financed by special interests whose motives, not surprisingly, are increased profits and further energy exploration. It is anticipated that a deregulation of natural gas at the wellhead will increase the cost of natural gas to the consumer by approximately 300%. The regulation policies of the Federal Power Commission have been cost of production plus 15%. So if the cost of natural gas goes up 300%, we see that there is a substantial margin for profit, and, inasmuch as there are very few producers, one could say that they have us by the throat. It is a monopolistic industry. I certainly believe in the free enterprise system and would like to see a gradual deregulation of natural gas where it is possible, but we cannot deregulate natural gas overnight without very serious consequences to the consumer.

Now, we need to move and move quickly on our energy problems. But if we do, if we take the crucial policy steps now, we can avert the crisis that some of the special interests tell us are already at hand. The resolution of our energy problems is an issue so crucial that our decision may literally determine our future as a nation. The United States' energy consumption is enormous. With only 6% of the world's population, we consume about one third of the world's energy production. There is good reason for this. Cheap and abundant energy supplies have fueled our rise to a position of world political and industrial leadership. And we have given our citizens a standard of living second to none.

Yet, suddenly, we have been brought up short. This year saw widespread fuel rationing for home heating in the Midwest and blackouts in Florida. Threats of brownouts occur with depressing regularity along the entire East Coast. Our wasteful chaotic and outmoded energy policies have finally caught up with us. Nor can we expect relief in the immediate future. It has been widely predicted that in the next 30 years we will consume more energy than in our entire previous history. That kind of increase in energy demand would place us in a very serious dilemma. To meet this exploding demand, we could make massive increases in our imports of foreign energy resources, but this would subject us to the political dictates of a small group of countries, particularly in the Middle East, and would generate severe deficits in foreign trade. It is anticipated that, if our imports of Middle East oil continue at present growth rates, we will be importing $25 billion worth of oil by 1985. Already Saudi Arabia is threatening to withhold oil shipments if we do not reverse our position on the Israeli question.

To avoid these problems of national security and balance-of-payments deficits, we should choose a policy of domestic self-sufficiency. Such a policy would emphasize domestic development but would threaten our environment if we are not very careful in the way this policy is implemented. We know all too well the unfortunate results of allowing unchecked resource development at the expense of environmental concerns.

NATIONAL ENERGY POLICY

Now what can we do in these circumstances? There are several policy alternatives that will allow us to avoid an energy crisis without drastic economic or environmental consequences. First, we need an overhaul of our federal policy-making structure. At the present time we have 64 agencies that are responsible for establishing policy for energy. The differing responsibilities and the conflicting mandates of these agencies have meant that the United States does not have a coherent energy policy. Instead, we have a multitude of conflicting policies that confound one another and confuse our efforts to deal with our energy needs. We will not, and cannot, have a coherent national energy policy until we have an agency responsible for developing that policy. We urgently need a focal point for decision making.

I am a sponsor of legislation pending before the Congress that would create a Council on Energy Policy to develop a long-range comprehensive plan for energy utilization while taking into full account environmental considerations. I believe that this legislation deserves the highest priority in Congress. In his energy message, the President recommended the creation of a Department of Natural Resources as the coordinating branch of national energy policy. This approach will work only if the new department has the authority to coordinate its efforts with its sister departments and other agencies and if it has the power to enforce its will upon those other agencies.

Second, we must formulate policies to enable us to have enough energy to meet future needs without having to make a choice between reliance on foreign resources and environmental chaos. The President in his energy message really avoided those stark alternatives by proposing policies to facilitate energy imports while at the same time facilitating increased domestic production. Presidential aide Peter M. Flanigan characterized the thrust of the President's message like this: Everything must give a little, national security, environmental quality, and price. A policy of giving a little may seem to the President and to his aides the best that we can do. But if we act quickly and wisely and in more effective ways than was proposed in the President's message, we can tide this country over short-term shortages. And we can lay the ground work for sensible long-term policies that will enable us to use the clean, modern energy processes that we will be developing in a more intelligent, less wasteful manner.

The key point is that we face a short-term gap between our demand for energy and our capacity to supply it. If we can develop a policy to bridge that gap, we can look forward to a new era of abundance. A rational policy for the short and long term must take into account certain key factors: (1) projections for increased energy demand are in many cases far too high; (2) energy conservation measures can greatly decrease the need for increased energy supplies; (3) new domestic energy supplies and processes can be developed to increase greatly our reservoir of clean, readily available energy; and, most importantly, (4) the public and the politicians must become sufficiently concerned about energy conservation to take steps to conserve energy until alternative sources are available.

A close analysis of most energy projections for the United States suggests that the crystal balls used by many prognosticators are cloudy. Most of the projections forecast a growth in energy demand in the next 30 years based upon a continued population growth such as we have had in the 1940s and the 1950s and the early part of the 1960s. It seems clear that that is just not going to occur if demographic trends of the last few years continue. Electrical demand in particular is cited as the fastest growing sector, and some say it would double every 10 years until the end of the 20th century. This would mean that we would duplicate our entire present generating capacity every decade, which is a staggering thought. There is one problem with these projections. They are, as I have indicated, based on past increases in energy demands, which may not be accurate indicators of our future needs. Besides the flattening out of the growth in population, we also see that the cost of energy is rapidly increasing, and everyone agrees that these prices will continue to climb and that this trend clearly will dampen demand.

CONSERVATION PROGRAMS

Whether the projections are correct or not, we must implement massive programs for energy conservation if we are to avoid a collision course with the energy shortages. The President mentioned this issue only briefly in his energy message. He called for "a new national energy consideration ethic," but he said it can be undertaken most effectively on a voluntary basis. Voluntary action is a welcome change from the past history of inaction in this area, but it is clearly inadequate. We must have wide ranging, broadly based programs throughout our society if we are to come to grips with our historical pattern of profligate and inefficient energy use.

There are several areas in which we can take major steps in conserving energy. Transportation is one. About one fourth of our energy at present is used in moving people and goods around our nation. Significant savings could be made through the development of mass transportation and more efficient automobile engines. For those of you who have had the opportunity to drive in southern California during a rush hour, you will note that out of tens of thousands of cars that are on the freeways, very very few have more than two people in the car and most have only one. So it is clear that this is the most inefficient use of energy imaginable. The notion of shifting large numbers of commuters from personal autos to mass transit is an idea that sooner or later is going to come to pass. Our only choice lies in our timing. Will this shift occur only after fuel shortages and environmental effects have reached the crisis proportions, or will we be farsighted enough to make the change while we still have time to do so in a coherent and in a rational manner? I think that the Senate of the United States has forthrightly faced this issue with the highway bill last year and again this year. We passed legislation that would provide that the Highway Trust Fund could be tapped by local communities to build mass transit systems. The House of Representatives last year refused to go along and, as a result of a stalemate in the conference, there was no transportation bill, there was no highway bill. This year once again the House has rejected an amendment to tap the Highway Trust Fund, and the matter now goes to conference. The question is whether the conferees on the Senate side will hang tough. The issue is joined, and I just don't know what is going to happen.

This week the Senate Commerce Committee will hold hearings on legislation that I have introduced to create a federal effort to develop a clean, durable, energy-efficient auto engine. This development alone could have a huge impact in conserving our reserves of petroleum and other energy resources. Enormous decreases in energy usage could also be effected through minor changes in individual energy consumption in homes, offices, and factories. The industrial sector can eliminate production processes that use far more energy than necessary to get the job done. As Chairman of the Senate Subcommittee on Science, Technology, and Commerce, I am going to be holding hearings soon to investigate these and other alternatives for reducing energy demands. It is my hope that this subcommittee will be a continuing forum for discussion and evaluation of energy policies.

CLEAN DOMESTIC ENERGY

Fortunately, we are also taking first steps towards development of such previously untapped resources as geothermal power, solar power, tides, winds, advanced coal power cycles, and fusion energy. These processes and others like them offer exciting potential for clean domestic energy. I have joined Senator Jackson of Washington in sponsoring legislation that will create federal corporations to undertake development of these promising resources. Again, the President's energy message falls disappointingly short. He proposes such small amounts of funds for the development of these important alternatives that we may not have them when we need them.

Let me say a final word at this point about the relationship between our energy needs and our environmental policies. In many ways the policies of energy conservation in the development of new energy sources are complementary with the goals of maintaining a clean and healthy environment. Increasing our commitment to mass transit has the dual effect of reducing energy demands and cutting down emission of pollutants. Developing clean energy sources expands our energy pool and reduces the need for sole reliance on environmentally harmful fuels and processes; it is of critical importance to remember that solving our energy problems can, and should, go hand in hand with our environmental concerns. It is quite clear that we have vast resources of crude petroleum in oil shale, particularly in the Rockies, but one can imagine if in an unrestrained fashion we were to strip-mine these resources without giving any thought to the environmental impact. That would present, in my mind, a devastating environmental impact upon the region concerned.

It seems clear to me that there is a need for future development of fission reactors. But, coming from California, which is earthquake land, I certainly do not want a fission reactor built on a fault line and I would hope that most, if not all, other policy makers would feel exactly the same way. Now there has been a substantial challenge in California to any new fission reactors and this has been true in other parts of the country as well. I do not think that we can blind ourselves to the possibility that fission technology is with us and can provide a source of energy that is clean. It is a very low risk but high consequence form of energy and it seems to me that, when we build these fission plants, they have got to be built in areas where there are no fault lines and where we do not have major population centers, just in case the cooling system goes awry and you do have the release of these radioactive gases and radioactive particles that would be devastating to surrounding populations.

In the case of off-shore drilling we do have vast reserves of crude oil on the continental shelf. But that does not mean that we should allow the oil companies to drill wherever they want to without regard for the environmental consequences. The same thing is true with the movement of oil from Alaska. We do need the oil from Alaska, but we have to make sure that, when we bring it down by pipeline, it follows a route that is not going to scar for centuries the tundra of Alaska.

It is unfortunate that the administration is apparently reducing its funding support for programs of research and study of environmental health effects, which is most pertinent to all of you who are here today. The President's budget for fiscal 1974, for example, calls for a cut of approximately $4 million in funding for the National Institutes of Environmental Sciences, the primary agency for conducting research on environmental health effects. It ought to be expanding dramatically, but it is being cut.

We can hardly hope to come up with effective answers to our environmental and energy problems without extensive information on the relationship between the state of our environment and the state of our health. We must know when our health will be threatened by energy production or usage. Otherwise we risk pitting the hard figures of dollars and cents of kilowatts and BTUs against vague imprecise considerations of health and the environment. What I think this country faces is less an energy crisis than a need for an energy policy reassessment. We have time to make the decisions than can prevent a genuine energy crisis. But we must go further and faster in formulating a policy to meet our energy needs, or we may be faced with problems of unforeseeable magnitude and complexity. This is the choice that we must face. I am confident that we will make it correctly and in time to allow us to face the future with an intelligent and a comprehensive energy position, if we are willing to take some political chances.

I am fully aware of the political risks involved in trying to change people's patterns of behavior. There is nothing that is more difficult than doing that. If you tell a person, for instance, that he may not be able to use his car to drive by himself to work every day, but that he is going to have to have a car pool or that at some future point in some cities he is going to have to ride on mass transit, you are risking the ire of that proud possessor of the steel chariot. On the other hand, somebody has got to stand up and address these issues forthrightly. And I think that we do have men in the Congress and men in the fields of public health who are prepared to do just that because they have done it in the past, and, increasingly, you hear voices of support around the country. I feel that the time for the decision is now.

Discussion of Senator Tunney's Paper

Q: The bill that you talked about sponsoring with regard to a number of futuristic sources of energy, none of which is liable to make any significant impact for centuries, seems to be much less important than a bill or a policy to get energy conservation off the ground.

Senator Tunney: The bill not only talks about fusion and solar energy and tides and winds, it also goes into the area of gasification of coal, the development of oil shale, and the more traditional sources of energy, the fossil fuels. But we need to develop new technologies so that these fossil fuels can be used in a way that will be compatible with our environmental needs. Insofar as conservation of energy goes, development of mass transit clearly is one need, one that I think is as important as any.

Secondly, requirements should be instituted in the insulation of housing. The federal government has begun to move in this area. The Federal Housing Administration (FHA) is presently requiring insulation that was not required two years ago. It is anticipated that within the next year the FHA will come out with much stricter standards regarding insulation. It is not only the federal government that has to do this but local government as well. Of course, the policy mandate must come from the federal government, but, in all of our major cities, the highrise architecture is an energy conservation nightmare. All that glass and no windows, and the lights are kept on all night because apparently it is cheaper to keep the lights on than turn them off. And as long as energy is cheap, they can get away with it.

I think that you have to address the conservation issue in different ways. I suppose that there will be a time when each electrical product that is sold will have to describe the amount of energy that it consumes. But there is such a vast panoply of problems and areas where action would have to be taken that it would be impossible for me to recite them all today. But we are moving in certain areas, as I have indicated, and I think more has to be done.

Dr. F. Rieke: Do you see any evidence that the automobile industry might somehow quit making 300-horsepower (hp) engines and go back to 100-hp cars? The American public seems to be interested in smaller cars. Second, I wonder if you see an increasing awareness of voters that this is a serious problem and that they are interested in what you are talking about.

Senator Tunney: I feel that the automotive industry has demonstrated in the past 20 years at least, but most particularly in the last three years, that it is unprepared to spend the money on research and development that needs to be spent in order to provide an energy efficient and low polluting vehicle. As a matter of fact, I would say that I have said that about as euphemistically as a man could. I think that the policies that it has followed are an outrage and it is about time that we forced it to do that which it felt it would be able to avoid, namely to develop an alternative to the internal combustion engine. One of the great hoaxes that has been perpetrated upon the American people is the research and development effort of the automotive industry in the past three years. Now the industry has decided that it is going to go the catalytic converter route and maintain the internal combustion engine.

The National Academy of Sciences, in a report published on February 15, 1973, indicated that, if we had all of the vehicles in the country switched to the catalytic converter system of pollution control, it would cost the consumers in America, the car owners and the taxpayers, only $23 billion a year. And the reason that it would cost only $23 billion a year is because there is a one-third increase in consumption of gasoline plus the instability of the system itself, since it only lasts about 20,000 miles. It is wiped out if you put in one tank of leaded gasoline. The cost is about $375 for the converter, and, in addition, there will be inspection stations. Hundreds of thousands of inspectors will be needed because more people will become backyard mechanics and will remove the mechanisms which consume so much more fuel. So you are talking probably somewhere between $400 and $500 a car per car owner. I just feel that the reason that the automotive industry did it was because it knew that that would be economically unacceptable to the American people so that then they could go back to business as usual. If you talk to these men, as I have talked to them, they say there is no real problem in Los Angeles basin, no problem at all. People can get along. They can learn to live with it. That is what they are saying, and I have had them say it in my office. And the reason that they say it is because they live near the lakes where there is a nice wind blowing and where they have got lots of land around them and don't have the same problems as the person does who lives in a city like Pasadena or Riverside or other cities in the country.

The automotive industry has to be forced into research and development. My legislation would do just that. It would provide money to develop an alternative to the internal combustion engine. I have had people who are really knowledgeable and who have spent their own money on it tell me that for $50 million or $100 million you could get a Rankine cycle engine, meaning the old steam engine, that could perform almost as efficiently and with as much pickup as an internal combustion engine. Not quite. You are going to lose some of the efficiency of the internal combustion engine, but you are going to have a much lower polluting car. As I understand it, one of the major technological problems is to get the heat of the steam from 800 C to 1,600 C and that represents an incredibly difficult technological problem. But, on the other hand, it is my understanding that when the Caterpillar Company decided to add two extra cylinders to their diesels, they spent $200 million dollars on research and development to put in those two extra cylinders. So we are obviously going to have to spend some money to get an efficient alternative to the internal combustion engine. But the automotive industry has made its money for the past 70 years from the internal combustion engine. It is wedded to it and does not want to change.

Q: What is the relation between world politics and energy conservation in the United States?

Senator Tunney: The reason that we are talking about energy conservation and about developing our in-country energy resources is because it puts the United States in an extremely vulnerable position to have to be importing $25 billion worth of oil from the Middle East. At the present time, the United States is importing about $3 billion worth of oil and that represents roughly, as I recall, 15% to 16% percent of our total consumption of petroleum products. By 1985, probably 38% to 40% of the total consumption of petroleum products will be coming from the Middle East unless we have a switch away from present policy trends.

Q: Are you becoming more isolationist from world politics?

Senator Tunney: We are not becoming more isolationist from world politics. I think I am becoming realistic when I say that the United States ought to have as much freedom of action as possible, and certainly we cannot allow our international political stands to be based upon the domestic political considerations in the countries from which we are purchasing our petroleum products.

Q: What is the Senate going to do about the soaring need for money for environmental health research?

Senator Tunney: We have to order our priorities. We cannot afford to spend as much as we would like to spend. I am very much in favor of seeing a budget ceiling. I think that we have real problems with the way that we have managed our budget in this country. My ordering of priorities, however, would be a little different than some. I do not see, for instance, any reason why we ought to be increasing military expenditures by $4.5 billion now that the war is ended. There is no reason whatsoever why we should maintain a 2.5 million-man standing army. I believe in good salaries, living salaries for servicemen, and I believe that they ought to be able to bring their families with them. But we do not need 2.5 million. We need about 1.5 million, and that would save about $12 or $13 billion right there. Now, when we have that kind of savings, I would like to see some of this money shifted into some of the matters that are of concern to me. Child day care centers is one area, Headstart is another area, and research and development, particularly for medical services and health services, is another. I would like to see environmental pollution research expanded. I would like to see us spend more money on basic research. I happen to be research oriented in the sense that I think that we have got to have a strong research effort in this country if we are going to be able to maintain our preeminence in technology. I like to think of myself as a humanist, and I do not think that there necessarily has to be a confrontation between humanism and technology. I think that technology can serve man.

Q: As a practical politician, what do you think are your chances of coordinating these 64 or so agencies responsible for energy in this country?

Senator Tunney: Very tough. Very, very difficult. But I am strongly in support of the proposal, and I just cannot answer the question. There are so many variables that are involved. One determinant is the amount of lost credibility of the President and his capacity for moral suasion. Another determinant is the realization on the part of individual congressmen and senators that we do have an impending energy crisis and that this is closely related to environment and the need for a body to coordinate all the energy problems coupled with environmental considerations. Those are the main determinants, and I hope that the majority of the Congress would have recognized by this time that it is absolutely essential to coordinate the energy policy of this country.

VII

LONG-TERM ENERGY USE POLICIES

21

Rational Long-Term
Energy Use Policy

Ralph E. Lapp, Ph.D.

The key to a rational energy policy should be the avoidance of crisis in any sector of the U.S. energy economy. In the medical sense, a crisis is a point of change toward recovery or death. In the economic sense it is useful to recall that the word derives from the Greek and signifies a "turning point or separation." An energy crisis is a separation of demand and supply producing a gap.

There is general agreement that gaps are developing in a number of energy sectors. Projecting ahead to the year 2000, we may take the estimates for annual demand of the Department of the Interior [1] as follows:

Table 26
Annual Demand Projections, 2000 A.D.

Petroleum plus natural gas liquids	66 X 10¹⁵ BTU	12 billion bbl
Natural gas	50 " "	49 Tcf
Coal	26 " "	1 billion tons
Hydropower	5 " "	632 billion kw-hr
Nuclear power	44 " "	5,440 billion kw-hr
Gross energy inputs	192 X 10¹⁵ BTU	

Without quarreling with these estimates or arguing that we do not need that much energy, one way of framing a rational energy policy is setting national goals and implementing programs to supply these quantities of energy. If this is done then the planning must focus on:

1. resource availability
2. environmental impact of resource exploitation
3. capital requirements
4. continuity of fuel supply
5. balance of payments

There is an additional factor to consider in this energy projection—namely, the specification of the energy form. It is assumed that fuel inputs into generation of electricity will dominate the energy scene with the generation of 9,000 kilowatt-hours (kw-hr) of electric energy in the year 2000. This is one of the most fundamentally planned aspects of U.S. energy policy even though it is a Topsy-like growth policy that has never been given an adequate public referendum.

DEMAND-SUPPLY GAPS

Given the premium fossil fuel requirements of 12 billion barrels (bbl) of petroleum and 49 trillion cubic feet of (Tcf) of natural gas for the year 2000, the most severe task facing the U.S. energy industry is the provision of these premium fuels that are so essential to our mobility and our economy. Figure 30 represents the problem in the oil sector of the U.S. energy economy. The uppermost curve is one obtained by projection of demand on the historic pattern of the past quarter century (i.e., a 4% annual growth rate). Growth was even higher in the preceding decades. The middle curve is the postulated demand curve we shall use; note that it reflects a considerable deviation from the pattern of past growth.

The demand-supply curves began separating after World War II, and, as the lowest curve in Figure 30, we have plotted production of petroleum liquids from the Lower 48 states. Production from domestic sources is now at full capacity and can be increased only by new discoveries that add to proved reserves. The National Petroleum Council [2] has provided a series of 1975, 1980, and 1985 estimates, including production from Alaskan fields, a very optimistic one being plotted to 1985 and then extended to 2000. This 1985 to 2000 extension is highly problematic—to be taken with a kilogram of salt—depending as it does on many variables. But for our purposes we can project a domestic supply of 107 billion barrels (Bb) for the 1975 to 2000 time period. Demand for the same quarter century will total 227 Bb, leaving an oil deficit of 110 Bb.

The supply of this 110 Bb of petroleum liquids constitutes the most vexing issue in the U.S. energy future. It can be argued that we do not need all this oil—that we can tighten our belts and use less. And, of course, this argument can be applied to all energy sources. The pacing factor in U.S. oil demand is the automobile with its immense demand for gasoline. This demand is soaring because of engine changes and pollution controls on automotive emissions. Standard and luxury model cars feature high horsepower power plants that are gas gulpers. Remember that Detroit sells its automobiles by the pound. So if horsepower is cut back there will be concomitant decreases in the dollar value of product sales. Now there is no question but that we do not need road monsters for essential transportation. Volkswagens can get us where we need to go. But the heavy automobile is imbedded in the economy and major political surgery will be required to extirpate it. But over the long run, meaning more than two decades in the future, the demands of the motor car and the jet plane are in contest for the finite resources of our domestic petroleum.

United States proved reserves have held at above the 30-Bb level for about 15 years, jumping up to 38 Bb with the recent Alaskan finds. If no new oil were to be found, then production from present reserves in the Lower 48 would drop off as shown by curve D in Figure 30.

Figure 30
United States Oil Demand and Supply, 1930–2000

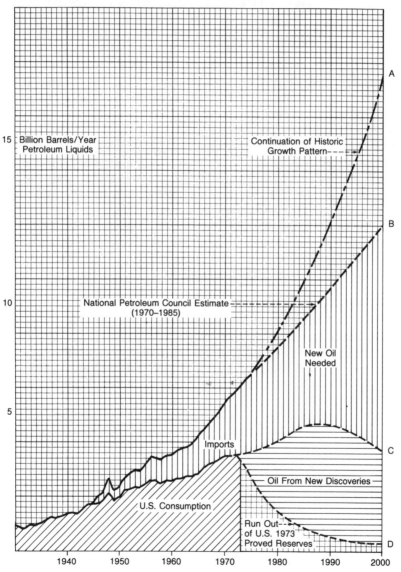

Assuming that the shaded area in the chart represents oil to be supplied as natural petroleum, there is only one source for the United States—namely, imports of foreign oil. Saudi Arabia as chief producer of the Middle East has the reserves in adequate supply to sell us oil required to fill the gap from 1975 to 2000. The question is: can we afford it? There are environmental costs to be reckoned. These include oil loss from tankers most of which will be much larger than the *Torrey Canyon,* and the terminal problem of accommodating these huge tankers. No eastern ports can take a really deep draught tanker so that off-shore islands will have to be created. A loss-of-oil accident (LOOA) on the Atlantic coast involving a supertanker could spill 70 million gallons of oil.

The dollar drain associated with oil payments of $20 billion in the 1980s could spell financial crisis for the United States unless some means were found to compensate by way of valuable exports. If the United States were to become dependent on the Oil Sheiks for its oil supply it could well be forced to pay severe penalties for this energy source.

Much the same kind of analysis may be made for the demand and supply of natural gas. About the same amount of energy is in deficit for the period from 1975 to 2000 as for oil. Thus the two premium fuels add up to roughly the equivalent of 200 Bb of oil required to meet demand on the assumption of a vigorous stimulation of the gas and oil industry.

The United States possesses the domestic resources of solid fossil fuels to allow their premiumization (i.e., conversion to gaseous and liquid fuels) in amounts sufficient to fill the oil-gas gap. Less than 100 billion tons of coal would be required, and U.S. reserves are more than adequate to supply such tonnages. There are serious obstacles to coal gasification and liquefaction, and these begin with the mining operation. Exploitation of our solid fossil fuels would require strip mining on a large scale, and much of this would have to be done in the Upper Missouri Basin where the environmental impact will have to be assessed with care. The conversion plant technology is not mature, and cost data are not firm, although it is clear that the synthetic premium product will be fairly costly. Nonetheless, the price structure for motor fuels could accommodate a federal tax, say 6¢ per gallon or $2.52 per barrel that could be used for price support of the synthetic fuel.

The capital costs involved in creating a coal-based substitute for Texas and Louisiana will be high, but the resources are there, the technology is attainable, and there is no balance of trade dilemma. Furthermore the inability of fuel synthetics to fill the oil gap in the next two decades can be accommodated on an interim basis by imports. It should be obvious that the existence, indeed, the preexistence of a U.S. fuel synthesis industry, will be a powerful deterrent to runaway Mid East oil prices.

The United States has not as yet gotten serious about coal-derived premium fuel, and it would appear that any rational analysis of the energy issues would have to assign a much higher funding priority to coal conversion technology.

CONSUMPTION PATTERNS

United States energy needs will not reach a plateau in the year 2000, but it is probable that fossil fuel exploitation will reach a maximum at about that time and then decrease throughout the 21st century. Advocates of zero power growth do not reckon with the inequities in energy use in our democracy and with the difficulty of applying a freeze to it. Many of us have almost reached the saturation point in our residential use of energy but much larger numbers of our population lack air conditioners and many energy-consuming devices. One must not assume that population will stop growing although much reduced rates of growth appear probable in industrialized countries. Per capita consumption of energy will undoubtedly increase steadily in the United States, particularly in the electric energy sector.

The following table would appear to be a reasonable accounting of electric energy consumption in the United States on a per capita basis over the course of a full century:

Table 27
Electricity Consumption

Population (in millions)	Electric Energy (billion kw-hr)	Generation (kw-hr per capita)
(1900) 76	2	26
(1910) 92	8.5	92
(1920) 105	40	380
(1930) 123	90	730
(1940) 131	140	1,060
(1950) 151	330	2,200
(1960) 178	760	4,300
(1970) 203	1,550	7,700
(1980) 230	3,200	14,000
(1990) 255	6,000	23,000
(2000) 280	9,000	32,000

As a rule of thumb, electric energy has doubled every decade, but this phenomenal growth rate cannot be sustained. As indicated in Table 27 the generation will taper off at the end of the century.

Utilities burned up 0.3 billion tons of coal, 0.3 billion barrels of oil and 4 trillion cubic feet of natural gas in 1972 to produce electric energy. They know that their days of natural gas burning are numbered, that boiler feed oil is hard to get and that tough Environmental Protection Agency (EPA) emission standards restrict the use of much coal. The result is that utilities are switching to nuclear power and "burning" uranium in a reactor core to produce heat as a substitute fire-box for a steam boiler. The U.S. electric power industry, according to the latest Atomic Energy Commission estimates, will have on line the following nuclear generating capacity:

1980	132 million kilowatts
1990	500 million kilowatts (est.)
2000	1200 million kilowatts

AEC projects that nuclear plants will provide 60% of all U.S. electric power by the year 2000.

Figure 31
United States Energy Consumption, 1960–2100

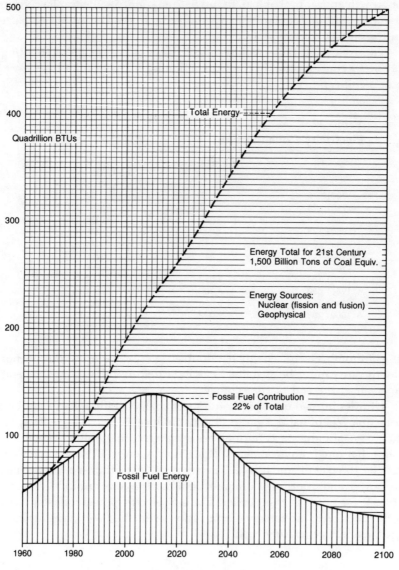

In the year 2000 the national fuel inputs should be allocating close to 100 quadrillion BTUs to the production of electric energy so that fossil fuels will account for a total of roughly 130 quadrillion BTUs in the nation's energy ledger. This estimate means that somewhat more than the energy equivalent of 5 billion tons of coal will be expended. That amount is about 14 times more energy than was used up in 1900 when coal was the mainstay of U.S. energy, and oil and gas were just making an appearance on the energy scene. Looking back, it is evident that the 20th century represents a century of conflagration of chemical fuel. In it the United States will manage to burn up almost all of its easily exploited oil and natural gas. It is, therefore, of great importance that we gain some glimpse of the energy profile for the 21st century. Nothing could be more important for a rational energy policy.

The cardinal parameter in energy projections is Q, the quantity of heat released in burning fuel. Q has been doubling every 21 years on an average, an increase corresponding to a 3.6% per annum growth rate. Such a growth rate cannot be sustained in the 21st century. Extrapolation on this basis would mean an energy consumption of over 5,000 quadrillion BTUs in the year 2100. A tenfold lower projection has been sketched in Figure 31.

The profile of this energy curve changes significantly at the turn of the century because population growth is assumed to slow down and per capita consumption of energy also abates. Whereas population will grow from 76 million in 1900 to perhaps 280 million in 2000, it is assumed to flatten out at 400 million in 2100. The energetics of the two centuries are as follows:

Table 28
Growth Projections

	20th Century	*21st Century*
Energy growth	21 x	2.6 x
Per capita growth	5.8 x	1.8 x
Population growth	3.7 x	1.4 x
Total energy use	5.6 quintillion BTUs	37.5 quintillion BTUs
Coal equivalent	225 billion tons	1,500 billion tons

FUTURE RESOURCE POTENTIALS

Our energy policy of drill, dig, and burn will have left the citizens of the next century with a legacy of solid fossil fuels and only the "tail of the curve" of depleted natural gas and oil. The latter will be insignificant energy sectors, and the real issue confronting people of future generations will be the environmentally safe extraction of solid fossils. The particular fossil fuel profile stipulated in Figure 40 calls for the use of fossil energy equivalent to 330 billion tons of coal during the century—and this would be almost exclusively coal, lignite, and oil shale. There is much more solid fossil fuel in U.S. reserves, but this energy scenario assumes that they will reach their peak exploitation in the first quarter century and thereafter decline. The environmental challenge inherent in the projection is disguised by the shape of the curve since, at the year 2000 only a fraction of the total fossil fuels will be removed from the ground as solids.

At this point in time it is impossible to define the prime limiting factors in use of fossil fuels in the next century but the environmental impact of strip-mining required to exploit underground coal must rank high on the list. The ability of the Upper Missouri Basin to produce strip-mined coal will depend on reclaiming soil in semiarid regions.

If the projection made in Figure 30 is approximately correct, then the United States will be dependent upon nonchemical sources of energy, and most experts agree that nuclear energy will be the dominant source in the next century. Early in the century the fission reactors will produce this nuclear power and the design now favored, the power breeder, is expected to produce nuclear fuel in larger amounts than consumed in the devices. This breeding potential allows some two thirds of the fission energy in heavy elements to be tapped. On this basis mineral resources are not a limiting factor in nuclear power. Furthermore, the condensed nature of the nuclear fuel (energy release 1.7 million-fold greater per pound than for fossil solids) means fewer acres disturbed in mining even though uranium ores may average a small fraction of 1% in uranium content (0.2% average).[3]

RESEARCH AND DEVELOPMENT

In the long term the dedication of U.S. research and development funds to nuclear power on the scale of past and current levels makes sense. Nuclear power planning appears to be rationally planned by the U.S. government. The federal research and development energy budget [4] is as follows:

Table 29
Energy Research and Development, Fiscal Year 1974

Fossil fuel energy	
Production and utilization of coal	$120 million
Production of other fossil fuels	9
	$129 million
Nuclear energy	
Liquid-metal fast-breeder	323
Nuclear fusion	88
Nuclear fuels process development	62
Other nuclear power	90
	563
Solar and geothermal energy	16
Other energy related programs	63
Total	$771 million

There are three basic questions to ask about this research and development activity:

1. *Is the dollar total adequate?* Any company oriented to research and development assesses its commitment to research and development in terms of probable return on the investment. The U.S. Government has yet to reckon its research and development budget in these terms, but in the energy area it ought to project ahead to the future and make some assessment of the national value of the product (i.e., BTUs). Since electric energy will demand 50% of the energy inputs in the year 2000 and since this is premium energy yielding the highest revenue, the electric sector of the energy economy can be singled out in such an assessment. The present almost $30 billion revenues in the electric power and light industry will increase tenfold by the year 2000. Anticipating this, research and development outlays ought to reflect the potential. Viewed in this light the present level of funding energy research and development is inadequate.

2. *Is the research and development dollar split appropriate?* The 73% nuclear split on the research and development energy dollar shortchanges research and engineering in the nonnuclear energy sectors. In such areas as coal liquefaction and gasification the dollar commitment is woefully inadequate. Real progress here requires going to scale in conversion plants and this is expensive business. The U.S. allocation of energy funds is paradoxical because it neglects the fossil fuels that will be so important to the economy in the rest of the century.

3. *Is the money being used effectively?* Apart from analyzing each energy project individually, there is the issue of how federal dollars are used in the framework of the government-vendor-utility complex. There is much to be said for the wartime expedient of a Manhattan Project approach to technical problems. Something of this character is retained by the Atomic Energy Commission but the power-breeder program is only partially of the Manhattan Project species. When we come to the fossil fuel research and development activity the situation is far from optimal. In this important sector the dollar is cost-ineffective and there would be great value in adopting a Manhattan Project approach to coal conversion.

In sum, the U.S. energy scene today is a cluttered landscape of bits and pieces of *ad hoc* policy. It is a prime candidate for rational analysis that would treat the energy problem as a national issue of enduring significance. Long-term rational planning should include:

1. Primary dependence on domestic fuel resources.
2. Development of national energy systems analyses as part of a governmental high-level energy planning agency.
3. Conservation of premium fossil fuels.
4. Exploitation of fossil solids in premiumized form.
5. Full payment of all environmental costs of energy exploitation.
6. Invigoration of energy research and development.
7. Creation of a single congressional committee to deal with energy issues.

278

References

1. *US Energy—A Summary Review,* Table 2, p 12. US Dept of Interior, Jan 1972

2. *US Energy Outlook,* chap 4. National Petroleum Council, Jan 1973.

3. *Environmental Survey of the Nuclear Fuel Cycle,* sec A. Per acre-disturbed uranium mining may involve 40 times more fuel production than the equivalent energy from coal that is strip-mined. US Atomic Energy Commission, Nov 1972.

4. *Special Analyses—Budget of the United States Government,* Table P-3, p 254. Fiscal Year 1974.

22

Environmental and
Social Implications of
Nuclear Energy

Alvin M. Weinberg, Ph.D.

As our population increases and as our easily available resources diminish, more and more energy will be required to maintain our current standard of living. Let us therefore take the 11-billion world population projected by Ralph Lapp for the year 2100 and assume a per capita rate of expenditure of energy in the entire world equal to 5 kilowatts (kw) per person (i.e., one half the present per capita expenditure of the United States). This comes to about 10 times the present world-wide energy consumption. Let us then assume this to be the asymptotic energy expenditure of the world. Can we cope, forever, with energy production at a rate 10 times larger than present energy production?

Before dwelling on that point, I should make the following comment about rational energy use policy. We have acquired an energy conservation ethic. Even I, an energy optimist, have acquired this ethic. But I would oppose those who say that the way to conserve energy is to place some kind of arbitrary limit on its per capita use. This is irresponsible unless those who espouse this position also provide a plausible answer to the social and economic dislocations such an arbitrary policy implies. This is not an unimportant point. I do not accept some of the bland statements from environmentalists, who wish to curb the use of energy, to the effect that means must be found for taking care of the poor people. If limiting growth of energy causes more people to be poor, then one has to outline an acceptable scenario for dealing with those poor people, not merely urge that something be done about them.

But let me proceed to the longer range question: How do we cope with this almost inevitable increase in man's energy budget? How will we cope with it environmentally, biologically, and socially?

ENERGY PRODUCTION LIMITS

Man's present energy consumption represents 1/20,000 of the amount of energy that we receive from the sun. (This is not to be confused with the estimate in Frank Parker's paper where he gave the figure of 1/2,000 of what is called the net radiation balance. That radiation balance is the amount of the sun's energy that is involved in moving the winds and evaporating waters from the oceans.) The ultimate limit on the amount of energy that man can produce is, of course, the thermal load that the earth can sustain. If one increases that energy load by, say, 50-fold, to be somewhat on the safe side, one is then up to 1/400 of the solar insolation. The figure of 1/20,000 leads to an average increase of the earth's temperature of .004 C. At 1/400, this number is about 0.2 C on the assumption—a very big assumption—that the energy is distributed uniformly, and that there is no change in the earth's albedo as a result of this energy production.

Two years ago when I, with R. Philip Hammond,[1] first made these very elementary calculations, we felt fairly comfortable about them because in geological times there were swings in the earth's temperature of 2 C; therefore, an increase of 0.2 C ought to be tolerable. Before publishing our belief that a 0.2 C increase would be safe, we asked the National Center for Atmospheric Research (NCAR) in Boulder, Colorado, to run their world-wide atmospheric model to see how much the isotherms would be changed by this amount of man-made energy. It was the NCAR staff's contention at that time that this would be a safe amount.[2] However, this contention has now been challenged by a number of people, particularly by the Russian climatologist, M. I. Budyko.[3] He argues that, if the average temperature of the earth is increased by a few tenths of a degree centigrade (by approximately 0.8 C), then there is some danger, because of subtle feedback effects, that the polar icecaps might melt. This matter is of such immense importance that it is now being studied seriously by such institutions as NCAR.

If one concedes Ralph Lapp's scenario that in 100 years we will have used up our fossil fuels, with what are we left? We are left with the possibility of solar energy, geothermal energy, fusion, and fission.

With respect to solar energy, I would again agree with Victor Reinemer that it would be great if we could use solar energy at a price that is close to the present price of fission energy or coal energy. The best estimate I have seen for the price of solar energy from any of the proposed systems exceeds present prices by perhaps a factor of five. Therefore, until we see a major new invention, I believe society will not choose solar as its primary energy source unless we must turn away from fission for some reason other than economics. Society may decide, perhaps because of questions of safety, perhaps because of problems of waste disposal, that it does not want fission; but I repeat that, short of basic (and presently unknown) discoveries in solar energy, society will not choose solar as its primary energy source.

With respect to geothermal energy, again one of the main objections is that we really do not know whether we can mine heat from hot rocks (as opposed to naturally occurring hot steam or hot water). I hope experiments on mining hot rocks are tried as quickly as possible, even though geothermal is not a truly inexhaustible energy source. An interesting point is that the average geothermal heat flux is the same as what man is now using—1/20,000 of the sun's energy reaching the earth, a convenient number to remember. Nevertheless, Professor Robert Rex of the University of California, Riverside,[4] estimates that, from the hot rocks in the western part of the United States, we have available some 10^8 megawatt (Mw) centuries of heat; this amount would be enough to maintain our present levels of consumption for about 50 centuries. So, I think geothermal energy is great; but we do not really know whether the hot-rock version is practical, and this is the only version that is really a very large source of energy.

With respect to fusion, David J. Rose has told you that it is great, is inexhaustible, is not entirely devoid of environmental difficulties, but is cleaner than fission. Again, we do not yet know whether fusion is practical; therefore, it is impossible to base public policy on the availability of fusion at any given time in the future. Perhaps five to ten years from now I will see things somewhat differently.

RELIANCE ON NUCLEAR FISSION

It seems to me, therefore, that of these four inexhaustible energy sources the only one we can seriously count on at this time is fission. Let us assume what in some respects may be the most pessimistic of the scenarios: that the other three possibilities—solar, geothermal, fusion—will never work. This assumption forces us to confront the question: can man live forever with fission? You have heard discussions about the advantages and disadvantages of fission. In Ralph Lapp's asymptotic world, with most or all of its energy based on fission, there would be 10,000 reactors, each producing 5,000 Mw of heat. The radioactive wastes in equilibrium would amount to some 5,000,000 megacuries (not counting the long-lived ^{99}Tc). Man must ask squarely and without equivocation whether he can deal with these potential dangers from fission, without causing a very serious dislocation of his environment.

While nobody really knows the answer, I am optimistic about the outcome. Thus, the routine release of radioactivity is not an issue; these releases, as Ralph Lapp points out, are too small to be a serious matter. The real issue as far as nuclear reactors are concerned is the very remote but not zero possibility that there might be a bad accident. How low does the possibility of serious accident have to be for us to be comfortable with fission as an energy source? I suppose one would say that once every 1,000 years, perhaps once every 100 years, a serious reactor accident could be tolerated. One can then count backward and see what the probability per reactor per year would have to be. But we are always left with an uneasy feeling that no matter how well one makes such calculations, as Peter Morris implied, one worries not about the accident we can predict in advance but rather about the unpredictable accident one has not thought of. One gradually excludes these freakish accidents as one acquires more and more experience with reactors. Merril Eisenbud pointed out, significantly, that there are some 700 reactors in operation, but, perhaps more revelant, there are about 200 power reactors that have operated very successfully in the nuclear navy. Our confidence in the wide-spread deployment of nuclear power reactors relies heavily on our good experience in the nuclear navy.

Let me close with two points. Regardless of how good one's method of energy production is, with the possible exception of solar energy, it is inconceivable that there will not be some kind of low-level physical insult to the environment as a result of energy production. These physical insults, almost without exception, do have deleterious effects on the biosphere, even though one often cannot measure them. Medical science must somehow respond to these low-level, but unavoidable, physical insults to the biosphere.

It seems that biomedical research is now entering an enormously fruitful new era with respect to physical insult to the biosphere that may match the era that culminated in the control of disease caused by pathogenic organisms. Looking back to the time of Louis Pasteur, there is an interesting and relevant analogy between society's attitude toward pathogens in the environment and society's attitude toward physical insults to the environment. One hundred years ago, until pathogens were eventually discovered, doctors did not know what killed people. Two things then happened: First, and most important, methods of sanitation and public hygiene were greatly improved. This was a technological resolution of the issue, probably more important than anything the medical profession did. Second, we began to understand how at a cellular level the biosphere protects itself against assault by microbial and bacterial pathogens; in addition, we were able to intervene with antibiotics and chemotherapy.

DEVELOPING BIOMEDICAL STABILITY

In analogous fashion, we are now aware of the biomedical impact of physical insult, particularly of physical insults from production of energy. Again, there are two ways of dealing with these insults. One is to clean up; and, as John Goldsmith, Marvin Goldman, and Merril Eisenbud pointed out, we are cleaning up both with respect to fossil fuels and nuclear fuels. But there will always be a residuum of physical insult, just as there is always a residuum of pathogenic insult despite our best sanitation methods.

Where does biomedical research stand with respect to residual physical insult to the organism? We seem to be finding mechanisms *at the molecular level* for repairing physical insults! We all know about the genetic effects of radiation, and that ultraviolet or x-rays will produce genetic damage and will cause cancer. But what is the molecular mechanism of these lesions? Perhaps one of the most important lesions is the production of thymine dimers formed either between adjacent strands of DNA or within a single strand. This lesion damages the DNA and presumably can cause genetic damage. R. B. Setlow and W. L. Carrier [5] at Oak Ridge National Laboratory have found, remarkably, that at this molecular level there is an enzyme that recognizes and excises the imperfection in the DNA. A second enzyme then comes along and uses the undisturbed strand of DNA as a template to reconstruct the DNA that has been damaged by the injury or by the ultraviolet. Thus, Setlow has discovered a molecular basis for stability against physical environmental insults, just as there is at the cellular level a mechanism for stability against pathogens. As we succeeded with antibiotics finally in dealing with the residuum of pathogenic environmental insults, which technology could not cope with, so I believe medical science will ultimately be able to do much more than it now can with the residuum of physical insults that technology is not able to cope with.

From what I see of the situation, the most probable scenario 10 to 15 years hence is that the world's energy production will increase; population will increase, perhaps by another billion; we won't find anything better than fission; and the fission breeder will prove to be the asymptotic energy source. Can man live with fission? I think that man *can* live with fission, but I believe that in order to live with fission he will have to make certain social commitments of an unprecedented order. He will have to figure out a way of achieving at least a modicum of stability in society over a long enough time to be able to deal fully with the residues of fission.

What does one do about plutonium that has a half-life of 24,400 years? What does one do about maintaining a cadre of people with sufficient expertise to exercise the quality assurance and the care that is necessary to keep reactors out of trouble? These require social commitments. There are those who say that this kind of social commitment is unprecedented, and therefore impossible to achieve; this is the reason that the Nobel Prize-winning physicist Professor Hannes Alfven, for example, says that fission is unacceptable. I can only say that I think man really has no valid and acceptable alternative. The bargain is sometimes called a Faustian bargain—that in return for this inexhaustible energy source we promise to be careful for a very long time. Others say a Faustian bargain is a bargain with the devil, and they will have nothing to do with it. But in Goethe's *Faust* you will recall that Faust is finally redeemed by making a deal with God, and part of the redemption involves his acquiring additional wisdom. I would only point out that fission technology is really a new technology, and that there are always methods of improving technology One would hope that, as we master the technology, the magnitude of the required social commitment will gradually diminish and thus become acceptable, even to the skeptics.

References

1. Global Effects of Increased Use of Energy, Proceedings of the Fourth International Conference on the Peaceful Uses of Atomic Energy, vol 1, pp 171–184, United Nations, New York, and International Atomic Energy Agency, Vienna, 1972.

2. Washington WM: On the Possible Uses of Global Atmospheric Models for the Study of Air Pollution, National Center for Atmospheric Research, Boulder, August 1970.

3. Possibility of Changing the Climate by Acting on the Polar Ice, Modern Problems of Climatology, Main Geoplup Observatory, Moscow, 1967.

4. Summary Report of the Cornell Workshop on Energy and the Environment, Feb 22–24, 1972, sponsored by the National Science Foundation Research Applied to National Needs Program, US Government Printing Office, Washington, May 1972.

5. Setlow RB, Carrier WL: The Disappearance of Thymine Dimers from DNA: An Error-Correcting Mechanism, Proceedings of the National Academy of Sciences, vol 51, pp 226–231, Feb 1964.

Discussion

Q: Dr. Weinberg, is it really wise to put all our eggs in one basket? We will always need all of the energy sources and resources that can do the job best. I do not believe that one single source can really do all our jobs.

Dr. Weinberg: I did not convey my message quite accurately. I agree completely with everything you have said. I was envisaging the situation when fossil fuels have been used up, which Ralph Lapp says will happen by 2100. We will then be left with solar, geothermal, fusion, and fission energy sources. Solar we will use just as widely as we can. We will try to use it to heat buildings. We will use geothermal if it works. If fusion works, then we will go out of the fission business. But from what I see of the situation now, it is most likely that fission will be the primary system. I visualize this world of the future as having a primary energy system that will probably be fission but will perhaps be fusion. I hope that the *secondary* energy system will be based on hydrogen or one of its derivatives, with fission energy producing hydrogen, and hydrogen being the basis for the mobile fuel.

Q: There has been a controversy as to whether the global temperature is increasing as a result of the clouds of CO_2 in the atmosphere or whether it is decreasing as a result of the particulate matter in the atmosphere. Data that were given to us yesterday suggest that in recent years the temperature is decreasing. Is this consistent with what you have said?

Dr. Weinberg: I said that man's present energy production, assuming there is no change in the albedo, no change in the carbon dioxide, no change in the particulates, would (according to the Stefan-Boltzmann law) lead to a .004 C temperature increase.

Dr. Forrest E. Rieke: It has been said that we might choke on some of the products of fossil fuels within the atmospheric envelope. Do you have a comment as to how this may go during the next 100 years or so?

Dr. Lapp: I do not think that the suffocation level would be reached on the basis of the controlled releases. You mean worldwide?

Dr. Rieke: Well, you are predicting the using up of all the fossil reserves, and there are alarmists who say that as that happens, along with the population increase, the CO_2 build up, and some other problems, that we might not last to get into this era that Dr. Weinberg contemplates.

Dr. Lapp: No, the level of CO_2 would not be physiologically significant in terms of the atmospheric dilution. The projection I made was that we will burn up all of the premium fossil fuel, meaning the oil and natural gas, because that is the way we have done it in this century. We have stuck pipes in the ground instead of mining. Now there is a very significant thing happening and very few people have commented on it. The profile of fuel use in the United States is now shifting back to solids from liquids and gases. This change is fraught with many difficulties because it means that you have to go mining instead of putting pipes in the ground. And that is where our troubles may lie since I assume the solid fossil fuels to be limited on an extraction basis.

Dr. Weinberg: Dr. Lapp, you did say that you project 400 million people and an energy consumption of 1,500 billion tons of coal equivalent in the year 2100? If that is all in coal, it will about exhaust the U.S. reserves.

Dr. Lapp: Yes, I had assumed it would be mostly nuclear. The split there for the world would be 70–30.

Dr. Rose: I just want to emphasize that it is the biological consequences of a bad nuclear accident that really makes it bad; the energy release, the physical destruction, per se, is really rather modest as various explosions go. So for the long run, then, as a sort of life insurance policy for mankind in the fission era, basic biomedical research should be supported for all it is worth in order to exploit every possible means of altering and ameliorating the biological consequences of radiation exposure.

A very different point has to do with the long-range disposal of all the fission products that will come if we are in the fission rather than the fusion era. Eugene Robinson, when he was alive, pointed out that a very hot source, a reactor buried in the earth, would melt its own way down but, in the process, would leave behind it a fused, glassy track that would be quite impermeable. Now I understand that one of the problems of a nuclear accident, when all the water systems fail, is that the fission products continue to generate heat. It is possible to use this glassy track for the disposal of fission products? I do not think anyone really knows whether this proposal will really work or whether it is really acceptable for disposal of fission products. I personally happen to be a salt man. I think that bedded salt is a great idea. The only thing that I can see wrong with salt is that salt beds do occur where oil tends to be and so you have a minimal social commitment to prevent people from digging holes in salt beds. Now there are ways of getting even around this by reducing the social commitment from many hundreds of thousands of years to say 800 or so years if you can make a sharp separation between the so-called actinides, which are the 100,000-year ones, and the other fission products, which are the 800-year ones instead of the 100,000-year ones.

Dr. Lapp: I think that the China Syndrome was a little overstated. The China Syndrome is characterized by the dropped core going through containment and as it goes into the base, usually 8 to 10 feet of concrete, it would simply eat into it and incorporate more and more of it into a large viscous mass, if in fact it goes this far. At that point what happens depends upon what the substratum is under the concrete. Calculations have shown that, depending upon the substratum, sand or granite, the combined mass would reach about 80 or 100 feet in diameter, at which point it presumably would come into equilibrium and could have only one means of heat transfer away from it—conduction. It would remain in a viscous condition for perhaps 10 years and be environmentally embarrassing for the utility.

But the real problem would have been the puff of the radioactive gases coming off in the initial drop through the bottom of the core and that is the matter on which there is so much uncertainty. The report that was mentioned by Dr. Peter Morris (Wash-740,1957), which has never been updated by the Atomic Energy Commission and which was for a reactor eight times smaller than those of today, was really critical to the whole concept of reactor safety because it does pertain to the question of how safe is safe enough. We heard today a discussion of all the paper work the AEC goes through in order to make these reactors safe. But that paper work does not protect you, because safety is a matter of how good the design is, how well the research and development behind the design is implemented, how well quality control is exercised by the vendor, by the architect-engineer, by the utility, and by the Atomic Energy Commission. When you are all through, it then comes down to how well the utility operates the reactor. Then I fully agree with Dr. Weinberg when he says that, even if you come up with 10^{-8} chance per reactor per year, that does not assume that some nut is not going to try to crash a plane into a reactor. Nobody knows what will happen if a plane crashes into, let us say, a Dresden reactor. It is not so much a matter of directly hitting the reactor but of the jet fuel burning and knocking out the control room, a matter that can be very nasty.

Dr. Robert S. Pogrund: Dr. Weinberg, while you have considered the nearly inexhaustible supply of energy from fission, I wonder if you would comment on another potential hazard during the transmission of all this power—the extremely low frequency electromagnetic radiation that would be emanating from these transmitters.

Dr. Weinberg: I have been aware of the ozone problem from transmission lines, but I was not aware of the demonstration that electromagnetic radiation at 60 cycles indeed is hazardous. Perhaps you can tell us a little more about that.

Dr. Pogrund: People have been reported to be vulnerable to these particular frequencies and animals have been vulnerable. People who are on the sensitive side can convert these kinds of energies into audible sounds.

Dr. Weinberg: Do you mean that people can convert it or that they are sensitive to the audible sounds that come along with the 60 cycles?

Dr. Pogrund: They are sensitive to the energies that are normally inaudible to most people but that do become audible in certain individuals. Certain animals have receptors that are sensitive to these energies. One of my graduate students at UCLA determined the sensitivity of these individuals by measuring electroencephelographic alterations during exposures to these transmission energies. Now if we are going to allow for energy development there will be far more people showing evidence, depending upon their proximity to the energy sources. People working on radar. . . .

Dr. Weinberg: Radar is different; the frequency is very different. But what you say is quite extraordinary. This is indeed a very interesting and almost startling phenomenon that you report. I would like to know more about it.

Acknowledgment is made to Pitman Publishing Ltd. (publishers for the Royal College of Physicians of London) for permission to reproduce Figure 9 from *Air Pollution and Health* 1970.

Acknowledgment is also made to the American Association for the Advancement of Science (publisher of *Science*) for permission to reproduce a portion of Figure 8, page 108, Volume 109 of *Science,* for February 1949.

Acknowledgment is also made to The Johns Hopkins University Press (publishers for Resources for the Future) for permission to reproduce Table 12, pp. 186–187 and Table 16C, page 206, from the book *Energy, Economic Growth, and the Environment,* edited by Sam H. Schurr, for which it holds the copyright.